# 365
# All-American
# Favorites

Sarah Reynolds

A JOHN BOSWELL ASSOCIATES BOOK

HarperCollins*Publishers*

HarperCollins books may be purchased for educational, business, or sales promotional use. For information please write: Special Markets Department, HarperCollins Publishers, Inc., 10 East 53rd Street, New York, NY 10022.

FIRST EDITION

Series Editor: Susan Wyler
*Design: Nigel Rollings*
Index: Maro Riofrancos

Library of Congress Cataloging-in-Publication Data

Reynolds, Sarah.
    365 all-American favorites / Sarah Reynolds. — 1st ed.
        p.    cm.
    "A John Boswell Associates book."
    Includes index.
    ISBN 0-06-017294-0
    1. Cookery, American.    I. Title.
TX715.R46    1997
641.5973—dc20                                                    96-28422

97  98  99  00  01  HC  10  9  8  7  6  5  4  3  2  1

# Contents

# Introduction: The American Culinary Cauldron

When you think about American food, what comes to mind? A sizzling steak, barbecued chicken, corn on the cob, or a slice of apple pie? These are a few favorites, but our cooking has come to represent much more than these classics.

America has a rich and fascinating culinary history, with food made up from many cultures and many influences. First there were our country's original inhabitants, the native Americans, who grew corn, pumpkins, and squash. Spanish, English, Dutch, and French explorers came to our shores, bringing their European vegetables and seasonings. African slaves brought okra and yams. Italian, Portuguese, Scotch, Irish, German, Jewish, Swedish, Norwegian, Danish, Indian, Mexican, Hungarian, Armenian, Chinese, Japanese, Russian, Korean, Vietnamese, and Thai are just some of the other immigrants who have made the long hard trip to America. All of these cultures have left their mark in our cooking and on our supermarket shelves. Recipes—once unfamiliar—have been adapted and changed and assimilated into mainstream American culture.

*365 All-American Favorites* includes the best recipes from our past, which I've updated with an eye to our knowledge of good nutrition, modern time pressures, and new ingredients that constantly become available. Also included are contemporary favorites, which have become new American classics. America is one big melting pot as far as food goes. Some of the classics that at one time belonged to other cultures but have now been absorbed into American cooking are Spaghetti and Meatballs, pizza, Guacamole, salsa, burritos, lasagna, Chicken Soup with Matzoh Balls, and gingerbread.

The fact that we have had so many influences on our food and cooking is what makes American cuisine so interesting. We have foods that are dictated by what region of the country we live in. Some of these regional recipes, such as tacos from the Southwest or clam chowder from New England, have traveled around and become popular everywhere. Regional recipes are dictated by what foods are native to a region. For instance, blueberries, lobsters, and clams in Maine; blackberries, hazelnuts, and salmon in Oregon; or okra, crayfish, and rice in Louisiana. Because of today's transportation systems, these ingredients are now shipped all over the country in peak condition in a matter of hours or days.

In *365 All-American Favorites* I've gathered recipes from every region of the United States. You can cross the country with recipes like Savannah Red Rice, Cincinnati Five-Way Chili, and San Francisco Cioppino. Almost all ingredients used are commonly found in supermarkets. Convenience products have been used wherever possible to save time for today's busy cooks. There are many good-quality prepared products available now. New ones come out all the time; so take a few extra moments in the grocery store every once in a while to see what's there. Also, contemporary concern for health and sensible nutrition has been taken into consideration. Fat has been reduced where possible, without sacrificing flavor.

In selecting recipes to include in this book, I incorporated some traditional recipes, in part because I sometimes see a trend that is taking us away from simple, homemade, good food. Having enough time is a concern of everyone today, but I don't think a lack of time means we have to make compromises in the quality of our food. I love to read cookbooks, and some of my favorites are about cooks from all over America. They tell their stories and include traditional down-home favorite recipes. Sometimes I get the feeling that these recipes are being lost. Let's hope we keep our traditions alive and don't lose our culinary history by one day relying solely on frozen dinners or food from mixes.

If you can't travel through this glorious country to see the rocky Maine coast, the Maryland shores, the Texas plains, the Iowa cornfields, or the crashing waves of the Pacific coast, then do it by sampling some of *365 All-American Favorites*. Try a home-style favorite, like New England Clam Chowder, Maryland Shore Crab Cakes, Texas All-Beef Chili, Iowa Corn Pudding, or Oregon Blackberry Cobbler. Discover some of America's remarkable recipes. It's the next best thing to being there.

## A FEW NOTES ON INGREDIENTS

BUTTER: Butter used for testing was salted unless specified as unsalted in the recipe. Use butter in stick form, not tub, light, or whipped. In most cases margarine can be substituted for butter, but I prefer to use butter in baking for the best taste. Again, use only margarine in stick form, not reduced fat, light, or whipped.

EGGS: Eggs are Grade A Large. Do not use cracked eggs. If a recipe calls for separated eggs, separate them while cold and let sit to room temperature if specified in the recipe.

FLOUR: Flour used in testing the recipes was all-purpose flour unless specified otherwise in the recipe. I prefer bleached, except for breads.

MAPLE SYRUP: Use pure maple syrup, not a blend.

NUTS: Store nuts in the freezer, as they can become rancid quickly. To toast nuts, spread them on a baking sheet and toast in a preheated 350° F oven 7 to 10 minutes, until fragrant and golden in color. Time will vary depending on the kind of nut.

VANILLA EXTRACT: Use pure vanilla extract, not imitation.

## On Measuring Ingredients

Using the right equipment to measure is one of the steps that leads to successful cooking. Measure dry ingredients in graduated dry measuring cups or graduated measuring spoons. Liquids should be poured into clear glass or plastic measuring cups with a spout.

FLOUR: One of the most important steps to successful baking is to measure flour correctly. This is my method: Stir the flour a few times to aerate, as it can settle in the bag or when it is turned into a canister. Lightly spoon or scoop the flour into the measuring cup; do not pack it down. Level it off by sweeping across the top with a chopstick or the flat side of a knife.

LIQUIDS: When measuring liquids, use a clear glass or plastic liquid measuring cup with a lip and be sure to check the amount at eye level.

My experience both in my own home kitchen and in various magazine test kitchens has taught me a trick or two that makes cooking much easier. The first is to read through a recipe from beginning to end. The second is to assemble a prep tray. This means to measure, cut, prepare, and set all ingredients out on a tray before you start cooking or preparing the recipe. It can be the difference between success and disaster. You'll find that you spend less time cooking because you don't have to stop to find this or that or measure something out. And if you've ever put a cake in the oven only to discover you forgot to add the sugar because it wasn't sitting in front of you, you'll know what I mean.

# Chapter 1

# All-American Snacks and Starters

As a nation, admit it, we like to snack. These days, with the fast pace at which we live, sometimes a snack is all we have time for, and it replaces what once was a sit-down dinner.

One of my favorite family "dinners" was on New Year's Eve, and it was made up of just appetizers. This chapter is full of starters and snacks, such as Chorizo Cheese Quesadillas, Easy Cheesy Nachos, spicy Cajun Chicken Nuggets, or the ever popular Buffalo Wings, to satisfy anyone's cravings anytime.

There are some cocktail party favorites—Fresh Vegetable Cream Cheese Dip, Spicy Chili Snack Mix, Sausage and Spinach Meatballs—and what I believe is still the most popular party appetizer: Shrimp with Zesty Cocktail Sauce. I've even included a recipe for making your own little square cheese crackers. Many of these recipes such as Smoked Fish Spread, Chicken Liver Spread with Pistachios and Dried Cranberries, California Rolls, or Crunchy Cheese Straws, are make-ahead.

When planning a cocktail party, don't overload yourself with work. Prepare one or two appetizers that can be made ahead and fill in with purchased ingredients. Rely on great cheeses, olives, pâtés, or even take-out dim sum from your local Chinese restaurant. Place appetizers on platters around the room and let guests help themselves. This way you won't have to be racing around the kitchen while your guests are out having all the fun.

# 1    CAJUN CHICKEN NUGGETS

*Prep: 10 minutes    Stand: 30 minutes*
*Cook: 3 to 4 minutes per batch    Serves: 6 to 8*

These slightly spicy morsels can be made ahead and reheated. Kids and adults love them. They're good with a quick dip made of barbecue sauce, mayonnaise, Creole or coarse mustard, and chopped scallions.

| | |
|---|---|
| 4 skinless, boneless chicken<br>    breast halves (about<br>    5 ounces each) | 1 garlic clove, crushed<br>    through a press<br>½ cup flour |
| 1 tablespoon Creole<br>    Seasoning (page 152) | ⅓ cup cornmeal<br>½ teaspoon salt |
| ½ cup buttermilk | Vegetable oil, for frying |

**1.** Cut chicken into 1-inch chunks. In a medium bowl, combine chicken, 2 teaspoons Creole seasoning, buttermilk, and garlic. Stir to mix. Refrigerate 30 minutes. Drain chicken in a colander, stirring a few times.

**2.** Place remaining Creole seasoning, flour, cornmeal, and salt in a 1-gallon plastic food storage bag. Shake to mix. Add chicken to bag a few pieces at a time. Shake to coat. Place in a single layer on a sheet of wax paper. Repeat until all pieces are coated. Line a baking sheet with a few layers of paper towels.

**3.** In a large skillet, heat ½ inch vegetable oil over medium-high heat until hot. Add chicken to skillet in batches without crowding. Cook, turning once, until golden brown and cooked through, 3 to 4 minutes. Remove with a slotted spoon to paper towels. Serve warm.

# 2    SHRIMP WITH ZESTY COCKTAIL SAUCE

*Prep: 10 minutes    Cook: 1½ to 2 minutes    Chill: 1 hour*
*Serves: 4 to 6*

| | |
|---|---|
| 1 tablespoon salt | 2 tablespoons prepared white<br>    horseradish |
| ½ teaspoon cayenne | |
| ½ teaspoon freshly ground<br>    pepper | 2 tablespoons fresh lemon<br>    juice |
| 1 pound medium shrimp,<br>    shelled and deveined | 2 teaspoons honey<br>½ teaspoon hot pepper sauce |
| 1 cup ketchup | 1 teaspoon grated lemon zest |

**1.** In a large saucepan, bring 8 cups water, salt, cayenne, and pepper to a boil over high heat. Add shrimp and cook until pink and just cooked through, 1½ to 2 minutes; drain. Place shrimp in a bowl of ice water to stop cooking. When cool, remove and pat dry. Place in a bowl, cover, and refrigerate until cold, at least 1 hour.

**2.** In a small bowl, combine ketchup, horseradish, lemon juice, honey, hot sauce, and lemon zest. Stir until blended. Cover and refrigerate until chilled. Serve shrimp with cocktail sauce.

## 3     CALIFORNIA ROLLS
*Prep: 25 minutes     Cook: 20 minutes     Serves: 6 to 8*

These sushi rolls are great to make ahead and slice up for a party. These have crabmeat or smoked salmon instead of the traditional raw fish. Sushi rice and nori are available at health food stores.

1 cup sushi rice
2 tablespoons rice vinegar
2 tablespoons toasted sesame
  seeds
1 small firm, ripe avocado,
  thinly sliced, or 8 thin
  cooked asparagus spears
4 (7 × 8-inch) sheets sushi
  nori
½ medium cucumber, peeled,
  seeded, and cut into thin
  strips

¼ pound fresh crabmeat,
  surimi, or strips of
  smoked salmon
1 tablespoon wasabi powder
  Pickled ginger and
  soy sauce, as
  accompaniments

**1.** Bring 2 cups water to a boil in a medium saucepan. Stir in rice. Cover and simmer until water is absorbed, about 20 minutes. Remove pan from heat, uncover, and let rice cool to room temperature. Stir in vinegar and sesame seeds.

**2.** On a piece of wax paper, lay 1 sheet of nori with a 7-inch side facing forward. Place one fourth rice (about ¾ cup) on nori and with wet fingers spread to cover nori up to 2 inches from far edge. Place one fourth avocado slices or asparagus spears on rice along front edge. Lay one fourth cucumber and crabmeat on avocado. Brush uncovered edge of nori with water. Using wax paper to help, roll up tightly toward uncovered edge. Repeat with remaining ingredients, making 3 more rolls. Serve or wrap tightly in plastic wrap and refrigerate overnight.

**3.** To serve, with a serrated knife and a sawing motion, cut each roll crosswise into 8 slices. Mix wasabi powder with 1 tablespoon water to make a paste. Serve sushi with small bowls of wasabi paste, pickled ginger, and soy sauce.

## 4    CLAMS CASINO
*Prep: 10 minutes    Cook: 13 minutes    Serves: 6*

4 slices of bacon, finely
   chopped
1 garlic clove, crushed
   through a press
2 tablespoons minced onion
2 tablespoons minced red bell
   pepper
2 tablespoons minced green
   bell pepper

1 tablespoon butter, softened
1 tablespoon chopped Italian
   flat-leaf parsley
1 tablespoon lemon juice
¼ teaspoon freshly ground
   pepper
24 littleneck clams, on the half-
   shell

**1.** In a medium skillet, cook bacon over medium heat until cooked but not crisp, about 5 minutes. Stir in garlic, onion, and red and green bell pepper. Cook until softened, about 2 minutes. Pour into a small bowl. Let cool.

**2.** Add butter, parsley, lemon juice, and pepper to bowl. Stir with a fork to mix.

**3.** Preheat broiler. Crumple foil and place on a jelly-roll pan to hold clams in place. Spoon bacon mixture over clams, dividing evenly. Place clams on foil.

**4.** Broil clams 4 to 5 inches from heat about 6 minutes, until topping is bubbly and clams are just cooked through.

## 5    OYSTERS ROCKEFELLER
*Prep: 10 minutes    Cook: 11 to 14 minutes    Serves: 6 to 8*

This classic was created at Antoine's restaurant in New Orleans in the 1890s and is named after John D. Rockefeller because it's so rich. This is a somewhat streamlined version.

2 scallions, cut into 1-inch
   pieces
¼ cup chopped celery
¼ cup packed parsley sprigs
1 cup packed fresh basil
2 cups loosely packed fresh
   spinach
6 tablespoons butter, softened

2 garlic cloves, crushed
   through a press
¼ teaspoon dried tarragon
¼ teaspoon salt
¼ cup heavy cream
¼ teaspoon Tabasco sauce
1 cup fresh bread crumbs
24 oysters on the half-shell

**1.** In a food processor, combine scallions, celery, parsley, basil, and spinach. Process until very finely chopped.

**2.** In a medium skillet, melt 2 tablespoons butter over medium heat. Add garlic and cook 1 minute. Stir in chopped vegetable mixture, tarragon, and salt. Cook until softened, 2 to 3 minutes. Stir in cream. Remove from heat. Stir in 2 tablespoons butter and Tabasco sauce.

**3.** Preheat oven to 450°F. In a small saucepan, melt remaining 2 tablespoons butter over low heat. Stir in bread crumbs. Crumple foil to hold oysters steady and place in 2 (15 × 10-inch) jelly-roll pans. Place oysters on foil. Spoon spinach mixture over oysters. Sprinkle bread crumbs on top.

**4.** Bake 8 to 10 minutes, or until oysters are hot and topping is lightly browned.

---

## 6   SAUSAGE AND SPINACH MEATBALLS
*Prep: 20 minutes    Cook: 20 to 25 minutes    Makes: about 90*

These little meatballs are simple to make. You don't need to squeeze the spinach dry; just make sure it's completely thawed. If you're a sauce fan, serve these with heated marinara sauce for dipping.

1¼ **pounds lean ground beef**
¾ **pound hot Italian sausage, casing removed**
1 **(10-ounce) box frozen chopped spinach, thawed**
2 **eggs, lightly beaten**
½ **cup grated Parmesan cheese**
⅓ **cup dry bread crumbs**
3 **tablespoons minced oil-packed sun-dried tomatoes**

1 **garlic clove, crushed through a press**
¾ **teaspoon freshly ground pepper**
½ **teaspoon salt**
**Olive oil**

**1.** Preheat oven to 400°F. Crumble ground beef and sausage into a large bowl, breaking sausage up into small pieces. Add spinach, eggs, Parmesan cheese, bread crumbs, sun-dried tomatoes, garlic, pepper, and salt. Mix until well blended.

**2.** Shape meat mixture into 1-inch balls. Place meatballs in single layers on 2 oiled jelly-roll pans without touching.

**3.** Bake 20 to 25 minutes, until meatballs are cooked through and lightly browned. Drain on paper towels. Serve hot.

## 7  BUFFALO WINGS
*Prep: 20 minutes    Cook: 40 minutes    Serves: 6*

This popular snack has become a modern American classic. The story goes that they began in a bar in Buffalo, New York, thrown together by the owner.

18 chicken wings (about 3½ pounds)
½ cup flour
½ teaspoon cayenne
½ teaspoon salt
3 tablespoons butter

¼ cup Durkee's Red Hot Sauce or other mild hot pepper sauce
Blue Cheese Dressing (page 42)
Celery sticks

**1.** Preheat oven to 425° F. Rinse and dry wings. Cut off and discard tips. Halve wings at joint.

**2.** In a large plastic food storage bag, shake flour, cayenne, and salt to mix. Add wings to seasoned flour a few at a time and shake to coat. Place in a single layer on 2 greased jelly-roll pans.

**3.** Bake wings 40 minutes, or until browned, turning with a spatula halfway through cooking time and reversing pans in oven. Drain on paper towels.

**4.** Meanwhile, in a small saucepan, combine butter and hot sauce. Cook over low heat until butter melts; keep warm. To serve, place wings on a large platter. Stir sauce and drizzle over wings with a spoon. Serve while hot with blue cheese dressing and celery sticks for dipping.

## 8  EASY CHEESY NACHOS
*Prep: 10 minutes    Cook: 5 minutes    Serves: 6*

1½ cups shredded Monterey Jack cheese
1 cup shredded sharp Cheddar cheese
2 plum tomatoes, seeded and cut into ¼-inch dice

¼ cup sliced pickled jalapeño peppers, minced and patted dry
2 scallions, finely chopped
1 teaspoon ground cumin
40 round tortilla chips

**1.** Preheat oven to 400°F. In a large bowl, combine Monterey Jack and Cheddar cheeses, and plum tomatoes, pickled jalapeños, scallions, and cumin. Toss to mix.

**2.** Arrange tortilla chips on 2 large baking sheets in single layers. Top with cheese mixture, dividing it evenly among chips and mounding in center of each.

**3.** Bake until cheese is melted and bubbly, about 5 minutes. Serve immediately while hot.

## 9    CRUNCHY CHEESE STRAWS

*Prep: 25 minutes    Bake: 20 to 22 minutes per batch    Makes: 60*

These crunchy snacks are like a cheesy bread stick. Although 60 sounds like a lot, they store well and won't last long because you can't eat just one.

| | |
|---|---|
| 1  envelope (¼ ounce) active dry yeast | 3  tablespoons grated Parmesan cheese |
| 1  teaspoon sugar | ½  teaspoon salt |
| ½  cup warm milk (105° to 115°F) | ¼  teaspoon cayenne |
| 1½  cups flour | 1½  cups finely shredded Cheddar cheese |
| 4  tablespoons butter | |

**1.** Sprinkle yeast and sugar over warm milk. Stir and let stand 5 minutes to soften.

**2.** In a food processor, combine flour, 2 tablespoons butter, Parmesan cheese, salt, and cayenne. Process 15 seconds, or until butter is blended into flour. With machine on, pour in milk mixture until dough forms into a ball. If too dry, add water 1 teaspoon at a time; if too wet, add flour 1 teaspoon at a time until ball forms. Process 45 seconds to knead dough.

**3.** In a small saucepan, melt remaining 2 tablespoons butter. Divide dough in half. On a lightly floured surface with a floured rolling pin, roll out 1 piece to a 14 × 12-inch rectangle. Brush half of long side of rectangle with about ½ tablespoon melted butter. Sprinkle one fourth of Cheddar cheese over buttered half of dough, pressing cheese lightly to stick. Fold dough over from longer side so edges meet. Brush with another ½ tablespoon butter and sprinkle on one third of remaining cheese. Sprinkle lightly with flour and roll with floured rolling pin to a 16 × 7-inch rectangle. Cut crosswise into 30 (½-inch) strips. Repeat with remaining half of dough.

**4.** Preheat oven to 325°F. Grease 2 large baking sheets. Twist strips and place 1-inch apart on baking sheets, pressing ends so sticks remain twisted.

**5.** Bake 1 sheet at a time in upper third of oven until golden brown, 20 to 22 minutes. Remove with a spatula while hot and let cool on wire racks. Store in an airtight container at room temperature.

## 10    CHEDDAR CHEESE CRACKERS
*Prep: 20 minutes    Cook: 9 to 11 minutes per batch    Makes: 160*

These spicy cheesy crackers are great to snack all by themselves. They store well and are fun to bring out and impress people with. They really are not time consuming to make.

1½  cups flour
¾  cup shredded sharp
    Cheddar cheese
1  tablespoon solid vegetable
    shortening
¼  cup plus 2 tablespoons
    grated Parmesan cheese

½  teaspoon salt
¼  teaspoon cream of tartar
¼  teaspoon baking soda
¼  teaspoon cayenne

**1.** In a food processor, combine flour, Cheddar cheese, shortening, ¼ cup Parmesan cheese, salt, cream of tartar, baking soda, and cayenne. With machine on, pour ⅓ cup plus 1 tablespoon warm water through feed tube. If dough does not form a ball, add additional water 1 teaspoon at a time until it forms a ball. Process 45 seconds to knead.

**2.** Preheat oven to 400°F. Divide dough in half. Roll out 1 piece of dough on a lightly floured surface with floured rolling pin to a rectangle measuring 20 × 7 inches. Fold in thirds like a business letter and roll to a 22 × 8-inch rectangle. Trim uneven edges. Cut crosswise into 16 strips and then lengthwise into 5 to make 80 squares. Prick each square 3 times with a fork. Sprinkle 1 tablespoon Parmesan cheese over squares. Roll rolling pin lightly over dough to press in cheese so it sticks. Transfer squares to large greased baking sheets, placing them ½ inch apart. Repeat with remaining dough.

**3.** Bake 1 sheet at a time 9 to 11 minutes, or until just golden brown in spots, removing crackers to cooling rack if some brown faster than others. Repeat with remaining dough. Let cool completely. Store in an airtight container.

## 11    CHILE CON QUESO DIP
*Prep: 5 minutes    Cook: 10 minutes    Makes: 2 cups*

1  tablespoon olive oil
½  small onion, minced
1  (4½-ounce) can chopped
    green chiles
1  garlic clove, crushed
    through a press
1  teaspoon ground cumin
1  cup light cream
2  tablespoons cornstarch

1¼  cups shredded sharp
    Cheddar cheese
½  cup shredded Monterey
    Jack cheese
1  large plum tomato, seeded
    and finely chopped
½  teaspoon Tabasco sauce
    Tortilla chips and raw
    vegetables, for dipping

**1.** In a medium saucepan, heat oil over medium heat. Add onion and cook, stirring, until softened, about 3 minutes. Add chiles, garlic, and cumin. Cook 2 minutes, stirring occasionally.

**2.** In a small bowl, whisk cream and cornstarch until smooth. Add to saucepan and cook, stirring, until mixture comes to a simmer and thickens, about 3 minutes. Reduce heat to low.

**3.** Gradually add Cheddar and Monterey Jack cheese, stirring until melted. Stir in tomato and Tabasco sauce. Cook, stirring, until heated through, about 2 minutes. Do not allow mixture to simmer, as cheese will separate. Serve at once with tortilla chips and vegetables for dipping.

---

## 12    DEVILISH EGGS
*Prep: 10 minutes    Cook: 12 minutes    Chill: 2 hours    Serves: 12*

Dust off that cut-glass deviled egg plate that's been hidden in a closet and serve this classic at your next picnic or barbecue. The recipe can be easily halved if you're serving a small group, but leftovers for lunch the next day are awfully good.

12 eggs
¼ cup grated carrot
3 tablespoons minced
   pimiento-stuffed olives
2 tablespoons minced fresh
   chives
2 tablespoons chopped
   parsley

¼ cup mayonnaise
2 teaspoons Dijon mustard
1 teaspoon cider vinegar
¼ teaspoon pepper
⅛ teaspoon salt

**1.** Place eggs in a large saucepan and cover with cold water. Bring to a boil over medium-high heat. Reduce heat to medium-low and cook 12 minutes. Rinse eggs under cold water. Peel off shells.

**2.** Cut eggs lengthwise in half. Cut a paper-thin slice off bottoms so whites stay flat. Remove yolks to a medium bowl and mash with a fork. Add carrot, olives, chives, parsley, mayonnaise, mustard, vinegar, pepper, and salt. Stir well with a fork.

**3.** Spoon filling back into whites, mounding to fill. Place on a platter, cover, and refrigerate at least 2 hours.

## 13 CHICKEN LIVER SPREAD WITH PISTACHIOS AND DRIED CRANBERRIES

*Prep: 10 minutes     Cook: 16 to 18 minutes     Chill: overnight*
*Makes: 2¼ cups*

1 **pound chicken livers**
3 **slices of bacon, cut into**
   **½-inch dice**
1 **medium onion, finely**
   **chopped**
1 **garlic clove, crushed**
   **through a press**
2 **tablespoons bourbon**
4 **ounces cream cheese**

¼ **cup sour cream**
½ **teaspoon salt**
½ **teaspoon freshly ground**
   **pepper**
⅓ **cup dried cranberries,**
   **chopped**
½ **cup shelled pistachios,**
   **chopped**

**1.** Rinse and dry chicken livers. Cut each in half, removing membrane.

**2.** In a large skillet, cook bacon over medium heat until crisp, about 6 minutes. Remove to small bowl with a slotted spoon. Add onion to skillet. Cook, stirring occasionally, until golden, 5 to 7 minutes. Add chicken livers and garlic. Cook, stirring occasionally, until livers are brown outside but still rosy pink inside, about 5 minutes. Scrape into a food processor.

**3.** Return skillet to heat, add bourbon, and stir to scrape up brown bits. Add to livers; puree until smooth. Add cream cheese, sour cream, salt, and pepper. Process until blended. Turn into a medium bowl. Stir in reserved bacon, cranberries, and pistachios. Cover and refrigerate overnight to allow flavors to blend.

## 14 GUACAMOLE

*Prep: 10 minutes     Cook: none     Makes: 3 cups*

This makes a generous amount of dip for a party. Of course, the recipe can be halved easily. If you like it spicy, leave some of the seeds and ribs in the jalapeños.

¼ **cup fresh lime juice**
¼ **cup finely chopped red**
   **onion**
1 **teaspoon salt**
4 **ripe avocados**

2 **plum tomatoes, finely**
   **chopped**
3 **jalapeño peppers, seeded**
   **and minced**
¼ **cup chopped cilantro**

**1.** In a medium bowl, combine lime juice, red onion, and salt. Stir to mix. Let stand 20 minutes.

**2.** Cut avocados in half and remove pits. Using a soup spoon, scoop avocados into bowl with onion mixture. Mash with a potato masher or fork until as coarse or smooth as you like it. Stir in tomatoes, jalapeños, and cilantro. Serve at once, or cover tightly with plastic wrap directly against surface and refrigerate until serving.

## 15  CHORIZO CHEESE QUESADILLAS
*Prep: 5 minutes    Cook: 22 to 26 minutes    Serves: 6 to 8*

½  pound chorizo sausage,
   casing removed
½  cup chopped scallions
1½ teaspoons ground cumin

8  large (8-inch) flour tortillas
2  cups shredded hot pepper
   Monterey Jack cheese
¼  cup chopped cilantro

1. Spray a large skillet with vegetable cooking spray and heat over medium heat. Add chorizo and cook, stirring to break meat into bits, until browned and cooked through, about 5 minutes. Pour off any fat. Stir in scallions and cumin and cook, stirring, 1 minute. Turn into a small bowl.

2. Lay 4 tortillas on a flat work surface. Spoon chorizo mixture on each up to ½ inch from edges. Sprinkle cheese and cilantro over chorizo. Top with remaining tortillas, pressing lightly at edges.

3. Spray clean skillet with cooking spray, place over medium-low heat, and add 1 quesadilla. Cook until lightly browned on bottom, 2 to 3 minutes. Turn carefully and cook until cheese melts, about 2 minutes. Repeat with remaining quesadillas. Cut each into 6 wedges and serve hot.

## 16  FRESH VEGETABLE CREAM CHEESE DIP
*Prep: 10 minutes    Cook: none    Makes: 3 cups*

This is a creamy, crunchy dip that takes just a few minutes longer to make than stirring together a mix and sour cream. It's worth the extra time and tastes refreshing. If you have a food processor, use it to mince the vegetables to save time. If the dip has been refrigerated, you may need to stir in 1 to 2 tablespoons of milk to thin it a little. Serve with cut-up vegetables and potato chips.

3  large radishes, minced
1  medium carrot, peeled and
   minced
1  medium celery rib, minced
2  scallions, minced
¼  cup jarred roasted red
   pepper, minced and well
   drained

1  (8-ounce) package
   Neufchâtel cheese, at
   room temperature
1½ cups sour cream
1  teaspoon grated lemon zest
½  teaspoon salt
½  teaspoon freshly ground
   pepper

In a large bowl, combine radishes, carrot, celery, scallions, and roasted pepper. Add cheese and stir to mix well. Add sour cream, lemon zest, salt, and pepper. Stir until blended. Serve or cover and refrigerate up to 2 days.

## 17    SMOKED FISH SPREAD
*Prep: 5 minutes    Cook: none    Chill: 2 hours    Makes: 2 cups*

If you can't find smoked bluefish, this can be made with an equal amount of smoked trout or whitefish. It's great to have on hand for impromptu gatherings. Serve with crackers.

½ **pound smoked bluefish,
    skin and bones removed**
1 **(8-ounce) package
    Neufchâtel cheese, at
    room temperature**
4 **tablespoons butter, at room
    temperature**

2 **scallions, minced**
1 **tablespoon minced parsley**
1 **tablespoon fresh lemon
    juice**
1 **teaspoon grated lemon zest**
¼ **teaspoon freshly ground
    pepper**

**1.** Flake fish into a small bowl.

**2.** In a medium bowl, beat cheese and butter with an electric mixer on medium speed until fluffy. Beat in scallions, parsley, lemon juice, lemon zest, pepper, and half of fish. Stir in remaining fish.

**3.** Cover and refrigerate at least 2 hours to allow flavors to blend.

## 18    FRESH TOMATO SALSA
*Prep: 5 minutes    Cook: none    Makes: 3 cups*

Make this with ripe, red tomatoes. If available, use a sweet yellow onion such as a Vidalia or Texas sweet. This is best the same day it's made. Serve as a dip with tortilla chips or use as a sauce or topping.

½ **cup minced sweet yellow
    onion**
2 **tablespoons lime juice**
4 **ripe medium tomatoes,
    (about 1½ pounds), finely
    chopped**

1 **large jalapeño pepper,
    seeded and minced**
¼ **cup chopped cilantro**
½ **teaspoon salt**

In a medium bowl, combine onion and lime juice. Let stand 10 minutes. Stir in tomatoes, jalapeño, cilantro, and salt. Serve or cover and let stand at room temperature up to 2 hours or in refrigerator up to 6 hours.

## 19 BAKED POTATO SKINS
*Prep: 10 minutes    Cook: 38 to 44 minutes    Serves: 6 to 8*

You won't have to wait to bake some potatoes in this version. Use the insides for mashed potatoes.

4 large Idaho potatoes
1 tablespoon olive oil
1 teaspoon Cajun seasoning

½ cup shredded Cheddar
  cheese
¼ cup chopped scallions

**1.** Quarter potatoes lengthwise to make 4 wedges. Cut out centers, leaving ¼-inch shells. Reserve centers for another use.

**2.** Preheat oven to 425°F. Blot cut sides of potatoes with paper towels. In small bowl, combine oil and Cajun seasoning; stir to blend. Brush over cut sides of potatoes. Cut each quarter crosswise in half. Place on a large greased baking sheet oiled side up.

**3.** Bake potato skins 35 to 40 minutes, or until browned and crisp. In a small bowl, toss cheese and scallions together. Sprinkle over potatoes. Bake until cheese melts, 3 to 4 minutes. Serve hot.

## 20 SPICY CHILI SNACK MIX
*Prep: 10 minutes    Cook: 32 to 33 minutes    Makes: about 16 cups*

4 tablespoons butter
2 tablespoons olive oil
1 tablespoon chili powder
1 teaspoon ground cumin
1 teaspoon hot pepper sauce
4 cups thin pretzel sticks
1 (6-ounce) bag small
  goldfish-shaped crackers

2 cups unsalted dry-roasted
  peanuts
1 (8-ounce) bag baked tortilla
  chips, broken into large
  pieces
3 cups Chex cereal (corn or
  rice)

**1.** Preheat oven to 300°F. In a small saucepan, combine butter, olive oil, chili powder, cumin, and hot sauce. Cook over low heat, stirring occasionally, until butter melts, 2 to 3 minutes.

**2.** In a large roasting pan, combine pretzels, goldfish crackers, peanuts, tortilla chips, and cereal. Toss to mix. Stir seasoned butter. Drizzle slowly over mixture in roasting pan while stirring. Stir well until evenly coated.

**3.** Bake, stirring once, 30 minutes, or until tortilla chips are very lightly toasted in spots. Let cool completely. Store in airtight containers.

## 21  ALMOND COCONUT CARAMEL CORN

*Prep: 10 minutes    Cook: 77 to 79 minutes    Makes: about 4 quarts*

3½  quarts freshly popped
    popcorn
1  cup sliced almonds
1  cup flaked coconut
1  cup packed light brown
    sugar

1  stick (4 ounces) butter,
    cut up
¼  cup light corn syrup
½  teaspoon salt
½  teaspoon baking soda

1. Place popcorn in a large bowl or roasting pan.

2. Preheat oven to 350°F. Place almonds on a jelly-roll pan. Bake 6 to 8 minutes, or until lightly toasted. Place on a plate to cool. Spread coconut on baking sheet. Bake 6 minutes, stirring once, or until golden. Add to almonds. Reduce oven temperature to 200°F.

3. In a small saucepan, combine brown sugar, butter, and corn syrup. Cook over medium heat, stirring, until mixture comes to a boil. Boil 5 minutes. Remove from heat and stir in salt, baking soda, almonds, and coconut. Mixture will foam up. Pour over popcorn, stirring well until popcorn is evenly coated.

4. Divide popcorn evenly between 2 jelly-roll pans. Bake 1 hour, stirring 3 times. Let cool. Break apart and store in an airtight container up to 2 months.

## 22  BACK PORCH LEMONADE

*Prep: 10 minutes    Cook: 5 minutes    Makes: about 2 quarts*

Part of the lemonade may be tinted pink with grenadine syrup and frozen in ice cube trays; this way the lemonade isn't diluted by ice cubes made with water.

1¾  cups sugar
2¼  cups fresh lemon juice
2  teaspoons grated lemon zest

1  tablespoon grenadine
    (optional)

1. In a small saucepan, combine sugar and 1 cup water. Bring to a boil, stirring to dissolve sugar. Let cool. Cover and refrigerate syrup until cold.

2. Remove seeds from lemon juice but leave pulp. In a pitcher, stir together cold syrup, lemon juice, lemon zest, and 7 cups cold water. Stir well. If desired, remove 2½ cups to a small bowl and stir in grenadine. Pour into 2 ice cube trays and freeze. Cover lemonade and refrigerate until cold.

3. Serve lemonade in tall glasses filled with lemonade cubes.

## 23   HOT CHOCOLATE

*Prep: 3 minutes    Cook: 10 minutes    Serves: 4*

The best hot chocolate I've ever had was in a pastry shop in Annecy, France. I'm sure it was made with heavy cream. This comes close, but it uses milk instead of cream. If you like hot chocolate on the sweet side, omit the cocoa powder.

4  cups milk
6  ounces best-quality
    semisweet chocolate,
    chopped
2  tablespoons unsweetened
    Dutch-process cocoa
    powder

½  teaspoon vanilla extract
   Marshmallows (optional)

In a medium saucepan, combine milk, chocolate, and cocoa powder. Heat over medium heat, whisking occasionally, until chocolate melts and mixture is hot and steaming, about 10 minutes. Whisk in vanilla extract. Serve while hot in mugs, with a marshmallow, if desired.

---

## 24   CHOCOLATE MILK SHAKES

*Prep: 5 minutes    Cook: 6 minutes    Serves: 2*

There will be extra syrup, but it lasts and makes a great fat-free ice cream sauce.

1¼  cups sugar
1  tablespoon instant espresso
    powder
½  cup unsweetened Dutch-
    process cocoa powder

1  teaspoon vanilla extract
¼  cup milk
2½  cups vanilla ice cream

**1.** In a medium saucepan, combine sugar, espresso powder, and 1 cup water. Bring to a boil, stirring to dissolve sugar. Place cocoa in a small bowl. Whisk some sugar syrup into cocoa until smooth. Whisk cocoa mixture into remaining syrup in saucepan. Bring to a boil. Reduce heat slightly and boil, whisking, until slightly thickened, about 4 minutes. Pour into a bowl and stir in vanilla. Let cool. Cover and refrigerate until cold.

**2.** In a blender, combine 3 tablespoons chocolate syrup, 2 tablespoons milk, and 1¼ cups ice cream. Blend until smooth. Pour into a glass and add 1 tablespoon syrup, stirring just to swirl it in. Repeat to make second drink.

*Chapter 2*

# Simmering Stove-top Soups and Chowders

What's more soothing than a bowl of hot soup? Or easier to put together and have on hand? Soups are convenient to make because much of their cooking time is unattended, with an occasional check to stir the pot. So even if a soup does take 2 hours to simmer, you can be off doing other things while it cooks. In fact, many of the recipes here cook in 30 minutes or less. There are soups that take just a few minutes to make—Speedy Black Bean Soup with Cilantro-Lime Cream, Oyster Stew, or Cold Avocado Soup, for example. Others, which take longer and benefit from some time spent simmering, like old-fashioned Beef and Barley Soup with Squash and Swiss Chard or Sausage and Kale Soup, are substantial enough to make a meal. Many are even better if made ahead and refrigerated overnight to let the flavors develop. A technique I like to use is to puree part of the soup. It improves the texture by thickening the soup and eliminates the need to add cream or other thickening ingredients. Salsa, pesto, sour cream, and yogurt make nice additions, swirled in or dolloped on, to dress up a soup.

The base of most soups is the broth, and while homemade is, of course, best, there are some good canned chicken, beef, and vegetable broths on the market. The only exceptions are Chicken Noodle Soup and Chicken Soup with Matzoh Balls, which I think are best made from scratch with a whole chicken.

Some regional favorites you'll find here are New England Clam Chowder, U.S. Senate Bean Soup, Tortilla Soup with Roasted Vegetables, Wisconsin Cheddar Cheese Soup, and Charleston She-Crab Soup. If you are not familiar with some of these, then give one a try. You're in for one delicious bowl of soup.

## 25    COLD AVOCADO SOUP

*Prep: 5 minutes    Cook: none    Chill: 2 hours    Serves: 4*

Make this refreshing soup ahead so it can be chilled until ice cold. Fresh tomato salsa makes a perfect, pretty garnish.

3  ripe avocados, halved and
    pitted
¼  cup fresh lemon juice
2  cups chicken broth
¾  teaspoon chili powder
1  teaspoon salt

½  teaspoon ground cumin
¼  cup sour cream
½  cup Fresh Tomato Salsa
    (page 16) or 1 large plum
    tomato, seeded and diced

**1.** Scoop avocados from skin with a spoon into a food processor. Add lemon juice and puree until smooth. With machine on, add 1 cup chicken broth. Process until smooth. Add chili powder, salt, and cumin and process to blend. Pour into a medium bowl.

**2.** Whisk in remaining chicken broth and ½ cup water. If too thick, stir in ¼ cup more water. Cover tightly and refrigerate until cold, at least 2 hours.

**3.** To serve, ladle soup into bowls. Top each bowl with 1 tablespoon sour cream and 2 tablespoons salsa.

## 26    BEEF AND BARLEY SOUP WITH SQUASH AND SWISS CHARD

*Prep: 25 minutes    Cook: 2 hours 3½ minutes    Serves: 8 to 10*

2  tablespoons olive oil
1  pound lean beef chuck, cut
    into ½-inch pieces
4  garlic cloves, minced
1  teaspoon dried thyme
1  bay leaf
½  teaspoon salt
½  teaspoon freshly ground
    pepper
2  (13¾-ounce) cans beef broth
1  large onion, chopped
¾  cup pearl barley, rinsed

1  (28-ounce) can diced
    tomatoes in juice
½  medium butternut squash,
    peeled, seeded, and cut
    into ½-inch cubes
1  (15-ounce) can chickpeas,
    rinsed and drained
½  bunch of Swiss chard,
    coarsely chopped
¾  teaspoon curry powder
¼  teaspoon ground cinnamon

**1.** In a large soup pot, heat 2 teaspoons oil over medium-high heat. Add half of beef and cook, stirring, until well browned, about 3 minutes. Remove beef to a plate and repeat with 2 teaspoons oil and remaining beef. Return beef to pot. Add garlic, thyme, bay leaf, salt, pepper, beef broth, and 4 cups water. Bring to a boil, reduce heat to medium-low, cover, and simmer 1 hour.

**2.** Skim off any fat from surface of broth. Add onion, barley, and tomatoes with their juices to pot. Bring to a boil. Reduce heat and simmer, covered, 30 minutes.

**3.** Add squash and chickpeas to pot. Simmer, uncovered, 15 minutes. Stir in Swiss chard. Simmer until chard is tender, about 12 minutes.

**4.** In a small skillet, heat remaining oil over medium-low heat. Add curry powder and cinnamon. Cook, stirring constantly, until fragrant, about 30 seconds. Stir into soup. Remove and discard bay leaf and serve.

---

## 27  U.S. SENATE BEAN SOUP

*Prep: 10 minutes    Soak: overnight    Cook: 2 hours    Serves: 8 to 10*

This was a family recipe brought to the Senate restaurant in Washington, D.C., by Senator Henry Cabot Lodge.

| | |
|---|---|
| 1 **pound navy beans, rinsed and picked over** | 2 **medium celery ribs, finely chopped** |
| 2 **smoked ham hocks** | 5 **medium carrots, peeled and finely chopped** |
| 1 **bay leaf** | |
| 5 **garlic cloves, minced** | 2 **tablespoons chopped flat-leaf parsley** |
| 2 **medium baking potatoes, peeled and diced** | 1¼ **teaspoons salt** |
| 2 **medium onions, finely chopped** | ¼ **teaspoon freshly ground pepper** |

**1.** Soak beans overnight covered by at least 2 inches cold water. If there's not enough time, place in a soup pot, cover with cold water, bring to a boil, remove from heat, and let stand 1 hour.

**2.** Drain beans. Return to pot. Add 2 quarts cold water, ham hocks, bay leaf, and garlic. Bring to a boil and add potatoes. Cover and simmer 1 hour.

**3.** Stir in onions, celery, and carrots. Simmer, covered, 30 minutes. Uncover and simmer, stirring occasionally, 30 minutes longer, or until beans are soft.

**4.** Remove ham hocks to a plate to cool. Remove 2 cups soup to a small bowl. Mash with a potato masher until smooth. Stir back into pot. When hocks are cool enough to handle, remove meat and finely chop. Return meat to pot. Stir in parsley, 1 teaspoon salt, and pepper. Reheat if necessary and taste for salt, adding remaining ¼ teaspoon if needed. Remove and discard bay leaf before serving.

## 28   SPEEDY BLACK BEAN SOUP WITH CILANTRO-LIME CREAM

*Prep: 10 minutes    Cook: 21 to 23 minutes    Serves: 6*

Made with canned beans, this is a fast version of the traditional soup. Instead of a lemon slice garnish, it's served with a drizzle of lime and cilantro-flavored sour cream.

4  slices of bacon, chopped
1  medium onion, finely
   chopped
2  garlic cloves, crushed
   through a press
1  teaspoon ground cumin
3  (15-ounce) cans black beans,
   rinsed and drained
1  (14½-ounce) can diced
   tomatoes in juice

1  (13¾-ounce) can chicken
   broth
¼  cup sour cream
4  teaspoons lime juice
1 ` tablespoon minced cilantro
½  teaspoon jalapeño Tabasco
   sauce

1.  In a large soup pot, combine bacon, onion, and garlic. Cook over medium heat, stirring occasionally, until onion is golden, 10 to 12 minutes. Drain off any fat. Stir in cumin and cook 1 minute.

2.  Add beans, tomatoes with their juices, and chicken broth. Bring to a boil. Cover, reduce heat to medium-low, and simmer 10 minutes. Uncover and let cool 10 minutes.

3.  Puree 2 cups soup in a blender or food processor. Stir back into pot. Stir in ½ cup water if soup is too thick. Keep hot over low heat.

4.  In a small bowl, stir together sour cream, lime juice, cilantro, and jalapeño sauce. Serve soup in bowls, drizzled with cilantro-lime cream.

## 29   CHICKEN SOUP WITH MATZOH BALLS

*Prep: 5 minutes    Cook: 35 minutes    Chill: 4 hours    Serves: 6*

Many ethnic specialties have entered the American melting pot kitchen repertoire. These exceptionally light matzoh balls are the creation of California chef and friend Joseph Costanzo. Although Joe is Italian, he makes a mean matzoh ball.

4  eggs
2½  quarts homemade chicken
   broth
¾  teaspoon salt
¼  teaspoon freshly ground
   pepper

⅔  cup matzoh meal
2  tablespoons chopped
   parsley

1.  In a small bowl, beat eggs, 2 tablespoons broth, salt, and pepper with a fork. Gradually beat in matzoh meal, beating until blended and smooth. Cover and refrigerate 4 hours or overnight.

**2.** Bring a large pot of generously salted water to a boil. Reduce heat so water just simmers. Shape matzoh balls with wet hands by rounded teaspoonfuls, adding to simmering water as they're shaped, making 18 balls. Mixture will be very soft. Rinse hands frequently while shaping. Cover and simmer gently 30 minutes, without lifting cover.

**3.** Meanwhile, in a large soup pot, bring remaining chicken broth to a boil. Reduce heat to low. With a slotted spoon, transfer matzoh balls to chicken soup. Simmer 5 minutes. Serve piping hot, garnished with parsley.

---

## 30   CHICKEN NOODLE SOUP
*Prep: 15 minutes    Cook: 2 hours 41 minutes to*
*2 hours 43 minutes    Chill: overnight    Serves: 6*

Onion skins were used as a natural dye at one time, and leaving the skin on the onions is an old trick for giving the soup a golden color.

| | |
|---|---|
| 1  (4- to 5-pound) chicken, quartered | 3  medium carrots, peeled and cut into 1-inch pieces |
| 1  pound chicken wings | 12  parsley sprigs |
| 4  garlic cloves, smashed with a knife | 1½  to 2 teaspoons salt |
| 2  medium onions, peel scrubbed and left on, halved | ½  teaspoon whole black peppercorns |
| 3  medium celery ribs, cut into 1-inch pieces | 3  cups medium egg noodles |
| | 2  tablespoons chopped parsley |

**1.** Rinse and remove any excess fat. In a large soup pot, combine chicken and chicken wings. Add 3 quarts cold water. Bring to a boil, reduce heat to a gentle simmer, and skim off foam as it rises to surface. Add garlic, onions, celery, 2 carrots, parsley sprigs, 1½ teaspoons salt, and pepper. Reduce heat to low, partially cover, and cook 2½ hours. Strain soup into a colander set over a large bowl. Remove chicken to a plate. Cover broth and chicken and refrigerate separately overnight.

**2.** Remove and discard fat from surface of broth. Place broth in a large soup pot. Thinly slice remaining carrot and add to broth. Bring to a boil, reduce heat to medium-low, and cook until carrot is tender, about 5 minutes. Taste broth and add remaining salt if necessary. Remove chicken from bones and cut enough small pieces to make 2 cups; add to broth. Reserve remaining chicken for another use, such as chicken salad.

**3.** While broth heats, bring a medium pot of salted water to a boil. Add noodles and cook until just tender, about 5 minutes. Drain and rinse briefly under running water.

**4.** Add noodles to soup and simmer 1 to 2 minutes. Ladle into bowls, sprinkle with chopped parsley, and serve.

## 31    COUNTRY CORN CHOWDER
*Prep: 15 minutes    Cook: 20 to 22 minutes    Serves: 6*

This simple soup lets the flavor of fresh corn shine through. The corn-cobs are boiled in the soup base for extra flavor and then removed.

6    ears of corn
3    tablespoons butter
1    medium onion, finely
     chopped
2    cups chicken broth
3    large all-purpose potatoes
     (1½ pounds), peeled and
     cut into ¾-inch cubes

1    teaspoon minced fresh
     thyme or ½ teaspoon
     dried
¾    teaspoon salt
⅛    teaspoon pepper
2    cups milk

1. Husk corn. With a large sharp knife, cut kernels off cobs. Set corn kernels and cobs aside separately.

2. In a large Dutch oven, melt butter over medium heat. Add onion and cook, stirring occasionally, until golden, about 5 minutes. Add chicken broth, potatoes, 1 cup water, and corncobs. Bring to a boil. Reduce heat to medium-low, cover, and simmer about 10 minutes, or until potatoes are tender.

3. Remove corncobs. Add corn kernels, thyme, salt, and pepper to pot. Return to a simmer. Cover and cook 5 to 7 minutes, or until corn is tender. Remove from heat.

4. Remove 1½ cups soup and puree in a blender or food processor until smooth. Stir back into pot. Stir in milk. Cook over low heat just until hot; do not boil. Serve chowder hot.

## 32    CHARLESTON SHE-CRAB SOUP
*Prep: 10 minutes    Cook: 16 minutes    Serves: 4*

This specialty of Charleston, South Carolina, usually is made with the roe from female crabs. In lieu of roe, hard-cooked egg yolks are substituted.

4    tablespoons butter, at room
     temperature
¼    cup minced onion
2    cups milk
1    cup light cream
2    tablespoons medium-dry
     sherry
½    teaspoon salt

¼    teaspoon freshly ground
     pepper
⅛    teaspoon cayenne
2    tablespoons flour
½    pound fresh lump crabmeat,
     picked over
2    hard-cooked egg yolks
1    tablespoon chopped parsley

1. In a large saucepan, melt 2 tablespoons butter over medium heat. Add onion and cook, stirring occasionally, until softened, about 3 minutes. Stir in milk, cream, sherry, salt, pepper, and cayenne. Cook over low heat until hot, about 3 minutes.

**2.** In a small bowl, stir together remaining 2 tablespoons butter and flour until smooth. Gradually whisk into milk mixture until blended. Stir in crab. Bring to a gentle simmer. Simmer 10 minutes, stirring occasionally. Ladle into bowls and sieve egg yolks over each to garnish. Sprinkle with parsley.

---

## 33  NEW ENGLAND CLAM CHOWDER
*Prep: 20 minutes    Cook: 32 to 38 minutes    Serves: 6*

3 dozen littleneck or
  cherrystone clams,
  scrubbed
1 cup clam juice
¼ pound sliced bacon, cut into
  ¼-inch dice
1 medium onion, finely
  chopped
4 large all-purpose potatoes,
  peeled and cut into
  ½-inch dice

¼ teaspoon freshly ground
  pepper
2 cups milk
½ cup light cream
1 tablespoon flour
1 tablespoon butter

**1.** Place clams and clam juice in a large soup pot. Bring to a boil over high heat. Cover and cook just until clams begin to open, 5 to 8 minutes. Remove clams as they just open to a large bowl. Discard any clams that do not open. Strain broth through a sieve lined with cheesecloth and reserve.

**2.** Let clams cool. Pry open shells and remove clams to a small bowl; discard shells. Finely chop clams and return to bowl.

**3.** In soup pot, cook bacon over medium heat until crisp, about 5 minutes. With a slotted spoon, remove bacon to a small bowl. Pour off all but 2 table-spoons drippings in pan. Add onion and cook, stirring occasionally, until softened, 3 to 5 minutes. Add potatoes, reserved clam broth, and 1 cup water. Bring to a boil, reduce heat to medium-low, cover, and simmer until potatoes are tender, about 15 minutes. With a slotted spoon, remove 1 cup potatoes to a small bowl and mash until smooth. Stir back into pot.

**4.** Stir in pepper and milk. In a small bowl, whisk light cream and flour. Stir into pot. Bring to a boil, stirring, until slightly thickened, 2 to 3 minutes. Reduce heat to low. Add clams and butter, cook to heat through, about 2 minutes. Serve garnished with bacon.

# 34   GOLDEN FISH CHOWDER
*Prep: 15 minutes    Cook: 26 to 30 minutes    Serves: 6 to 8*

Some New Englanders think clam and fish chowders should *not* be served after being made, that they must mellow overnight in the refrigerator. After experimenting, I agree. This chowder is good, but definitely better if allowed to sit overnight. When reheating the soup next day, do it gently. Finnan haddie is Scottish for smoked haddock. Look for the product at fish markets.

3 tablespoons butter
1 medium onion, chopped
1 leek (white and tender green), halved lengthwise, rinsed, and thinly sliced
1 large carrot, peeled and shredded
1 medium celery rib, finely chopped
3 large Yukon Gold or all-purpose potatoes, peeled and cut into ¾-inch cubes
¾ teaspoon chopped fresh thyme or ½ teaspoon dried

1 teaspoon salt
¼ teaspoon freshly ground pepper
1½ cups milk
1½ pounds cod, haddock, halibut, or other firm white skinless, boneless fish fillets, cut into 1½-inch pieces
¼ pound finnan haddie, finely chopped

**1.** In a large soup pot, melt butter over medium heat. Add onion, leek, carrot, and celery. Cook, stirring occasionally, until onion begins to turn golden, 8 to 10 minutes. Add potatoes, thyme, ½ teaspoon salt, pepper, and 3 cups water. Bring to a boil, reduce heat to medium-low, cover, and simmer until potatoes are tender, 10 to 12 minutes.

**2.** Remove pot from heat. With a slotted spoon, remove and measure out 1 cup potatoes. Place in a small bowl and mash with a potato masher until smooth. Whisk in ½ cup milk.

**3.** Add fresh fish to pot and stir gently. Return pot to heat and simmer, covered, until fish is just cooked through, about 5 minutes. Add potato mixture, remaining milk, finnan haddie, and remaining salt. Reduce heat to low, cover, and cook until hot, about 3 minutes. Do not let boil.

# 35    OYSTER STEW
*Prep: 15 minutes    Cook: 9 to 10 minutes    Serves: 4*

Smaller oysters are best for this stew. If you like your soup richer, reduce the milk to 2½ cups and add ½ cup heavy cream.

3  cups milk
¼  teaspoon salt
¼  teaspoon freshly ground
   pepper
   Pinch of cayenne
1½ pints freshly shucked
   oysters, with their liquor

2  tablespoons butter, cut into
   4 pieces
   Oyster crackers, as
   accompaniment

1. In a medium saucepan, combine milk, salt, pepper, and cayenne. Place over medium-low heat and cook until very hot and steaming but not boiling, about 5 minutes.

2. In a medium saucepan, place oysters and liquor. Cook over medium-low heat until liquid is hot and edges of oysters begin to curl, 4 to 5 minutes. Pour into milk.

3. Taste and add additional salt if necessary. Ladle into warmed soup bowls. Add a lump of butter to each bowl and serve while hot, with oyster crackers alongside.

---

# 36    SUMMER GAZPACHO
*Prep: 15 minutes    Cook: none    Chill: 2 hours    Serves: 4 to 6*

4  ripe medium tomatoes
   (1½ pounds), halved
   crosswise and seeded
1  medium cucumber, peeled,
   halved, and seeded
3  cups tomato juice
1  garlic clove, minced
1  medium green bell pepper,
   cut into ½-inch dice
1  medium yellow bell pepper,
   cut into ½-inch dice

¼  cup diced red onion
¼  cup extra-virgin olive oil
3  tablespoons red wine
   vinegar
½  teaspoon salt
⅛  teaspoon cayenne
   Chopped cilantro or parsley,
   for garnish

1. In a blender, puree 1½ tomatoes, ¼ cucumber, 1 cup tomato juice, and garlic until smooth. Pour into a large bowl.

2. Finely dice remaining tomatoes and cucumber. Add tomatoes, cucumber, bell peppers, red onion, olive oil, vinegar, salt, cayenne and remaining tomato juice to bowl. Stir until blended.

3. Cover and refrigerate at least 2 hours, or until cold. Serve soup garnished with chopped cilantro.

## 37 LENTIL SOUP WITH SUN-DRIED TOMATOES AND LEMON

*Prep: 20 minutes    Cook: 66 to 67 minutes    Serves: 6 to 8*

This soup is a good choice on a cold fall day. Unlike other dried beans, lentils can be cooked quickly without presoaking. Sun-dried tomatoes, once only imported from Italy, are now produced in California. The easiest way to chop dry-packed tomatoes is to cut them into small pieces with scissors.

2  tablespoons olive oil
4  garlic cloves, crushed
   through a press
1  large onion, chopped
2  large celery ribs, chopped
2  large carrots, peeled and
   diced
1  pound lentils, rinsed and
   picked over

4  cups chicken broth
½  cup dry-packed sun-dried
   tomatoes, finely chopped
1  teaspoon dried thyme
½  teaspoon crushed hot red
   pepper
½  teaspoon salt
1  to 2 tablespoons lemon juice

**1.** In a soup pot, heat oil over medium heat. Add garlic and cook, stirring constantly, until golden but not brown, 1 to 2 minutes. Stir in onion, celery, and carrots. Cook, stirring occasionally, until vegetables soften, about 5 minutes.

**2.** Add lentils, chicken broth, dried tomatoes, thyme, hot pepper, and 4 cups water. Bring to a boil. Reduce heat to medium-low, cover, and simmer 1 hour, or until lentils are tender.

**3.** Puree 1 cup soup in a blender or food processor. Stir back into pot. Stir in salt and lemon juice to taste.

## 38 CURRIED SPLIT PEA SOUP WITH SWEET POTATOES

*Prep: 15 minutes    Cook: 1 hour 40 to 55 minutes    Serves: 6 to 8*

1  (1-pound) bag green or
   yellow split peas
3  smoked ham hocks
4  garlic cloves, minced
1  bay leaf
2  medium onions, chopped
1  tablespoon butter
2  large carrots, peeled and cut
   into ½-inch dice

1  small sweet potato or yam,
   peeled and cut into
   ½-inch dice
2  medium celery ribs, cut into
   ½-inch dice
1  teaspoon curry powder
¾  teaspoon salt
¼  teaspoon freshly ground
   pepper

**1.** Pick over peas and rinse in a colander; place in a large soup pot. Add ham hocks, garlic, bay leaf, 1 onion, and 2 quarts water. Bring to a boil, reduce heat to medium-low, cover, and simmer 1 hour.

**2.** In a medium skillet, melt butter over medium heat. Add remaining onion, carrots, sweet potato, celery, curry powder, salt, and pepper. Cook, stirring occasionally, until vegetables soften, about 10 minutes.

**3.** Stir vegetables into soup. Simmer, uncovered, 30 to 45 minutes, or until peas fall apart. Stir frequently as soup thickens to prevent sticking. Remove ham hocks. Cut meat off bone and finely chop. Stir meat into soup. Discard bay leaf. Season with additional salt to taste.

---

## 39 CREAM OF MUSHROOM SOUP
*Prep: 15 minutes    Soak: 30 minutes    Cook: 37 to 38 minutes*
*Serves: 6*

This soup is full of mushroom flavor from a combination of dried and fresh mushrooms. You can use dried imported or Polish mushrooms in place of the porcini to achieve a similar effect at a lower cost.

½ **ounce dried porcini mushrooms**
2 **cups boiling water**
3 **tablespoons butter**
3 **shallots, minced**
2 **garlic cloves, minced**
½ **pound shiitake mushrooms, stemmed, caps sliced**
½ **pound cremini mushrooms, sliced**

½ **pound white button mushrooms, sliced**
2 **cups chicken broth**
2 **tablespoons dry sherry**
1 **cup light cream**
1 **teaspoon salt**
¼ **teaspoon freshly ground pepper**
2 **tablespoons chopped parsley**

**1.** Place porcini mushrooms in a small bowl, pour on boiling water, and soak 30 minutes. Strain, reserving soaking liquid. Rinse mushrooms and finely chop.

**2.** In a soup pot, heat 2 tablespoons butter over medium heat. Add shallots and 1 garlic clove. Cook, stirring occasionally, until softened, about 3 minutes. Set aside ½ cup each sliced shiitakes, cremini, and button mushrooms for garnish. Add remaining sliced mushrooms and chopped dried mushrooms to pot and cook until softened, about 5 minutes. Add chicken broth, mushroom soaking liquid, and sherry. Bring to a boil, reduce heat to medium-low, cover, and simmer 20 minutes.

**3.** Remove ½ cup cooked mushrooms with a slotted spoon and set aside. Puree soup in batches in a blender or food processor until smooth. Pour mushroom puree back into pot. Finely chop reserved cooked mushrooms and return to pot. Stir in cream, salt, and pepper. Set over low heat to heat through, about 5 minutes.

**4.** Meanwhile, in a medium skillet, melt remaining 1 tablespoon butter over medium-high heat. Add reserved uncooked mushrooms and remaining garlic and cook until softened, 4 to 5 minutes. Remove from heat and stir in parsley. To serve, ladle soup into bowls and garnish with parsleyed mushrooms.

## 40   WISCONSIN CHEDDAR CHEESE SOUP
*Prep: 15 minutes    Cook: 27 to 29 minutes    Serves: 8*

3 tablespoons butter
1 large carrot, peeled and shredded
1 leek (white and tender green), halved lengthwise, sliced, and rinsed
1 medium onion, chopped
¼ cup flour
3 cups chicken broth
1 (12-ounce) bottle beer
2 large red potatoes, peeled and cut into ½-inch dice

½ cup heavy cream
2 cups shredded sharp Cheddar cheese
2 teaspoons Dijon mustard
¼ teaspoon salt
¼ teaspoon freshly ground pepper
⅛ teaspoon cayenne
Shredded Cheddar cheese and chopped parsley, for garnish

**1.** In a large soup pot, melt butter over medium heat. Add carrot, leek, and onion. Cook, stirring occasionally, until onion is golden, 8 to 10 minutes. Add flour; cook, stirring constantly, 1 minute. Stir in broth, beer, and 1 cup water. Add potatoes. Bring to a boil, reduce heat, and simmer, stirring occasionally, until potatoes are tender, about 15 minutes.

**2.** Stir in cream. Gradually stir in cheese, stirring until melted. Stir in mustard, salt, pepper, and cayenne until blended. Cover and cook until hot, about 3 minutes. Do not let boil. Serve garnished with cheese and parsley.

---

## 41   BUTTERNUT SQUASH AND PEANUT SOUP
*Prep: 15 minutes    Cook: 1 hour 22 minutes    Serves: 8*

1 large butternut squash (3 pounds), halved lengthwise and seeded
1 teaspoon salt
¼ teaspoon freshly ground pepper
2 tablespoons butter
1 medium onion, chopped
1 medium red bell pepper, cut into ½-inch dice

2 jalapeño peppers, seeded and minced
4 cups chicken broth
¼ cup creamy peanut butter
⅔ cup half-and-half
2 tablespoons fresh lime juice
Thinly sliced scallions and chopped peanuts, for garnish

**1.** Preheat oven to 350°F. Line a jelly-roll pan with aluminum foil. Season cut side of squash with ¼ teaspoon salt and ⅛ teaspoon pepper. Place cut side down on prepared pan. Bake 1 hour, or until soft. Turn halves cut side up and set aside until cool enough to handle. Scoop pulp into a bowl, stirring to break up.

**2.** In a soup pot, melt butter over medium-low heat. Add onion and cook, stirring frequently, until golden brown, about 10 minutes. Add squash, bell pepper, jalapeños, and chicken broth. Bring to a boil. Cover, reduce heat to medium-low and cook 10 minutes, stirring occasionally to break up squash.

**3.** Remove 1 cup soup and set aside. Puree remaining soup in a food processor, in batches if necessary, until smooth; return to pot. Add reserved soup, peanut butter, half-and-half, and remaining ¾ teaspoon salt and ⅛ teaspoon pepper. Cook over low heat, stirring, until peanut butter melts, about 2 minutes. Stir in lime juice. Serve hot, garnished with scallions and peanuts.

---

## 42    GARDEN VEGETABLE SOUP
*Prep: 25 minutes    Cook: 1 hour 13 minutes    Serves: 8 to 10*

This ingredient list may look long, but after you have chopped all the vegetables, the work is done. This is even better the next day. It can be dressed up by topping each bowl with a small spoonful of pesto.

| | |
|---|---|
| 2  tablespoons olive oil | ½  pound green beans, cut into |
| 1  large onion, chopped | ½-inch pieces |
| 2  leeks (white and tender | 3  cups shredded cabbage |
|    green), halved | 1  (14½-ounce) can diced |
|    lengthwise, thinly sliced, |    tomatoes in juice |
|    and rinsed | 5  cups chicken broth |
| 1  large celery rib, chopped | ¾  teaspoon salt |
| 2  garlic cloves, minced | ½  teaspoon freshly ground |
| 3  large carrots, peeled, halved |    pepper |
|    lengthwise, and sliced | 2  large zucchini, cut into |
| 3  medium all-purpose | ½-inch dice |
|    potatoes, peeled and | 2  cups shredded spinach |
|    diced | |

**1.** In a large nonreactive soup pot, heat oil over medium heat. Add onion, leeks, and celery. Cook, stirring occasionally, until vegetables are soft, about 5 minutes. Add garlic and cook 3 minutes, stirring occasionally.

**2.** Add carrots, potatoes, green beans, cabbage, tomatoes with their juices, chicken broth, salt, pepper, and 4 cups water. Bring to a boil. Reduce heat to medium-low and simmer, partially covered, 45 minutes.

**3.** Stir in zucchini and simmer 15 minutes. Remove 2 cups soup and puree in a blender or food processor until smooth. Stir back into pot. Stir in spinach and simmer 5 minutes. Serve hot.

## 43    MINNESOTA WILD RICE SOUP
*Prep: 15 minutes    Cook: 26 to 28 minutes    Serves: 6*

2    tablespoons olive oil
1    large onion, chopped
2    medium celery ribs, cut into
     ¼-inch dice
1    large carrot, peeled and cut
     into ¼-inch dice
½    pound fresh shiitake
     mushrooms, stems
     removed, caps sliced
1    apple, peeled, cored, and
     cut into ¼-inch dice
2    (13¾-ounce) cans chicken
     broth

2    cups cooked wild rice
½    cup frozen corn kernels
½    teaspoon dried thyme
1½   cups half-and-half
½    teaspoon salt
¼    teaspoon freshly ground
     pepper
¼    cup chopped toasted
     hazelnuts
1    tablespoon chopped parsley

**1.** In a large soup pot, heat oil over medium heat. Add onion, celery, carrot, shiitake mushrooms, and apple. Cover and cook, stirring occasionally, until softened, 6 to 8 minutes.

**2.** Add chicken broth, wild rice, corn, and thyme. Bring to a simmer. Cover and simmer 15 minutes.

**3.** Stir in half-and-half, salt, and pepper. Cook until hot, about 5 minutes. Ladle into bowls and garnish with hazelnuts and parsley.

## 44    CREAM OF TOMATO SOUP
*Prep: 15 minutes    Cook: 45 minutes    Serves: 4*

This soup pairs well with another classic—grilled cheese sandwiches—for a perfect winter lunch.

2    tablespoons olive oil
1    small onion, finely chopped
1    small celery rib, finely
     chopped
1    small carrot, peeled and
     grated
2    garlic cloves, minced
1    (28-ounce) can diced
     tomatoes in juice

1    (13¾-ounce) can chicken
     broth
1    teaspoon sugar
¼    teaspoon salt
⅛    teaspoon freshly ground
     pepper
½    cup heavy cream
⅛    teaspoon cayenne

**1.** In a large nonreactive saucepan, heat oil over medium-low heat. Add onion, celery, carrot, and garlic. Cover and cook, stirring once, 10 minutes, or until vegetables are soft. Stir in tomatoes with their juices, chicken broth, sugar, salt, and pepper. Bring to a boil, reduce heat to medium-low, and simmer, covered, 25 minutes.

**2.** In a small saucepan, bring cream and cayenne to a boil. Reduce heat to medium-low and simmer 10 minutes, or until cream is reduced to about ⅓ cup.

**3.** Set aside 1 cup soup. Puree remaining soup in batches in a blender or food processor until completely smooth. Return to pot. Stir in reserved soup and cream. Reheat, if necessary, but do not let boil.

---

## 45 TORTILLA SOUP WITH ROASTED VEGETABLES

*Prep: 15 minutes    Cook: 46 to 51 minutes    Serves: 4*

This Mexican classic is a light, intensely flavored soup, made more so by roasting the vegetables.

¼ cup olive oil
1 teaspoon chili powder
1 teaspoon ground cumin
½ teaspoon dried oregano
8 ripe plum tomatoes, sliced
   ¼ inch thick
1 medium onion, thinly sliced
4 garlic cloves, crushed
   through a press
2 jalapeño peppers, seeded
   and minced

2 (13¾-ounce) cans chicken
   broth
¼ teaspoon salt
6 corn tortillas, halved and cut
   crosswise into thin strips
Diced avocado, chopped
   cilantro, grated Monterey
   Jack cheese, and lime
   wedges, as
   accompaniment

**1.** Preheat oven to 450°F. In a small bowl, combine 2 tablespoons oil with chili powder, cumin, and oregano. Stir until blended. Spread tomatoes and onion in a single layer on a greased jelly-roll pan. Brush evenly with seasoned oil.

**2.** Bake 25 to 30 minutes, or until tomatoes are very soft and onion begin to brown in spots. Scrape into a food processor or blender and puree until very smooth. Reduce oven temperature to 400°F.

**3.** In a large nonreactive Dutch oven, heat 1 tablespoon oil over medium heat. Add garlic and jalapeños. Cook, stirring constantly, until garlic is golden but not brown, about 1 minute. Add broth, ½ cup water, and salt. Strain tomato-onion puree through a sieve into pot, stirring to press through all pulp, discarding skins and seeds. Bring to a boil, reduce heat to medium-low, cover, and simmer 10 minutes.

**4.** Meanwhile, on a large baking sheet, toss tortilla strips with remaining 1 tablespoon oil. Spread out in a single layer. Bake 10 minutes, stirring once, or until golden brown and crisp.

**5.** To serve, ladle hot soup into bowls. Garnish with tortilla strips, avocado, cilantro, and Monterey Jack cheese. Pass lime wedges to squeeze into soup.

## 46    SAUSAGE AND KALE SOUP
*Prep: 15 minutes    Cook: 1 hour 9 to 11 minutes    Serves: 8*

This soup was brought to this country by Portuguese fishermen who settled in the Fall River and New Bedford areas of Massachusetts. If you can't find chorizo sausage, substitute pepperoni.

1    tablespoon olive oil
½    pound chorizo sausage,
       casing removed, chopped
1    medium onion, chopped
3    garlic cloves, minced
4    medium carrots, peeled and
       thinly sliced
2    large red potatoes (1 pound),
       peeled and cut into 1-inch
       cubes
2    (13¾-ounce) cans reduced-
       sodium chicken broth

¼    teaspoon crushed hot red
       pepper
1    pound kale, tough stems
       removed, cut into thin
       strips
1    (15-ounce) can kidney
       beans, rinsed and
       drained
1½  cups tomato juice

**1.** In a large nonreactive Dutch oven, heat oil over medium heat. Add chorizo and cook, stirring frequently, 5 minutes. Add onion and cook until softened, 3 to 5 minutes. Stir in garlic and cook 1 minute. Add carrots, potatoes, chicken broth, hot pepper, and 2½ cups water. Bring to a boil. Stir in kale and kidney beans. Return to a boil. Reduce heat to medium-low, cover, and simmer 45 minutes.

**2.** Stir in tomato juice and return to a boil. Reduce heat and simmer, covered, 15 minutes.

*Chapter 3*

# Substantial Salads and Sides

Salads are one of my favorite foods because they have lots of crunch and textures and don't take a long time to prepare. There was a time in America when a salad consisted of a wedge of lettuce with a thick salad dressing. Those times have changed. A dazzling variety of lettuces are available these days: iceberg, romaine, Boston, radicchio, arugula, chicory, green leaf, red leaf, Belgian endive, and mesclun—my favorite—a mix of baby greens. Salads have become so popular, especially because of our concerns about healthier eating, that often a salad becomes the whole meal. Classic Cobb Salad or Chicken Taco Salad with Pinto Beans make great dinner salads.

Many grocery stores have salad bars, and even if you don't want to get your salad there, you can at least purchase all kinds of cut-up vegetables to use in recipes to save time. Supermarkets also now carry pre-cut lettuces and vegetables in bags, already rinsed, which are great time-savers for preparing salads. These are good, too, if you don't want to buy a whole head of cabbage or a bunch of broccoli.

This chapter also includes those all-American favorites often referred to on diner menus as "sides." Many of these are simply salads in another form and include All-American Potato Salad, My Favorite Macaroni Salad, Creamy Coleslaw, Five-Bean Salad, and even homemade Bread & Butter Pickles. I wouldn't think of having a picnic or barbecue without them. All these sides are served cool or at room temperature. For hot accompaniments, such as baked beans and stuffings, look in Chapter 10, "Vegetables, Beans, and Grains," on pages 181 to 203.

# 47   CHEF'S SALAD
*Prep: 15 minutes    Cook: none    Serves: 4*

Chef's salad is a classic, and here you'll find the traditional roast beef, turkey, and cheese, but I've omitted the usual ham and added a new, Thai-inspired twist with mango, peanuts, cilantro, and mint. If you're a traditionalist, simply omit those ingredients and substitute one of the dressings on pages 41 to 44 for the Lime-Pepper Dressing that follows.

10  cups packed torn leaf
    lettuce, romaine, or
    mesclun
    Lime-Pepper Dressing
    (recipe follows)
½  pound cooked roast beef,
    cut into thin strips
½  pound cooked turkey or
    chicken, cut into thin
    strips
¼  pound Monterey Jack
    cheese, cut into thin strips
1  medium cucumber, peeled,
    seeded, and cut into thin
    strips

1  small red bell pepper, thinly
    sliced
1  small ripe mango, peeled,
    pitted, and cut into thin
    strips
2  scallions, cut into thin strips
⅓  cup unsalted roasted
    peanuts, chopped
¼  cup packed cilantro leaves
¼  cup packed mint leaves,
    shredded

**1.** Place lettuce in 4 large individual salad bowls or on dinner plates. Stir dressing and drizzle 1 tablespoon over each bed of lettuce.

**2.** Arrange beef, turkey, cheese, cucumber, bell pepper, mango, and scallions over lettuce. Sprinkle on peanuts, cilantro, and mint. Pass remaining dressing separately.

# 48   LIME-PEPPER DRESSING
*Prep: 5 minutes    Cook: none    Makes: about ½ cup*

¼  cup olive oil
2  tablespoons fresh lime juice
1  tablespoon rice vinegar
1  teaspoon sugar
½  teaspoon grated lime zest

½  teaspoon salt
¼  teaspoon crushed hot red
    pepper
¼  teaspoon freshly ground
    black pepper

In a small bowl, combine oil, lime juice, vinegar, sugar, lime zest, salt, hot pepper, and black pepper. Whisk until blended.

# 49 GOAT CHEESE AND MESCLUN SALAD WITH ROASTED GARLIC VINAIGRETTE

*Prep: 15 minutes    Cook: 40 to 42 minutes    Serves: 4*

Here's another California classic that's swept across the country. Serve as a first course or as a light lunch. Mesclun, mixed baby lettuce leaves, is sold in many supermarkets, often labeled as field greens.

| | |
|---|---|
| 5 large garlic cloves, unpeeled | 1 (8-ounce) log of goat cheese |
| ⅓ cup olive oil | ½ cup fresh bread crumbs |
| ¼ cup fresh orange juice | 12 cups mesclun salad greens |
| 1 tablespoon minced sun-dried tomatoes | 1 ripe medium tomato, seeded and diced |
| 1 tablespoon balsamic vinegar | 6 kalamata olives, pitted and finely chopped |
| 1 teaspoon Dijon mustard | 1 tablespoon shredded fresh basil |
| ¼ teaspoon salt | |
| ¼ teaspoon freshly ground pepper | |

**1.** Preheat oven to 450°F. Wrap garlic cloves in foil and bake 30 minutes, or until soft. Unwrap and let cool.

**2.** Squeeze garlic pulp into a blender. Add ¼ cup of olive oil, orange juice, sun-dried tomatoes, vinegar, mustard, salt, and pepper. Blend until smooth. Set vinaigrette aside.

**3.** Increase oven temperature to 475°F. Cut goat cheese crosswise into 4 pieces and brush each piece with remaining oil. Place bread crumbs in a pie plate. Roll cheese in crumbs to coat completely. Freeze cheese 10 minutes. Place on a baking sheet.

**4.** Bake 10 to 12 minutes, or until cheese is hot and crumbs are golden.

**5.** In large bowl, toss salad greens with ⅓ cup of vinaigrette. Place on 4 plates. Place baked goat cheese in center of each. Sprinkle fresh tomato, olives, and basil over salads. Serve while cheese is hot. Pass remaining vinaigrette on the side.

# 50    EASY HOMEMADE KETCHUP
*Prep: 10 minutes    Cook: 1 hour    Makes: about 3½ cups*

Canned tomato puree and tomato paste make this a really simple recipe you can enjoy year-round. Small jars decorated with squares of printed cloth and tied with ribbon make a very nice gift to give, especially at holiday time.

| | |
|---|---|
| 1 **(28-ounce) can tomato puree** | 2 **teaspoons salt** |
| 1 **(6-ounce) can tomato paste** | 1 **teaspoon onion powder** |
| ⅓ **cup packed light brown** | ½ **teaspoon cayenne** |
| **sugar** | ½ **teaspoon ground cinnamon** |
| ½ **cup cider vinegar** | ⅛ **teaspoon ground cloves** |
| 1 **tablespoon Worcestershire** | 1 **garlic clove, crushed** |
| **sauce** | **through a press** |

**1.** In a nonreactive medium saucepan, combine tomato puree, tomato paste, brown sugar, vinegar, Worcestershire sauce, salt, onion powder, cayenne, cinnamon, cloves, and garlic. Whisk to mix.

**2.** Bring to a boil over medium-low heat. Reduce heat to low and simmer, partially covered to avoid spatters, stirring occasionally, until thickened, about 1 hour. Spoon into 2 (1-pint) jars. Let cool slightly, then cover and refrigerate at least 3 days before serving to allow flavors to blend.

# 51    ROAST CHICKEN SALAD WITH TOASTED PECANS
*Prep: 10 minutes    Cook: 6 to 8 minutes    Serves: 6*

My aunt Carol Poppel makes this chicken salad anytime she has leftover roast chicken. It is also perfect for a rotisserie chicken from the supermarket. Serve this over radicchio, garnished with some orange segments and grapes.

| | |
|---|---|
| ¼ **cup pecans** | 3 **cups shredded cooked** |
| ⅓ **cup light mayonnaise** | **chicken** |
| 1 **tablespoon Dijon mustard** | 1 **large celery rib, thinly sliced** |
| 1 **tablespoon red wine vinegar** | 2 **tablespoons finely chopped** |
| 1 **teaspoon grated orange zest** | **red onion** |
| ¼ **teaspoon freshly ground** | |
| **pepper** | |

**1.** Preheat oven to 350°F. Spread out pecans in a small baking dish or pie pan. Bake until fragrant and lightly browned, 6 to 8 minutes. Coarsely chop.

**2.** In a medium bowl, combine mayonnaise, mustard, vinegar, orange zest, and pepper. Whisk until blended. Add chicken, celery, red onion, and pecans. Stir until blended. Serve or refrigerate until serving.

## 52 STEAK AND POTATO SALAD WITH GRILLED PORTOBELLO MUSHROOMS

*Prep: 20 minutes    Marinate: 30 minutes    Cook: 18 to 20 minutes*
*Serves: 6*

¾ pound small red potatoes,
    halved or quartered
    Herb-Dijon Vinaigrette
    (recipe follows)
2 large portobello mushrooms
    (about 8 ounces each)

1 pound cooked steak, thinly
    sliced
2 scallions, cut into thin strips
1 head of Boston lettuce
4 medium tomatoes, sliced

1. Place potatoes in a medium saucepan, cover with water, and bring to a boil. Simmer until tender, 10 to 12 minutes; drain. While potatoes are still warm, place them in a medium bowl. Add 2 tablespoons of vinaigrette, stir to coat, and set aside to cool.

2. Trim stems from mushrooms. Brush mushrooms with 2 tablespoons vinaigrette. Heat a ridged grill pan over medium-high heat. Add mushrooms and cook, turning once, until tender, about 4 minutes per side. Place on a plate, brush with 1 tablespoon vinaigrette, and set aside to cool.

3. In a medium bowl, combine steak, scallions, and ¼ cup vinaigrette. Toss to combine and let marinate at room temperature 30 minutes. Slice mushrooms and add to steak; toss to mix.

4. Line a serving platter with lettuce. Arrange tomatoes around outside edge in a circle. Arrange potatoes next to tomatoes in a circle, leaving center of platter unfilled. Fill center with steak and mushroom salad. Drizzle any remaining vinaigrette over tomatoes.

## 53 HERB-DIJON VINAIGRETTE

*Prep: 10 minutes    Cook: none    Makes: about ⅔ cup*

2 tablespoons tarragon
    vinegar
1½ tablespoons Dijon mustard
1 tablespoon lemon juice
1½ teaspoons Worcestershire
    sauce
1 garlic clove, crushed
    through a press

½ teaspoon salt
½ teaspoon freshly ground
    pepper
6 tablespoons olive oil
3 tablespoons flat-leaf parsley
    leaves
2 tablespoons minced fresh
    chives

In a blender or mini food processor, combine vinegar, mustard, lemon juice, Worcestershire, garlic, salt, and pepper. With machine on, slowly add oil and process until vinaigrette is smooth and thickened. Add parsley and blend until chopped. Pour into a bowl and stir in chives.

## 54   TOSSED GREEN SALAD
*Prep: 15 minutes    Cook: none    Serves: 6 to 8*

Use whatever salad greens you like. I prefer a combination of sturdy and soft greens, such as romaine, iceberg, red leaf, Bibb, Boston, arugula, chicory, radicchio, or endive. This salad is my dad's specialty, always tossed with a tart vinegar and oil dressing. If this salad was not on the dinner table when he was growing up, it wasn't a meal worth eating.

8 cups torn, lightly packed
  salad greens
1 large carrot, peeled
1 cup cherry tomatoes, halved
½ medium cucumber, peeled,
  halved lengthwise, and
  sliced
½ medium red bell pepper,
  diced

1 large celery rib, thinly sliced
½ small red onion, sliced
  paper thin
Oil and vinegar or salad
  dressing of choice, such
  as Blue Cheese (page 42),
  Thousand Island (page
  43), or Vinaigrette
  (page 42)

Place salad greens in a large serving bowl. Run a vegetable peeler down carrot lengthwise to make long thin strips. Add carrot, tomatoes, cucumber, bell pepper, celery, and red onion to greens. Toss to mix. Serve in bowls. Pass cruets of olive oil and vinegar or salad dressing of choice at table.

## 55   BLUE CHEESE DRESSING
*Prep: 5 minutes    Cook: none    Makes: 2 cups*

½ cup mayonnaise
½ cup sour cream
½ cup buttermilk
1 cup crumbled blue cheese,
  preferably Gorgonzola

1 tablespoon fresh lemon
  juice
½ teaspoon coarsely ground
  pepper
¼ teaspoon garlic powder

In a medium bowl, combine mayonnaise, sour cream, buttermilk, blue cheese, lemon juice, pepper, and garlic powder. Stir until blended. Cover and refrigerate.

## 56   VINAIGRETTE DRESSING
*Prep: 2 minutes    Cook: none    Makes: ¾ cup*

2 tablespoons red wine
  vinegar
1 tablespoon lemon juice
1 small garlic clove, crushed
  through a press

½ teaspoon salt
½ teaspoon freshly ground
  pepper
2 teaspoons Dijon mustard
½ cup olive oil

In a small bowl, whisk vinegar, lemon juice, garlic, salt, and pepper. Whisk in mustard. Gradually whisk in oil until blended.

## 57 THOUSAND ISLAND DRESSING
*Prep: 5 minutes     Cook: none     Makes: 2¼ cups*

1 cup plain yogurt
½ cup mayonnaise
½ cup chili sauce
¼ cup minced celery
¼ cup minced roasted red
　pepper or pimiento

1 tablespoon sweet pickle
　relish
1 tablespoon minced onion
⅛ teaspoon cayenne

In a medium bowl, combine yogurt, mayonnaise, chili sauce, celery, red pepper, pickle relish, onion, and cayenne. Stir well until blended. Cover and refrigerate.

## 58 CHICKEN TACO SALAD WITH PINTO BEANS
*Prep: 15 minutes     Cook: 3 to 4 minutes     Serves: 6*

½ cup mayonnaise
¾ cup salsa
2 tablespoons lime juice
½ cup lightly packed cilantro
　leaves
1 tablespoon vegetable oil
1¼ pounds skinless, boneless
　chicken breasts, cut
　crosswise into thin strips
1 tablespoon chili powder
1 teaspoon ground cumin
1 medium head of romaine
　lettuce, cut into bite-size
　pieces

1 (15-ounce) can pinto beans,
　rinsed and drained
3 plum tomatoes, cut into
　½-inch dice
1 avocado, diced
3 scallions, thinly sliced
1 cup shredded red cabbage
1½ cups shredded Monterey
　Jack cheese
2 cups broken tortilla chips

**1.** In a blender or food processor, combine mayonnaise, salsa, and lime juice. Puree until smooth. Add cilantro and blend until chopped.

**2.** Heat a large skillet over medium-high heat. Add oil and swirl to coat. Add chicken strips and immediately sprinkle with chili powder and cumin. Cook, stirring constantly, until chicken is white throughout, 3 to 4 minutes. Remove from heat.

**3.** In a large bowl, combine lettuce, pinto beans, tomatoes, avocado, scallions, red cabbage, cheese, and tortilla chips. Toss to mix. Add chicken and toss again. Serve with dressing on the side.

# 59 CRUNCHY CHICKEN SALAD WITH CHOW MEIN NOODLES

*Prep: 20 minutes    Cook: 30 seconds    Serves: 4*

¼ pound snow peas
1 (3-ounce) can chow mein
   noodles
3 seedless oranges, sectioned
6 cups cut-up romaine lettuce
1 cup finely shredded red
   cabbage

3 cups thin strips of cooked
   chicken (about 12 ounces)
3 scallions, thinly sliced
1 tablespoon toasted sesame
   seeds
   Soy-Ginger Dressing
   (recipe follows)

**1.** Bring a small pot of water to a boil. Add snow peas. Cook 30 seconds. Drain and rinse with cold water until cool. Pat dry with paper towels. Cut diagonally in half.

**2.** In a medium bowl, combine chow mein noodles, snow peas, orange sections, romaine lettuce, and red cabbage. Toss to mix.

**3.** Arrange salad on 4 plates. Top with chicken. Sprinkle with scallions and sesame seeds. Drizzle on some dressing. Pass remaining dressing on the side. Serve immediately.

# 60 SOY-GINGER DRESSING

*Prep: 7 minutes    Cook: none    Makes: ½ cup*

2 tablespoons soy sauce
2 tablespoons balsamic
   vinegar
2 tablespoons vegetable oil
1 tablespoon honey
2 teaspoons Asian sesame oil

1½ teaspoons grated orange zest
1 teaspoon grated fresh ginger
½ teaspoon freshly ground
   pepper
⅛ teaspoon five-spice powder

In a small bowl, whisk soy sauce, balsamic vinegar, oil, honey, sesame oil, orange zest, ginger, pepper, and five-spice powder until blended.

# 61 CAESAR SALAD

*Prep: 15 minutes    Cook: none    Serves: 6*

It's amazing how popular this salad is! You see it on restaurant menus everywhere. It all started in Tijuana, Mexico, as the invention of Italian chef Caesar Cardini, and it's become an American classic. If you're a real garlic fan, double the amount in the dressing. This contemporary version omits the traditional coddled egg.

⅓ cup olive oil
2 tablespoons fresh lemon
    juice
2 tablespoons mayonnaise
1 tablespoon Dijon mustard
2 teaspoons balsamic vinegar
1½ teaspoons Worcestershire
    sauce
1 garlic clove, chopped
8 anchovy fillets, rinsed

½ cup finely shredded
    Parmesan cheese
¼ teaspoon salt
¼ teaspoon freshly ground
    pepper
1 large head of romaine
    lettuce, torn into large
    bite-size pieces
Crunchy Garlic Parmesan
    Croutons (recipe follows)

**1.** In a blender, combine oil, lemon juice, mayonnaise, mustard, vinegar, Worcestershire sauce, garlic, anchovies, ¼ cup Parmesan cheese, salt, and pepper. Blend well until dressing is smooth.

**2.** In a large bowl, combine lettuce and dressing. Toss to mix well. Add 1 cup croutons and remaining cheese and toss. Serve immediately with remaining croutons sprinkled on top.

# 62 CRUNCHY GARLIC PARMESAN CROUTONS

*Prep: 5 minutes    Cook: 15 to 20 minutes    Makes: 2 cups*

2 cups cubed (½-inch) French
    or sourdough bread
1 tablespoon garlic-flavored
    olive oil

2 tablespoons grated
    Parmesan cheese

**1.** Preheat oven to 350°F. In a medium bowl, combine bread cubes, oil, and 1 tablespoon cheese. Toss well until evenly coated. Spread on a lightly greased jelly-roll pan.

**2.** Bake 15 to 20 minutes, stirring once, until croutons are golden brown and toasted. Immediately toss with remaining cheese. Let cool.

## 63    ORANGE AND AVOCADO SALAD
*Prep: 20 minutes    Cook: 3 minutes    Chill: 30 minutes*
*Serves: 6*

If available, substitute 2 blood oranges for 1 of the navel oranges.

¼ cup fresh lime juice
⅓ cup olive oil
1 tablespoon honey
2 teaspoons grated orange zest
½ teaspoon salt
⅛ to ¼ teaspoon cayenne
⅛ teaspoon freshly ground
  pepper
1 small red onion, thinly
  sliced and separated into
  rings

1 head of romaine lettuce, cut
  into bite-size pieces
  (about 8 cups)
4 navel oranges, peeled,
  white pith removed, and
  sectioned
2 avocados, cut into ¾-inch
  dice
1 cup finely julienned jicama

**1.** In a small bowl, whisk together lime juice, oil, honey, orange zest, salt, cayenne, and pepper.

**2.** In a small skillet, heat 1 tablespoon dressing and red onion over medium heat. Cook, stirring frequently, until onion begins to soften, about 3 minutes. Scrape into a small bowl and refrigerate until cold, about 30 minutes.

**3.** Line serving platter with lettuce. Top with oranges, avocados, jicama, and red onion. Rewhisk dressing and drizzle over salad. Serve at room temperature.

## 64    DUNGENESS CRAB SALAD
*Prep: 35 minutes    Cook: 15 to 20 minutes    Chill: 1 hour    Serves: 4*

4 large artichokes
1 medium lemon, halved
1 shallot, minced
3 tablespoons olive oil
2 tablespoons fresh lime juice
½ teaspoon grated lime zest
¼ teaspoon salt
⅛ teaspoon freshly ground
  pepper
  Pinch of cayenne

1 avocado, cut into ½-inch
  dice
½ medium red bell pepper,
  chopped
2 cups lightly packed fresh
  spinach leaves
¾ pound cooked Dungeness
  crabmeat
2 tablespoons mayonnaise

**1.** Cut off artichoke stems and 1 inch from top of artichokes. Remove leaves. Using a teaspoon, scrape out hairy choke from bottoms. Trim bottoms and rub with cut halves of lemon to prevent discoloration. Add artichoke bottoms and lemon halves to a pot of boiling salted water. Cook 15 to 20 minutes, or until bottoms are tender when pierced with tip of a sharp knife. Remove artichokes and place in a small bowl.

**2.** In a small bowl, combine shallot, oil, lime juice, lime zest, salt, pepper, and cayenne. Whisk until blended. Drizzle 1 tablespoon of dressing over artichoke bottoms. Stir until coated. Cover and refrigerate until cold, about 1 hour.

**3.** In medium bowl, combine avocado, bell pepper, and 1 tablespoon dressing. Line 4 plates with spinach leaves. Place artichoke bottoms in center. Fill with avocado mixture. Surround artichokes with crabmeat. Whisk mayonnaise into remaining dressing and drizzle over salads.

---

## 65 COLD SESAME NOODLES
*Prep: 20 minutes    Cook: 8 minutes    Serves: 6*

The proliferation of Chinese restaurants has turned this Chinese classic into an American favorite. The addictive sauce can be made ahead and refrigerated. This salad is best served at room temperature. To turn it into a main course, add 2 cups shredded cooked chicken.

¾ **pound spaghettini**
1 **tablespoon grated fresh ginger**
1 **tablespoon brown sugar**
2 **tablespoons Asian sesame oil**
2 **tablespoons rice vinegar**
¼ **cup creamy peanut butter**
¼ **cup soy sauce**
1 **garlic clove, crushed through a press**

¼ **teaspoon salt**
⅛ **teaspoon cayenne**
1 **large cucumber, peeled, halved lengthwise, seeded, and cut into thin diagonal slices**
3 **scallions, thinly sliced**
1 **large red bell pepper, cut into thin strips**
1 **tablespoon toasted sesame seeds**

**1.** In a large pot of salted boiling water, cook spaghettini until tender but still firm, about 8 minutes. Drain and rinse with cold water until cool. Drain well.

**2.** In a food processor, combine ginger, brown sugar, sesame oil, vinegar, peanut butter, soy sauce, garlic, salt, and cayenne. Puree until sauce is smooth.

**3.** In a large bowl, combine spaghettini and sauce. Toss until combined. Place on a large serving platter.

**4.** In a medium bowl, combine cucumber, scallions, and bell pepper. Toss to mix. Mound vegetables on pasta and sprinkle sesame seeds on top. Serve at room temperature.

## 66 PEAR SALAD WITH HAZELNUTS AND BLUE CHEESE

*Prep: 15 minutes    Cook: 10 to 12 minutes    Serves: 4*

This salad, which can be offered either before or after the main course, is a combination of the Northwest, where pears and hazelnuts are grown, and the Midwest, where Maytag blue cheese is made.

⅓ cup hazelnuts
2 tablespoons sherry wine
   vinegar
3 tablespoons olive oil
1 shallot, minced
½ teaspoon salt
¼ teaspoon freshly ground
   pepper

1 bunch of watercress, tough
   stems removed
4 cups torn frisée or chicory
2 ripe pears, peeled, cored,
   and sliced
½ cup crumbled Maytag or
   other blue cheese
½ cup raspberries

**1.** Preheat oven to 350°F. Spread hazelnuts on a jelly-roll pan. Bake 10 to 12 minutes, or until toasted. While warm, rub in a clean dish towel to remove as much dark brown skin as possible. Coarsely chop hazelnuts.

**2.** In a small bowl, combine vinegar, oil, shallot, salt, and pepper. Whisk until vinaigrette is blended.

**3.** In a medium bowl, toss greens with 1 tablespoon vinaigrette. Place on 4 plates. Top with pears, blue cheese, and hazelnuts. Drizzle with remaining dressing. Garnish with raspberries.

## 67 WALDORF SALAD WITH BLUE CHEESE

*Prep: 15 minutes    Cook: none    Serves: 6*

I've lightened this classic salad by tossing it with lemon and oil. Just a thin drizzle of mayonnaise is spooned over the top before serving.

2 tablespoons lemon juice
1 tablespoon olive oil
¼ teaspoon salt
⅛ teaspoon freshly ground
   pepper
1 Granny Smith apple,
   quartered and cored
1 red apple, quartered and
   cored

1 large celery rib, thinly sliced
¼ cup golden raisins
2 tablespoons mayonnaise
3 cups torn salad greens
3 tablespoons crumbled blue
   cheese
½ cup chopped walnuts,
   preferably toasted

**1.** In a large bowl, whisk together lemon juice, olive oil, salt, and pepper. Cut apples into ½-inch-wide strips. Add apples, celery, and raisins to bowl. Toss gently to coat with dressing.

**2.** In a small bowl, whisk mayonnaise and 1 tablespoon water. Line plates with salad greens. Top with apple mixture. Drizzle with mayonnaise. Sprinkle with blue cheese and top with toasted walnuts.

## 68    FIVE-BEAN SALAD

*Prep: 15 minutes    Cook: 3 to 4 minutes    Chill: 2 hours    Serves: 12*

½ pound green beans
½ pound wax beans
¼ cup red wine vinegar
¼ cup olive oil
2 teaspoons honey mustard
¾ teaspoon salt
¼ teaspoon pepper
  Pinch of cayenne
1 medium red onion,
  quartered and thinly
  sliced

½ medium red bell pepper,
  diced
1 (15-ounce) can black beans,
  rinsed and drained
1 (15-ounce) can kidney
  beans, rinsed and
  drained
1 (8-ounce) can chickpeas,
  rinsed and drained

**1.** Trim stem end off green and wax beans and cut beans in half. In a medium saucepan of boiling salted water, cook beans until tender-crisp, 3 to 4 minutes. Drain and rinse under cold running water until cool. Drain; pat dry with paper towels.

**2.** In a large bowl, combine vinegar, oil, mustard, salt, pepper, and cayenne. Whisk until blended. Add green and wax beans, red onion, bell pepper, black beans, kidney beans, and chickpeas. Toss to combine. Cover and refrigerate at least 2 hours to allow flavors to blend. Let return to room temperature before serving.

## 69    CONFETTI COLESLAW

*Prep: 15 minutes    Cook: none    Chill: 2 hours    Serves: 8*

¼ cup olive oil
¼ cup cider vinegar
2 tablespoons Dijon mustard
2 teaspoons sugar
¾ teaspoon salt
¼ teaspoon freshly ground
  pepper
½ small green cabbage,
  preferably savoy,
  shredded (about 8 cups)
2 large carrots, peeled and
  shredded

½ medium red bell pepper,
  thinly sliced
½ medium yellow bell pepper,
  thinly sliced
½ small red onion, finely diced
1 Granny Smith apple, peeled
  cored, and cut into thin
  strips
1 tablespoon lemon juice

**1.** In a large bowl, combine oil, vinegar, mustard, sugar, salt, and pepper. Whisk until blended. Add cabbage, carrots, red and yellow bell peppers, and red onion. Toss well.

**2.** In a small bowl, toss apple with lemon juice. Add to cabbage mixture and toss well. Cover and refrigerate 2 hours to allow flavors to blend before serving.

## 70    MY FAVORITE MACARONI SALAD

*Prep: 15 minutes    Cook: 6 to 8 minutes    Chill: 2 hours*
*Serves: 8 to 10*

8 ounces elbow macaroni
¾ cup mayonnaise
¼ cup plain yogurt
2 tablespoons cider vinegar
1 tablespoon Dijon mustard
¾ teaspoon salt
½ teaspoon freshly ground
   pepper
1 large celery rib, cut into
   ¼-inch dice

1 large carrot, peeled and
   shredded
⅓ cup minced red onion
1 medium tomato, chopped
½ medium yellow bell pepper,
   cut into ¼-inch dice
1 cup frozen peas, thawed

**1.** In a large pot of salted boiling water, cook macaroni until tender but still firm, 6 to 8 minutes. Drain, rinse with cold water, and let drain well.

**2.** In a large bowl, combine mayonnaise, yogurt, vinegar, mustard, salt, and pepper. Stir until blended. Remove ¼ cup to a small container, cover, and refrigerate.

**3.** Add cooked macaroni, celery, carrot, red onion, tomato, bell pepper, and peas to remaining dressing in bowl. Stir well to combine. Cover and refrigerate 2 hours or overnight.

**4.** Just before serving, add reserved dressing to salad and stir to blend.

## 71    COOL AS A CUCUMBER SALAD

*Prep: 15 minutes    Stand: 30 minutes    Cook: none    Chill: 2 hours*
*Serves: 6*

4 medium cucumbers (about
   2 pounds)
1 tablespoon coarse (kosher)
   salt
1 small red onion, cut into
   ½-inch dice

¼ cup white wine vinegar
2 tablespoons sugar
¼ teaspoon crushed hot red
   pepper
1½ teaspoons grated lime zest

**1.** Peel and thinly slice cucumbers. Toss in a colander with coarse salt. Let drain 30 minutes.

**2.** In a large bowl, stir together onion, vinegar, sugar, and hot pepper. Let stand while cucumbers drain.

**3.** Pat cucumbers dry. Add to dressing in bowl. Add lime zest and toss. Cover and refrigerate at least 2 hours to marinate. Serve chilled.

## 72   DANDELION SALAD
*Prep: 10 minutes    Cook: 8 to 10 minutes    Serves: 6*

Look for young tender dandelion greens as they tend to be less bitter.

4  **slices of bacon, cut into**
    **½-inch dice**
½  **cup chopped red onion**
¼  **cup cider vinegar**
3  **tablespoons maple syrup**
½  **teaspoon salt**
½  **teaspoon freshly ground**
    **pepper**

3  **small bunches of young**
    **dandelion greens (about**
    **1¾ pounds), torn into**
    **bite-size pieces (12 cups)**
2  **hard-cooked eggs, chopped**

**1.** In a medium skillet, cook bacon over medium heat until crisp, 5 to 6 minutes. Remove bacon to paper towels to drain. Add red onion to drippings in skillet and cook, stirring occasionally, until softened, 3 to 4 minutes. Stir in vinegar, maple syrup, salt, and pepper. Bring to a simmer.

**2.** Place greens in a large bowl. While dressing is hot, pour it over greens and toss. Sprinkle with eggs and bacon, toss gently, and serve at once.

## 73   PICNIC PASTA SALAD
*Prep: 10 minutes    Cook: 10 to 12 minutes    Stand: 1 hour    Serves: 6*

½  **pound rotelle or bow-tie**
    **pasta**
¼  **cup olive oil**
2  **tablespoons red wine**
    **vinegar**
½  **teaspoon grated lemon zest**
½  **teaspoon salt**
½  **teaspoon freshly ground**
    **pepper**
1½  **cups cherry tomatoes,**
    **quartered**
1  **medium yellow bell pepper,**
    **cut into ½-inch dice**

1  **small cucumber, peeled,**
    **seeded, and cut in ½-inch**
    **dice**
½  **cup shredded carrot**
⅓  **cup minced red onion**
1  **medium celery rib, cut into**
    **½-inch dice**
12  **black olives, pitted and**
    **slivered**
2  **tablespoons chopped fresh**
    **basil**

**1.** In a large pot of salted boiling water, cook pasta until tender but still firm, 10 to 12 minutes. Drain, rinse with cold water, and drain well.

**2.** In a small bowl, whisk together oil, vinegar, lemon zest, salt, and pepper until dressing is blended.

**3.** In a large bowl, combine pasta, tomatoes, bell pepper, cucumber, carrot, onion, celery, olives, and basil. Pour on dressing and toss to combine. Let stand at room temperature 1 hour before serving, stirring occasionally. If refrigerated, let return to room temperature before serving.

# 74   ALL-AMERICAN POTATO SALAD
*Prep: 25 minutes    Cook: 25 to 30 minutes    Chill: 4 hours*
*Serves: 12 to 16*

This is potato salad at its best with all of the classic ingredients. If you have time, make this a day ahead to let the flavors blend.

4 pounds large red potatoes
½ cup cider vinegar
3 tablespoons vegetable oil
1½ teaspoons salt
¾ teaspoon freshly ground
   pepper
1½ cups mayonnaise
½ cup milk
1 tablespoon Dijon mustard
3 large celery ribs, chopped

½ cup finely chopped red
   onion
8 slices of bacon, cooked until
   crisp and crumbled
   (optional)
2 tablespoons chopped
   parsley
4 hard-cooked eggs,
   quartered (optional)
Parsley sprigs, for garnish

**1.** In a large saucepan or Dutch oven, cover potatoes with water. Bring to a boil, reduce heat to medium, and cook until potatoes are tender when pierced with a sharp knife, 25 to 30 minutes. Drain into a colander.

**2.** Meanwhile, in a large bowl, whisk vinegar, oil, salt, and pepper until blended. Peel potatoes when cool enough to handle but still warm, and cut into ¾-inch cubes. Add warm potatoes to dressing and stir gently to coat. Let cool to room temperature.

**3.** In a small bowl, whisk mayonnaise, milk, and mustard until blended. Pour over potatoes. Add celery, red onion, bacon, and chopped parsley. Stir gently to mix. Cover and refrigerate at least 4 hours or overnight.

**4.** Before serving, garnish with egg quarters and parsley sprigs.

# 75   CREAMY COLESLAW
*Prep: 10 minutes    Cook: none    Chill: 1 hour    Serves: 12*

½ cup mayonnaise
½ cup sour cream
3 tablespoons rice vinegar
1 tablespoon Dijon mustard
1 teaspoon salt
½ teaspoon pepper

9 cups shredded green
   cabbage
3 cups shredded red cabbage
2 large carrots, peeled and
   grated
2 scallions, thinly sliced

In a large bowl, whisk mayonnaise, sour cream, vinegar, mustard, salt, and pepper until blended. Add green and red cabbage, carrots, and scallions. Toss to mix well. Cover and refrigerate at least 1 hour to allow flavors to blend.

# 76    CORN AND BARLEY SALAD

*Prep: 15 minutes    Cook: 33 to 39 minutes    Serves: 6*

1    cup pearl barley
4    ears of corn, husked
1    large ripe beefsteak tomato,
        cut into ½-inch dice
½    cup thinly sliced scallions

¼    cup rice vinegar
¼    cup olive oil
¾    teaspoon salt
½    teaspoon freshly ground
        pepper

**1.** In a large saucepan of boiling water, cook barley until tender, 30 to 35 minutes; drain. In a large pot of boiling water, cook corn until tender, 3 to 4 minutes. Drain and rinse under cold running water.

**2.** Cut corn kernels from cobs. Place in a large bowl. Add barley, tomato, and scallions to corn.

**3.** In a small bowl, whisk vinegar, oil, salt, and pepper. Add to salad and stir gently to mix. Serve salad at room temperature. If refrigerated, remove from refrigerator and let return to room temperature.

# 77    BLACK-EYED PEA SALAD

*Prep: 15 minutes    Cook: 25 minutes    Serves: 6*

1    (10-ounce) package frozen
        black-eyed peas
⅓    cup olive oil
2    tablespoons cider vinegar
1    tablespoon spicy brown
        mustard
1    garlic clove, minced
½    to 1 teaspoon hot pepper
        sauce
½    teaspoon salt
¼    teaspoon freshly ground
        pepper
2    small celery ribs, cut into
        ½-inch dice

2    small carrots, peeled and
        shredded
½    medium red onion, finely
        chopped
½    medium red bell pepper, cut
        into ¼-inch dice
1    cup cherry tomatoes, halved
3    tablespoons chopped flat-
        leaf parsley
3    slices of bacon, cooked until
        crisp and crumbled

**1.** Cook peas in saucepan of boiling water according to package directions. Drain well. Pat dry with paper towels.

**2.** In a large bowl, combine oil, vinegar, mustard, garlic, hot pepper sauce, salt, and pepper. Whisk until dressing is blended and smooth.

**3.** Add black-eyed peas, celery, carrots, red onion, bell pepper, tomatoes, and parsley to dressing. Stir gently to combine. Cover and refrigerate. Before serving, sprinkle bacon on top.

## 78    SPINACH SALAD WITH ORANGES AND ALMONDS

*Prep: 15 minutes    Cook: 7 minutes    Serves: 4*

1  slice of bacon, cut into ½-inch dice
1  large shallot, minced
2  tablespoons olive oil
2  tablespoons red wine vinegar
1  teaspoon honey
½  teaspoon grated fresh ginger
¼  teaspoon salt
¼  teaspoon freshly ground pepper

8  cups torn spinach leaves (about 1 pound)
1  small red bell pepper, thinly sliced
1  medium celery rib, thinly sliced
2  blood or navel oranges, peeled, white pith removed, sectioned
⅓  cup slivered almonds, preferably toasted

**1.** In a small skillet, cook bacon over medium heat until crisp, about 5 minutes. Remove bacon to paper towels with slotted spoon. Pour off and discard fat. Add shallot to skillet and cook over low heat until softened, about 2 minutes. Remove skillet from heat and add oil, vinegar, honey, ginger, salt, and pepper. Return to heat and bring to a simmer, whisking. Remove from heat.

**2.** Combine spinach, bell pepper, celery, orange segments, almonds, and bacon in a large bowl. Add warm dressing and toss. Serve immediately.

## 79    THREE-RICE SALAD WITH ARUGULA AND FENNEL

*Prep: 15 minutes    Cook: 46 to 51 minutes    Stand: 1 hour    Serves: 8*

½  cup walnuts
2½  teaspoons salt
⅓  cup wild rice
½  cup brown rice
⅓  cup long-grain white rice
¼  cup olive oil
¼  cup lemon juice
½  teaspoon grated lemon zest
1  tablespoon Dijon mustard
½  teaspoon freshly ground pepper

1  fennel bulb, trimmed and cut into ½-inch dice
1  tart red apple, cored and cut into ½-inch dice
½  small red onion, minced
12  kalamata olives, pitted and slivered
1  small bunch of arugula, trimmed and cut into 1-inch pieces

**1.** Preheat oven to 350°F. Spread out walnuts in a small baking dish and toast 6 to 8 minutes, until fragrant and lightly browned. Let cool, then coarsely chop.

**2.** Bring a large pot of water to a boil. Add 2 teaspoons salt and wild rice. Boil 8 minutes. Add brown rice. Return to a boil, reduce heat to medium-low, cover, and cook 20 minutes. Add white rice, again return to a boil, simmer 12 to 15 minutes, or until all rices are tender. Drain well.

**3.** In a large bowl, whisk olive oil, lemon juice, lemon zest, mustard, remaining ½ teaspoon salt, and pepper until blended. Add rice and toss until coated.

**4.** Add fennel, apple, red onion, toasted walnuts, olives, and arugula to rice. Stir to combine. Let salad stand 1 hour to allow flavors to blend. Serve at room temperature.

---

## 80  GERMAN POTATO SALAD
*Prep: 15 minutes    Cook: 27 to 32 minutes    Serves: 6 to 8*

Because this type of potato salad contains no mayonnaise, it is ideal for a buffet or picnic. My lightened version of the original sweet-sour dressing is sweetened with maple syrup.

| | |
|---|---|
| **4 large red potatoes (2 pounds)** | **¼ teaspoon freshly ground pepper** |
| **4 slices of bacon, cut into ½-inch dice** | **1 medium celery rib, finely chopped** |
| **3 tablespoons olive oil** | **1 small carrot, peeled and shredded** |
| **3 tablespoons cider vinegar** | **½ medium red onion, finely chopped** |
| **2 teaspoons Dijon mustard** | |
| **2 teaspoons maple syrup** | |
| **½ teaspoon salt** | |

**1.** Cover potatoes with cold water in a large saucepan. Bring to a boil and cook until tender but not soft, 20 to 25 minutes; drain. Let stand until cool enough to handle but still warm.

**2.** While potatoes cool, cook bacon in a medium skillet over medium heat until crisp, about 6 minutes. With a slotted spoon, remove bacon to paper towels. Pour off and discard fat in skillet. Add oil, vinegar, mustard, maple syrup, salt, and pepper to skillet and set it aside.

**3.** Peel potatoes and cut in ¾-inch dice. Place in a large bowl. Add celery and carrot and toss lightly to mix.

**4.** Add red onion to dressing in skillet. Bring to a simmer over medium heat, whisking to scrape up brown bits. Simmer 1 minute. Pour over potatoes. Toss gently to combine. Let stand until cool. Serve at room temperature. If refrigerated, let return to room temperature before serving. Stir in bacon just before serving.

# 81    GARDEN TOMATO SALAD
*Prep: 15 minutes    Cook: 1 minute    Serves: 8*

This simple salad will be at its best when vine-ripened, juicy, summer tomatoes are available. Store tomatoes at room temperature.

½ **cup packed fresh basil leaves**
¼ **cup olive oil**
3 **tablespoons fresh lemon juice**
1 **shallot, minced**
½ **teaspoon salt**
½ **teaspoon freshly ground pepper**

3 **large beefsteak tomatoes, sliced**
1 **plum tomato, seeded and cut into ½-inch dice**
1 **pint yellow cherry tomatoes, halved**

**1.** Set aside 8 basil leaves for garnish. Finely chop remaining basil. In a small saucepan, heat 2 tablespoons oil over medium heat until warm, about 1 minute. Remove from heat and stir in chopped basil. Let basil oil cool.

**2.** In a small bowl, combine remaining 2 tablespoons olive oil, lemon juice, shallot, salt, and pepper. Whisk to blend dressing.

**3.** Just before serving, whisk basil oil into dressing. Arrange beefsteak tomatoes on a platter in a circle with slices overlapping and space in center. Drizzle half of dressing over slices. Add plum tomato and cherry tomatoes to remaining dressing. Stir to coat. Mound in center of sliced tomatoes. Cut reserved basil into thin strips and sprinkle over sliced tomatoes.

---

# 82    BREAD & BUTTER PICKLES
*Prep: 10 minutes    Cook: 10 minutes    Makes: 4 to 5 pints*

This recipe comes from my mom, tucked away with a bunch of recipes. I've added hot pepper flakes, which give these pickles some zip. They are really easy to make and are stored in the refrigerator, which eliminates the whole hot water bath processing procedure.

12 **small pickling cucumbers (2½ pounds), cut in ¼-inch-thick slices**
2 **medium onions, sliced**
2 **cups cider vinegar**
2 **cups sugar**
3 **tablespoons coarse kosher salt**

2 **tablespoons mustard seeds**
1 **teaspoon dry mustard**
1 **teaspoon turmeric**
1 **teaspoon crushed hot red pepper flakes**
½ **teaspoon celery seeds**

In a large pot, bring all ingredients to a boil, stirring occasionally. Remove from heat. Spoon cucumbers and onions into clean pint jars. Pour hot liquid over to cover. Cover loosely with lids and let cool. Tighten bands and refrigerate.

# 83  ROSY RED APPLESAUCE

*Prep: 15 minutes    Cook: 40 to 45 minutes    Makes: about 3 cups*

Spicy cinnamon candies, rather than apple skins, account for the pink color here. This sauce is not very sweet and makes a terrific accompaniment to roast pork or turkey.

| | |
|---|---|
| 3 **pounds cooking apples, preferably a combination of McIntosh, Macoun, and Cortland** | ¼ **cup sugar** |
| | ¼ **teaspoon grated nutmeg** |
| | ⅛ **teaspoon freshly ground pepper** |
| 1 **tablespoon fresh lemon juice** | ½ **teaspoon grated lemon zest** |
| 1½ **tablespoons cinnamon red-hot candies** | |

**1.** Peel, quarter, and core apples. Place in a large pot or Dutch oven. Add lemon juice, cinnamon candies, sugar, and nutmeg. Stir to mix.

**2.** Bring to a simmer over medium heat, stirring frequently. Reduce heat to medium-low and cook, breaking up apples with a wooden spoon, until softened and cooked down to a chunky sauce, 40 to 45 minutes.

**3.** Stir in pepper and lemon zest. Serve applesauce warm, at room temperature, or cold.

# 84  FRESH FRUIT SALAD

*Prep: 15 minutes    Cook: none    Stand: 1 hour    Serves: 8 to 10*

| | |
|---|---|
| 2 **tablespoons fresh orange juice** | 2 **kiwis, peeled, halved, and sliced** |
| 2 **tablespoons sugar** | 3 **cups cubed seedless watermelon** |
| ½ **teaspoon grated orange zest** | |
| ½ **teaspoon grated fresh ginger** | 1 **Granny Smith apple, quartered, cored, and cut into ½-inch dice** |
| 1 **pint strawberries, halved** | |
| 1 **ripe mango, peeled and cut into ¾-inch dice** | 2 **ripe peaches, sliced** |
| 1 **cup red and green seedless grapes** | ¾ **cup blueberries** |

**1.** In a small bowl, whisk together orange juice, sugar, orange zest, and ginger until sugar dissolves.

**2.** In a large bowl, combine strawberries, mango, grapes, kiwis, watermelon, apple, and peaches. Add orange juice mixture and stir gently to combine. Cover and let stand at room temperature 1 hour or cover and refrigerate up to 4 hours.

**3.** Just before serving, add blueberries and stir gently to mix in.

## 85  CRANBERRY FRUIT MOLD

*Prep: 15 minutes    Cook: 2 to 3 minutes    Chill: 3 hours    Serves: 8*

More than a few years back, gelatin molds were very popular in America. My grandmother had a whole assortment that she liked to serve, usually on salad greens with a dollop of mayonnaise.

1 cup fresh or frozen
   cranberries, picked over
1 (3-ounce) package
   cranberry-flavored gelatin
1 cup orange juice

½ cup chopped pecans
½ cup finely diced tart red
   apple (peel left on)
1 medium celery rib, finely
   chopped

1. In a nonreactive medium saucepan, bring cranberries and 1 cup water to a boil. Boil until cranberries pop, 2 to 3 minutes. Pour into a heatproof medium bowl. Add gelatin and stir until dissolved. Stir in orange juice. Place bowl in a large bowl of ice water. Stir occasionally until gelatin thickens and begins to mound. Stir in pecans, apple, and celery. Pour into a 1½-quart mold or bowl. Cover and refrigerate until firm, 3 hours or overnight.

2. To unmold, dip mold briefly in hot water; run a knife around edge. Place a serving plate over mold or bowl. Turn over and shake firmly to release. If mold does not release, dip again in hot water for a few seconds.

## 86  CRANBERRY SAUCE WITH PEARS AND PORT

*Prep: 10 minutes    Cook: 15 to 20 minutes    Makes: about 3 cups*

1 tangerine
1 (12-ounce) bag fresh or
   frozen cranberries,
   picked over
1 large pear, peeled, cored,
   and cut into ½-inch dice

1 cup sugar
½ cup port or red wine
¼ teaspoon ground cinnamon

1. Grate zest and squeeze juice from tangerine. In a medium nonreactive saucepan, combine tangerine juice, cranberries, pear, sugar, port, and cinnamon.

2. Bring to a boil over high heat. Reduce heat and simmer, stirring occasionally, until sauce thickens, 15 to 20 minutes. Stir in tangerine zest. Pour into a bowl. Let cool, then cover and refrigerate until cold.

# 87  CLASSIC COBB SALAD

*Prep: 15 minutes    Cook: 5 minutes    Serves: 4*

This salad was made famous at Hollywood's Brown Derby restaurant, a hangout for all the stars in the fifties, at a time when good food was okay and fat was not an obsession.

6  slices of bacon
⅓  cup olive oil
3  tablespoons red wine
    vinegar
1  shallot, minced
1  tablespoon chopped fresh
    tarragon or 1 teaspoon
    dried
1  teaspoon Dijon mustard
½  teaspoon salt

¼  teaspoon freshly ground
    pepper
12  cups torn salad greens
2  cups shredded cooked
    chicken (about 8 ounces)
2  ripe medium tomatoes,
    seeded and diced
1  ripe avocado, diced
2  hard-cooked eggs, chopped
½  cup crumbled blue cheese

**1.** In a large skillet, cook bacon over medium heat, turning, until crisp and lightly browned, about 5 minutes. Drain on paper towels. Crumble coarsely when cool.

**2.** In a jar with a lid, combine oil, vinegar, shallot, tarragon, mustard, salt, and pepper. Shake until dressing is blended.

**3.** In a large bowl, toss salad greens with ¼ cup of dressing. Divide greens among 4 plates and top with diagonal rows of chicken, tomatoes, avocado, bacon, eggs, and blue cheese. Serve with remaining dressing on the side.

# Chapter 4

# Sandwiches Dagwood Would Love

If I were stuck on a desert island and someone told me I had to pick one favorite food to eat, it would be sandwiches. For me, they are the perfect food—easy to make and eat; filled with any variety of meat, seafood, cheese, and or vegetables with all their different tastes and textures; and sandwiched (of course) between another great food—bread. For a great sandwich, it's essential to use good-quality bread or rolls that will hold up to fillings and won't become soggy. And we have access to such good breads today, from San Francisco's tangy sourdough to New York's chewy Jewish rye. While elsewhere in the book I've included recipes for baking your own, should you so choose, even supermarket bakeries are responding to the American demand for better bread, turning out sourdough and whole-grain European-style bread as well as rye and country white.

It's great fun to be creative with sandwiches. Like Dagwood, build your own and let your imagination run wild. Leftover salads, meats, and cooked marinated vegetables make great sandwich fillings. A few not-so-far-out, traditional favorite sandwiches in this chapter are Reuben's Reuben, New Orleans Oyster Po' Boy, Sloppy Joes, Sausage and Pepper Heros, and Philly Cheese Steak Sandwich. Two classics that might be tied for our all-time favorites are here, the Grilled Three-Cheese Sandwich and the BLT.

In true melting-pot fashion, some of the recipes I consider sandwiches contain no bread at all, but pizza dough or tortillas instead. They include Santa Fe Turkey Pizza, Roasted Vegetable and Bean Burritos, and Turkey Tacos.

## 88    MEDITERRANEAN TUNA MELT
*Prep: 15 minutes    Cook: 8 to 12 minutes    Serves: 4*

1 large red bell pepper
4 slices of sourdough bread,
   cut ¾ inch thick
1 garlic clove, halved
1 (6-ounce) can tuna packed in
   olive oil, drained, oil
   reserved
8 kalamata olives, pitted and
   slivered

2 tablespoons slivered basil
1 tablespoon minced red
   onion
3 ripe plum tomatoes, seeded
   and cut into ¾-inch dice
⅛ teaspoon freshly ground
   pepper
8 thin slices of mozzarella
   cheese

**1.** Roast bell pepper over gas burner or under broiler as close to heat as possible, turning, until skin is blackened, 5 to 7 minutes. Place in a paper bag, seal bag, and let stand until pepper is cool. Remove skin, stem, and seeds without rinsing pepper. Cut into ½-inch dice.

**2.** Preheat broiler. Place bread slices on a baking sheet. Broil 5 inches from heat, turning, until toasted on both sides, 1 to 2 minutes per side. Rub with garlic halves. Brush one side lightly with some reserved tuna oil.

**3.** In a medium bowl, combine roasted pepper, tuna, olives, basil, red onion, tomatoes, and pepper. Toss to combine and flake tuna. Top oiled side of bread with tuna mixture, dividing evenly. Drizzle each slice with ½ teaspoon reserved oil. Top each with 2 slices of mozzarella. Broil until cheese melts, about 1 minute. Serve hot.

## 89    GRILLED THREE-CHEESE SANDWICH
*Prep: 5 minutes    Cook: 10 to 16 minutes    Serves: 2*

1 tablespoon butter, softened
1½ teaspoons grated Parmesan
   cheese
4 slices of firm-textured white
   bread

4 slices of deli-sliced Cheddar
   cheese
¾ teaspoon Dijon mustard
2 slices of deli-sliced Swiss
   cheese

**1.** In a small bowl, stir butter and Parmesan cheese until blended.

**2.** Lay bread on a flat work surface and spread one side of each slice lightly with Parmesan butter. Turn over and top 2 slices with Cheddar cheese, folding cheese over to fit, if necessary. Spread mustard over cheese. Top with Swiss cheese. Top with remaining bread slices, buttered side up.

**3.** Place sandwiches in a large nonstick skillet over medium-low heat. Cook, turning once, 5 to 8 minutes per side, or until browned and cheese melts. Cut sandwiches in half and serve hot.

## 90 BLT
*Prep: 10 minutes    Cook: 8 minutes    Serves: 4*

12 thick slices of hickory-
 smoked bacon
8 slices of firm-textured white
 bread, toasted
⅓ cup mayonnaise

4 leaves of green leaf lettuce
2 ripe medium tomatoes,
 sliced
¼ teaspoon freshly ground
 pepper

**1.** In a large skillet, cook bacon over medium heat, turning occasionally, until crisp and brown, about 8 minutes. Drain on paper towels.

**2.** Lay toast on a flat work surface. Spread about 2 teaspoons mayonnaise over each slice of toast. Top 4 slices with lettuce, bacon slices broken in half to fit, and tomato slices, dividing evenly. Sprinkle with pepper and top with remaining slices of toast, mayonnaise side down. Cut in half with a serrated knife and serve at once.

## 91 GRILLED TURKEY CLUB
*Prep: 10 minutes    Cook: 4 to 8 minutes    Serves: 4*

This has a spicy lime-chili mayonnaise for extra flavor. It wouldn't be a club sandwich without the frilly toothpicks.

¾ cup mayonnaise
1 fresh jalapeño pepper,
 seeded and minced
¾ teaspoon chili powder
1 teaspoon lime juice
1 teaspoon grated lime zest
 Pinch of cayenne
4 turkey cutlets (about
 3 ounces each)

1 tablespoon olive oil
12 slices of bread, lightly
 toasted
4 leaves of Boston lettuce
2 small ripe tomatoes, thinly
 sliced
8 slices of bacon, cooked until
 crisp

**1.** In a small bowl, combine mayonnaise, jalapeño pepper, chili powder, lime juice, lime zest, and cayenne. Stir until blended.

**2.** Pound turkey cutlets between sheets of wax paper until ¼ inch thick. Brush cutlets with oil. Heat an oiled grill pan over medium-high heat until hot. Add cutlets in 2 batches and cook, turning, 1 to 2 minutes per side, or until cooked through. Remove to a plate to cool slightly.

**3.** Lay toast on a flat work surface. Spread with mayonnaise. Top 4 slices with lettuce and turkey. Place 4 slices of toast mayonnaise side down on turkey. Top with tomato slices and bacon. Place remaining slices of toast mayonnaise side down on bacon. Insert 4 toothpicks in each sandwich. Cut with a serrated knife diagonally to make 4 triangles and serve at once.

## 92    KENTUCKY HOT BROWN
*Prep: 15 minutes    Cook: 10 to 12 minutes    Serves: 4*

This sandwich classic is named after the Brown Hotel in Louisville, Kentucky. It's old-fashioned—and in this case, old-fashioned tastes *really* good.

3 tablespoons butter
2 tablespoons flour
1 cup hot milk
¼ teaspoon salt
¼ teaspoon Tabasco sauce
½ teaspoon spicy brown mustard
1 cup shredded sharp Cheddar cheese

2 medium tomatoes, thickly sliced
4 slices of white bread, toasted, cut in half diagonally
½ pound sliced roast turkey
¼ cup grated Parmesan cheese
4 slices of bacon, cooked until crisp, cut in half

**1.** In a small saucepan, melt 2 tablespoons butter over medium-low heat. Whisk in flour. Cook, whisking, 1 to 2 minutes. Whisk in hot milk. Cook, whisking, until sauce comes to a boil and thickens, about 2 minutes. Simmer, stirring occasionally, 3 minutes. Remove from heat and stir in salt, Tabasco sauce, mustard, and Cheddar cheese until cheese melts.

**2.** In a large skillet, melt remaining 1 tablespoon butter over medium-high heat. Add tomato slices and cook, turning once, until heated through, about 1 minute. Remove skillet from heat.

**3.** Preheat broiler. Place 1 slice of bread in each of 4 individual casserole dishes. Top with tomato slices and turkey. Spoon cheese sauce over, dividing evenly. Sprinkle Parmesan cheese over top.

**4.** Broil 5 to 6 inches from heat until sauce is bubbly and browned in spots, 3 to 4 minutes. Top each with 2 pieces of bacon. Serve hot.

## 93    TUNA SALAD SANDWICH
*Prep: 10 minutes    Cook: none    Chill: 1 hour    Serves: 6*

Here I've jazzed up the classic with pickled jalapeños and lime zest.

1 (12-ounce) can solid white tuna in water
2 tablespoons sliced pickled jalapeño peppers, minced
1 large carrot, peeled and shredded

½ small red onion, minced
½ teaspoon grated lime zest
¼ cup plain yogurt
¼ cup mayonnaise
12 slices of whole-grain bread
Leaf lettuce

**1.** Drain tuna. Place in a medium bowl and break up with a fork. Add pickled jalapeños, carrot, red onion, lime zest, yogurt, and mayonnaise. Stir to mix well. Cover and refrigerate at least 1 hour to let flavors blend.

**2.** Lay 6 bread slices on a flat work surface. Top with tuna salad, dividing it evenly. Top with lettuce leaves and remaining bread slices. Cut in half to serve.

# 94    EGG SALAD SANDWICH

*Prep: 10 minutes    Cook: none    Chill: 1 hour    Serves: 4*

6 hard-cooked eggs, peeled
1 medium celery rib, chopped
1 scallion, minced
1 tablespoon minced parsley
¼ cup mayonnaise
2 teaspoons spicy brown
   mustard
2 teaspoons cider vinegar

¼ teaspoon salt
¼ teaspoon pepper
4 onion rolls, halved
   horizontally
4 leaves of green leaf lettuce
   Cucumber and radish slices,
   if desired

**1.** Place eggs in a medium bowl and finely chop with a pastry blender or a fork. Add celery, scallion, parsley, mayonnaise, mustard, vinegar, salt, and pepper. Stir to mix. Cover and refrigerate at least 1 hour to allow flavors to blend.

**2.** Lay rolls cut sides up on work surface. Place lettuce on bottom halves. Top with egg salad and cucumber and radish slices, if desired. Cover with top halves and cut in half to serve.

# 95    TURKEY TACOS

*Prep: 10 minutes    Cook: 6 to 7 minutes    Serves: 4 to 6*

1 tablespoon vegetable oil
1 pound turkey cutlets, cut
   into ½-inch-wide strips
2 teaspoons chili powder
1 teaspoon ground cumin
1 large garlic clove, minced
1¼ cups thick and chunky salsa
12 white corn taco shells
1 large carrot, peeled and
   shredded

1 pickled jalapeño pepper,
   minced
3 scallions, thinly sliced
1 tablespoon rice vinegar
2 cups shredded iceberg
   lettuce
1½ cups shredded Monterey
   Jack cheese
2 medium tomatoes, cut into
   ½-inch dice

**1.** In a large skillet, heat oil over medium-high heat. Add turkey, chili powder, cumin, and garlic. Cook, stirring frequently, until turkey is lightly browned, 4 to 5 minutes. Stir in ¾ cup salsa and simmer 2 minutes, or until turkey is white throughout. Cover and set aside.

**2.** Heat taco shells according to package directions. In a small bowl, combine carrot, pickled jalapeño pepper, scallions, and vinegar. Stir to mix. Serve taco shells with turkey, carrot salad, lettuce, cheese, tomatoes, and remaining salsa to assemble at the table.

## 96   DOWN-EAST LOBSTER ROLLS
*Prep: 10 minutes    Cook: none    Serves: 4*

Pure delight and decadence, these rolls are heaped with a lobster salad that has a lemony mayonnaise dressing. Make these the next time there are leftover cooked lobsters, if that ever happens.

⅓ **cup mayonnaise**
¼ **cup finely chopped celery**
2 **teaspoons minced fresh chives**
1 **teaspoon lemon juice**
½ **teaspoon grated lemon zest**
⅛ **teaspoon salt**

⅛ **teaspoon freshly ground pepper**
3 **cups diced (¾-inch) cooked lobster meat**
4 **top-split hot dog buns**
2 **tablespoons butter, melted**

**1.** Preheat broiler. In a medium bowl, combine mayonnaise, celery, chives, lemon juice, lemon zest, salt, and pepper. Blend well. Add lobster and stir gently to mix.

**2.** Brush sides and insides of buns with melted butter. Place rolls on baking sheet and broil sides and insides until lightly toasted.

**3.** Fill rolls with lobster, heaping high in center. Serve at once.

## 97   SLOPPY JOES
*Prep: 10 minutes    Cook: 19 minutes    Serves: 4*

1 **tablespoon vegetable oil**
1 **large onion, chopped**
½ **red bell pepper, chopped**
3 **garlic cloves, crushed through a press**
1 **pound lean ground beef**
¾ **cup chili sauce**

1 **tablespoon Worcestershire sauce**
2 **teaspoons cider vinegar**
½ **teaspoon salt**
½ **teaspoon freshly ground pepper**
4 **hard rolls, split and toasted**

**1.** In a large skillet, heat oil over medium heat. Add onion and cook, stirring occasionally, until golden, about 8 minutes. Stir in bell pepper and garlic. Cook 2 minutes, or until softened. Increase heat to high and add beef, stirring to break it up. Cook, stirring frequently, until browned, about 4 minutes. Drain off fat.

**2.** Reduce heat to low. Stir in chili sauce, Worcestershire, vinegar, salt, and pepper. Bring to a simmer. Cover and cook, stirring occasionally, until slightly thickened, about 5 minutes.

**3.** To serve, spoon sloppy Joe mixture into split rolls.

# 98    NEW ORLEANS OYSTER PO' BOY

*Prep: 15 minutes    Cook: 12 minutes    Serves: 2 to 3*

In the nineteenth century, a New Orleans husband who spent the night in the French Quarter brought this sandwich home to his wife as a peacemaker. A poor-boy sandwich can have a variety of fillings, like fried soft-shelled crabs, catfish, meatballs, roast beef—just about anything you can fit inside a loaf of French bread.

1  loaf of French bread
   (18 inches long)
2  tablespoons melted butter
⅓  cup tartar sauce or
   mayonnaise
2  teaspoons Creole or coarse
   grainy mustard

1  cup shredded iceberg lettuce
2  small tomatoes, thinly sliced
   Crunchy Fried Oysters
   (recipe follows)

1. Preheat broiler. Halve bread lengthwise and pull out some of soft insides to make a tunnel in center. Toast cut sides under broiler until golden, about 1 minute. Brush cut sides with melted butter.

2. In a small bowl, stir tartar sauce and mustard until blended. Spread on cut sides of bread. On bottom half of bread, layer lettuce, tomatoes, and oysters. Replace top. Cut in half or thirds. Serve immediately.

# 99    CRUNCHY FRIED OYSTERS

*Prep: 10 minutes    Cook: 6 to 8 minutes    Serves: 4*

24  large freshly shucked
    oysters
 1  cup cornmeal
½  teaspoon salt

½  teaspoon freshly ground
   pepper
¼  teaspoon cayenne
 1  cup olive oil

1. Drain oysters. On a plate, combine cornmeal, salt, pepper, and cayenne. Stir well.

2. Heat oil in a medium skillet over medium heat until hot. While oil heats, coat oysters in seasoned cornmeal and place in a single layer on a piece of wax paper. Place paper towels on a baking sheet.

3. Fry oysters, in 3 or 4 batches without crowding, turning once, until golden brown and crisp, about 1 minute per side. Drain on paper towels. Serve while hot.

## 100    REUBEN'S REUBEN

*Prep: 10 minutes    Cook: 13 to 15 minutes    Serves: 4*

This recipe comes from my friend Elwin Greenwald, who owns a flourishing scone business in Royal Oak, Michigan. His friend Reuben created this lightened version of the classic sandwich.

| | |
|---|---|
| 3  tablespoons butter | 8  slices of rye bread |
| 2  medium onions, thinly sliced | ¾  pound thinly sliced corned beef |
| 1  Golden Delicious apple, halved, cored, and cut into thin strips | 1¼  cups shredded Swiss cheese |
| 1  (8-ounce) can sauerkraut, rinsed and well drained | 2  tablespoons coarse grainy mustard |

**1.** In a large skillet, melt 1 tablespoon butter over medium heat. Add onions and ¼ cup water. Cover and cook until softened, about 5 minutes. Uncover and cook, stirring frequently, until onions are golden brown, about 5 minutes. Stir in apple and cook until softened, 3 to 5 minutes. Stir in sauerkraut and remove skillet from heat.

**2.** Preheat broiler. Melt remaining 2 tablespoons butter. Lightly brush one side of each slice of bread. Lay buttered sides up on a baking sheet. Broil 4 inches from heat until toasted. Turn and broil until lightly toasted. Top 4 slices of bread with corned beef and cheese. Top remaining slices with sauerkraut mixture and spread with mustard. Broil until cheese melts. Sandwich halves together. Cut in half and serve while hot.

## 101    BARBECUED PORK SANDWICHES

*Prep: 20 minutes    Marinate: 8 hours    Cook: 1½ to 2 hours plus 5 minutes    Serves: 8*

| | |
|---|---|
| 1  teaspoon salt | 3  pounds lean boneless pork shoulder, cut into 2-inch chunks |
| ½  teaspoon freshly ground pepper | |
| ¼  teaspoon crushed hot red pepper | Tangy Tomato Barbecue Sauce (page 174) |
| 1  cup cider vinegar | Hamburger buns or hard rolls, split |
| 1  dried chipotle chile | |

**1.** In a large bowl, stir together salt, pepper, hot pepper, and cider vinegar. Add whole chile and pork and stir until coated with marinade. Cover and refrigerate at least 8 hours, or overnight.

**2.** Preheat oven to 375°F. Place pork and marinade in a nonreactive Dutch oven. Bring to a boil and cover pot.

**3.** Bake 1½ to 2 hours, or until very tender, stirring once about halfway through. Uncover and place pot over medium-high heat. Bring to a boil and cook, stirring frequently, until liquid evaporates but meat is still juicy, about 5 minutes. Spoon off any fat. Remove and discard chile. Using 2 forks, shred meat. Add 1 cup barbecue sauce to pork and stir to combine. Serve while hot on rolls, with remaining barbecue sauce on the side.

## 102 PHILLY CHEESE STEAK SANDWICH
*Prep: 15 minutes    Cook: 23 to 26 minutes    Serves: 4*

3 tablespoons butter
3 medium onions, thinly
   sliced
1 teaspoon balsamic vinegar
¼ teaspoon salt
¼ teaspoon freshly ground
   pepper
1 garlic clove, minced

1 teaspoon Dijon mustard
4 (7- to 8-inch) long, hard rolls
¾ pound deli-sliced roast beef
½ pound deli-sliced Muenster
   cheese
1 cup shredded sharp
   Cheddar cheese

**1.** In a large skillet, melt 1 tablespoon butter over medium heat. Add onions and ¼ cup water. Cook, covered, stirring occasionally, 10 minutes, or until softened. Uncover and cook, stirring frequently, until browned, about 10 minutes longer. Stir in vinegar, salt, and pepper. Set browned onions aside.

**2.** In a small saucepan, melt remaining 2 tablespoons butter with garlic over low heat, 1 to 2 minutes. Stir in mustard. Remove from heat.

**3.** Preheat broiler. Halve rolls lengthwise. Place cut sides up on a baking sheet. Brush cut sides lightly with garlic butter.

**4.** Broil 5 inches from heat until toasted, 1 to 2 minutes. Top 4 halves with roast beef and Muenster cheese. Top remaining halves with browned onions and Cheddar cheese. Broil until cheeses melt, 1 to 2 minutes. Sandwich halves together. Cut in half and serve hot.

## 103  MUFFULETTA
*Prep: 15 minutes    Cook: 17 minutes    Serves: 4 to 6*

A muffuletta is a New Orleans sandwich, filled with meats and cheeses and a great garlicky olive and vegetable salad.

¼ cup olive oil
1 small onion, finely chopped
1 large celery rib, chopped
3 garlic cloves, crushed
  through a press
½ teaspoon dried oregano
⅛ teaspoon crushed hot
  pepper
½ cup pimiento-stuffed green
  olives, coarsely chopped
½ cup kalamata olives, pitted
  and coarsely chopped

1 (6½-ounce) jar marinated
  artichoke hearts, drained
  and coarsely chopped
1 (8- to 10-inch) round loaf of
  crusty bread
¼ pound sliced mortadella
¼ pound sliced hard salami
¼ pound sliced provolone
  cheese
¼ pound sliced smoked baked
  ham

**1.** In a medium skillet, heat 2 tablespoons oil over medium heat. Add onion and celery; cook, stirring occasionally, until softened, about 5 minutes. Stir in garlic, oregano, and hot pepper. Cook 2 minutes, stirring. Remove from heat. Stir in remaining oil, green olives, kalamata olives, and artichokes.

**2.** Preheat oven to 450°F. Cut bread in half horizontally. Pull out some of soft bread in center of each half. Spoon half of olive mixture over bottom half, spreading it out evenly. Top with mortadella, salami, cheese, ham, and remaining olive mixture. Replace top. Wrap loaf tightly in foil.

**3.** Bake 10 minutes, or until warmed through. Unwrap and cut into wedges with a serrated knife.

## 104  CALIFORNIA VEGGIE SPROUT SANDWICH
*Prep: 15 minutes    Cook: none    Serves: 4*

¼ cup mayonnaise
2 teaspoons fresh lemon juice
1 teaspoon Dijon mustard
⅛ teaspoon salt
⅛ teaspoon pepper
8 slices of seven-grain bread
4 leaves of green leaf lettuce
1 large tomato, thinly sliced

4 thin slices of red onion,
  separated into rings
1 ripe avocado, sliced
½ cup shredded carrot
1 cup alfalfa or clover sprouts
8 slices of deli-sliced
  Muenster cheese

**1.** In a small bowl, combine mayonnaise, lemon juice, mustard, salt, and pepper. Stir until dressing is well blended.

**2.** Lay 4 slices of bread on a flat work surface. Spread half of dressing over bread. Top with lettuce, tomato slices, red onion, avocado, carrot, remaining dressing, sprouts, cheese, and remaining bread slices. Cut in half to serve.

# 105  SAUSAGE AND PEPPER HEROS
*Prep: 15 minutes    Cook: 29 to 34 minutes    Serves: 4*

1 tablespoon olive oil
1 pound hot Italian sausage
1 medium red bell pepper, thinly sliced
1 medium green bell pepper, thinly sliced
1 medium onion, sliced
¼ teaspoon salt
1 (15-ounce) can chunky Italian-style tomato sauce
1 garlic clove, minced

1 tablespoon red wine vinegar
1 teaspoon sugar
4 hero rolls (about 7 inches long)
1¼ cups shredded mozzarella cheese
2 tablespoons grated Parmesan cheese
¼ teaspoon freshly ground pepper

**1.** In a large nonstick skillet, heat oil over medium heat. Add sausage and cook, turning occasionally, until well browned and cooked through, 10 to 12 minutes. Remove sausage to a plate. Pour off all but 1 tablespoon drippings from pan.

**2.** Add red pepper, green pepper, onion, and salt to drippings in skillet. Cook over medium heat, stirring occasionally, until softened, 6 to 8 minutes. Stir in tomato sauce, garlic, vinegar, and sugar. Bring to a boil. Reduce heat and simmer until thickened, about 10 minutes. Remove sauce from heat.

**3.** Preheat broiler. Split rolls lengthwise; place cut sides up on a baking sheet. Broil rolls about 6 inches from heat until toasted, 1 to 2 minutes. In a small bowl, combine mozzarella and Parmesan cheese. Sprinkle over cut sides of rolls. Season with pepper.

**4.** Cut sausages into diagonal slices. Place on one side of each roll. Broil until sausage is hot and cheese melts, about 2 minutes. Top with tomato-pepper sauce, dividing evenly. Sandwich halves together and cut in half to serve.

# 106   BLACK BEAN TOSTADAS
*Prep: 15 minutes   Cook: 13 to 14 minutes   Serves: 6*

6 corn tortillas
1 tablespoon vegetable oil
½ teaspoon chili powder
½ teaspoon ground cumin
2 tablespoons lime juice
2 teaspoons jalapeño Tabasco
  sauce
¼ cup plain nonfat yogurt
2 tablespoons chopped
  cilantro
1 (15-ounce) can black beans,
  rinsed and drained

2 ripe plum tomatoes, seeded
  and cut into ½-inch dice
¼ pound jalapeño Monterey
  Jack cheese, cut into
  ¼-inch dice
½ small red onion, cut into
  ½-inch dice
1½ cups shredded romaine
  lettuce

**1.** Preheat oven to 400°F. Place tortillas on 1 or 2 large baking sheets. Bake until crisp, turning once, about 10 minutes. In a small cup, stir oil and chili powder. Brush on tortillas. Bake 2 minutes. Let cool.

**2.** In a small skillet, cook cumin over medium heat, stirring frequently, until fragrant, 1 to 2 minutes. Place in a small bowl. Add lime juice, jalapeño Tabasco, yogurt, and cilantro. Whisk until sauce is blended.

**3.** In a medium bowl, combine beans, tomatoes, cheese, and red onion. Stir to combine.

**4.** Top tortillas with lettuce and bean mixture. Drizzle with yogurt sauce. Serve immediately.

# 107   CALIFORNIA PIZZAS
*Prep: 10 minutes   Cook: 20 to 24 minutes   Serves: 4*

1 tablespoon olive oil
1 medium red onion, thinly
  sliced
1 medium red bell pepper, cut
  into ½-inch dice
¾ pound skinless, boneless
  chicken breasts, cut
  crosswise into ½-inch-
  wide strips
3 garlic cloves
¼ cup chopped basil
¼ teaspoon crushed hot red
  pepper

Easy Processor Pizza Dough
  (recipe follows) or
  1¼ pounds of your
  favorite refrigerated or
  frozen brand
Cornmeal
¼ cup sun-dried tomato pesto
1 cup shredded mozzarella
  cheese
1 cup shredded Monterey
  Jack cheese

**1.** In a large nonstick skillet, heat oil over medium-high heat. Add onion and bell pepper. Cook, stirring occasionally, 3 to 4 minutes, or until vegetables are crisp-tender. Set aside. Add chicken to skillet and cook, stirring, until chicken turns white but is not fully cooked, about 2 minutes. Drain chicken in a colander.

**2.** Bring a small saucepan of water to a boil. Add garlic and cook 3 minutes; drain. Peel and mince garlic. Place in a small bowl and stir in basil and hot pepper.

**3.** Preheat oven to 450°F. Divide dough into 4 pieces. On a floured surface, roll out to 8-inch rounds. Place on 2 large greased baking sheets sprinkled with cornmeal. Spread pesto over each round of dough, leaving a ¾-inch margin around edges. In a small bowl, combine cheeses. Sprinkle half of cheese over pizzas. Cover with onion mixture and then chicken. Top with basil mixture and remaining cheese.

**4.** Bake 1 sheet at a time on lowest oven rack 12 to 15 minutes, or until crust is browned. Slide onto cutting board and cut into wedges.

## 108 EASY PROCESSOR PIZZA DOUGH
*Prep: 5 minutes    Stand: 45 minutes*
*Makes: 1 (12- to 14-inch) pizza or 4 individual pizzas*

| | |
|---|---|
| 3  cups flour | 1  cup very warm water (120° to |
| 1  envelope (¼ ounce) quick- | 130°F) |
|    rising active dry yeast | 1  tablespoon olive oil |
| 1½  teaspoons salt | 1  teaspoon honey |

**1.** In a food processor, combine flour, yeast, and salt. In a measuring cup, combine water, oil, and honey. With machine on, gradually pour water mixture through feed tube. Process until dough forms a ball. If dough is too dry to form a ball, add water 1 tablespoon at a time. Process 45 seconds to knead. Dough should be soft and sticky.

**2.** Place dough in an oiled bowl. Turn oiled side up. Cover with greased plastic wrap. Let rise in a warm place 45 minutes.

*Variation:*

## CORNMEAL PIZZA CRUST

Replace ⅓ cup flour with ⅓ cup cornmeal.

# 109   SUPER SUBMARINE SANDWICH
*Prep: 15 minutes   Cook: none   Serves: 4 to 6*

Depending upon which region of the country you live in, this sandwich goes by many names: grinder, hoagie, bomber, hero, poor boy, and wedge. The ingredients that go inside vary also. This is a classic Italian combination.

3   tablespoons olive oil
2   tablespoons red wine
     vinegar
¼   teaspoon dried oregano
¼   teaspoon pepper
⅛   teaspoon salt
1   (18- to 20-inch) loaf of Italian
     bread
2   cups shredded romaine
     lettuce
2   ounces thin deli-sliced
     salami
1   large red bell pepper, sliced
     into thin rings

1   (6½-ounce) jar marinated
     artichoke hearts, drained
     and coarsely chopped
1   small red onion, sliced
     paper-thin, separated into
     rings
¼   pound deli-sliced provolone
     cheese
1   large tomato, thinly sliced
12   kalamata olives, pitted and
     slivered
¼   pound deli-sliced baked
     Virginia ham

**1.** In a small bowl, whisk together oil, vinegar, oregano, pepper, and salt until dressing is blended.

**2.** Cut bread in half lengthwise and turn cut sides up. Brush cut sides lightly with about one third of dressing. On bottom half of bread, layer lettuce, salami, red pepper, artichokes, and red onion. Stir remaining dressing and drizzle on half. Top with cheese and tomato. Drizzle on remaining dressing. Top with olives, ham, and top of loaf, cut side down. Cut into 3- to 4-inch sections with a serrated knife and serve at once.

# 110 ROASTED VEGETABLE AND BEAN BURRITOS

*Prep: 20 minutes    Cook: 39 to 40 minutes    Serves: 6*

3 tablespoons olive oil
1 large onion, chopped
3 garlic cloves, minced
3 jalapeño peppers, seeded and minced
1 pound Swiss chard, stems trimmed, coarsely chopped
½ teaspoon salt
1 (15-ounce) can black beans, rinsed and drained
1 large red bell pepper, cut into ½-inch dice
½ medium butternut squash, seeded, peeled, and cut into ½-inch dice

2 large all-purpose potatoes, peeled and cut into ½-inch dice
1 teaspoon ground cumin
1 teaspoon chili powder
½ cup shelled, unsalted pumpkin seeds
6 (10-inch) flour tortillas
Shredded Monterey Jack cheese
Guacamole, tomato salsa, and sour cream, as accompaniments

**1.** Preheat oven to 450°F. In a large skillet, heat 2 tablespoons oil over medium-high heat. Add onion and cook, stirring frequently, until onion begins to brown lightly, about 3 minutes. Stir in garlic and jalapeños. Cook 1 minute. Add Swiss chard, half at a time, stirring until wilted. Stir in ¼ teaspoon salt. Cook, stirring, until Swiss chard is tender, about 3 minutes. Stir in beans. Continue to cook, stirring, until any liquid evaporates, about 2 minutes. Remove skillet from heat and cover to keep warm.

**2.** In a medium bowl, combine bell pepper, squash, potatoes, cumin, and chili powder with remaining 1 tablespoon oil and ¼ teaspoon salt. Stir well to mix. Spread on a greased jelly-roll pan in a single layer.

**3.** Bake 15 minutes. Turn with a spatula. Bake 10 minutes longer, or until vegetables are tender and beginning to brown. Remove from oven. Reduce oven temperature to 350°F. Place pumpkin seeds on a baking sheet. Bake until toasted, about 5 minutes.

**4.** Heat tortillas by placing between dampened paper towels and heating in a microwave on high for 45 seconds, or until hot.

**5.** Serve burritos family-style for assembling at table. Spoon on some bean mixture, sprinkle with roasted vegetables, cheese, and pumpkin seeds. Top with guacamole, salsa, and sour cream. Roll up and eat.

# 111   SANTA FE TURKEY PIZZA

*Prep: 15 minutes    Cook: 20 to 25 minutes    Serves: 4 to 6*

For a vegetarian version, substitute a 15-ounce can of drained beans for the turkey.

Oil and cornmeal for pizza pan
½ pound ground turkey
2 teaspoons chili powder
1 teaspoon ground cumin
½ pound ripe plum tomatoes, seeded and diced
1 cup fresh or thawed frozen corn kernels
3 large scallions, thinly sliced
Cornmeal Pizza Crust (page 73)

1 cup shredded sharp Cheddar cheese
1 cup shredded part-skim mozzarella cheese
2 tablespoons chopped cilantro
2 tablespoons minced pickled jalapeño peppers
1½ cups shredded romaine lettuce
Salsa and sour cream, as accompaniments

1. Preheat oven to 450°F. Oil a large pizza pan or cookie sheet. Dust with cornmeal. Adjust oven rack to bottom. In a medium skillet, cook turkey over medium heat, stirring frequently to break up, until no longer pink and any moisture evaporates, about 5 minutes. Stir in chili powder and cumin. Remove from heat. Stir in tomatoes, corn, and scallions.

2. On a lightly floured surface, roll out pizza dough to a 13-inch circle. Place on prepared pizza pan. Sprinkle ½ cup each Cheddar cheese and mozzarella cheese over dough. Top with turkey mixture, leaving a ½-inch margin around edge. Sprinkle remaining cheeses over turkey.

3. Bake 15 to 20 minutes, or until bottom of crust is well browned. Sprinkle with cilantro, pickled jalapeño peppers, and lettuce. Pass bowls of salsa and sour cream on the side.

## Chapter 5

# Bright Breakfasts and Brunches

I think breakfast foods are among our all-time favorites. I also think it's fun to have breakfast for dinner once in a while. But there is nothing better than a stack of pancakes to get you going in the morning. My brother and I used to have pancake-eating contests when we were kids, and I think my mom lost count after a while. Speaking of pancakes, in this chapter there are Buttermilk Pancakes, Blueberry Cornmeal Flapjacks, Buckwheat Cakes, Sourdough Pancakes, and Gossamer Griddle Cakes, which are so light you practically have to hold them down with the spatula so they don't float away. If you have some left over, freeze them and pop them in the toaster on weekday mornings. Remember to mix pancake and waffle batters just until blended; like muffin and quick bread batters, they shouldn't be overmixed. I prefer to use a nonstick griddle for cooking pancakes. Nonstick cooking spray is all that is needed to grease the griddle, although sometimes I like to use a little butter for flavor. If you don't have a nonstick griddle, then a large nonstick skillet will work just fine.

If you're a waffle fan, there are Oatmeal Pecan Banana Waffles, light Crisp Sour Cream Waffles, and Overnight Raised Waffles to pick from. In testing the waffles, I used a square waffle iron with 4 grids, each grid being 4 inches wide. It's old and seasoned and doesn't need greasing, but do so if it's recommended for your iron; nonstick cooking spray works best. There are many waffle irons on the market, and not everyone has the same kind. So follow your manufacturer's directions, adding the amount of batter recommended. You may need to experiment with one to get the amount just right. Be sure to cook waffles long enough, until browned and crisp. Like pancakes, extra waffles make great weekday breakfasts if frozen and popped in the toaster. All of the waffle recipes make a generous amount.

They say that breakfast is the most important meal of the day. Some weekday choices would be a Strawberry-Banana Breakfast Shake, Golden French Toast, or Denver Omelet Sandwiches. When you have more time on the weekend, try Huevos Rancheros, Potato and Pepper Frittata, or for a real treat, Eggs Benedict. For a true Southern breakfast, try Ham and Red-Eye Gravy, with eggs, biscuits, and grits—when you're done, you might just be speaking with a Southern accent.

# 112    ROASTED TOMATO, CHEESE, AND SPINACH OMELETS

*Prep: 15 minutes    Cook: 1 hour 10 minutes    Serves: 4*

Prepare the roasted tomatoes the night or a few days before, if you like, so you can enjoy this omelet on the spur of the moment. This makes 2 omelets, which are cut in half to serve 4, saving time for the cook. For individual omelets, divide the ingredients accordingly and use a small skillet.

4  plum tomatoes, halved
    lengthwise
1  tablespoon olive oil
1  garlic clove, crushed
    through a press
½  teaspoon salt

½  teaspoon pepper
10  eggs
2  tablespoons butter
10  large spinach leaves
½  cup shredded fontina or
    Gruyère cheese

**1.** Preheat oven to 350°F. In a pie plate, place tomatoes cut sides up. In a small cup, combine oil and garlic. Spoon over cut sides of tomatoes. Sprinkle with ⅛ teaspoon salt and ⅛ teaspoon pepper. Bake 1 hour, or until soft. Let cool. (Refrigerate if not used within 3 hours. Let return to room temperature before using.)

**2.** In a large bowl, beat eggs, 1 tablespoon water, and remaining salt and pepper with a fork until blended. In a medium nonstick skillet, melt 1 tablespoon butter over medium heat. Swirl butter to coat skillet. When butter stops sizzling, pour in half of eggs. Cook, shaking skillet to swirl eggs. As eggs begin to set, lift edges with a spatula and tilt skillet to let uncooked eggs run underneath. Cook until eggs are set but still wet on top, about 3 minutes.

**3.** Lay 5 spinach leaves on half of omelet; top with 4 tomato halves and half of cheese. Cook until cheese begins to melt, about 1 minute. With a spatula, fold uncovered portion of eggs over onto cheese. Cover skillet and cook until cheese is melted, about 1 minute. Slide omelet onto a plate. Repeat with remaining ingredients. Cut omelets in half and serve at once.

# 113  HUEVOS RANCHEROS
*Prep: 15 minutes    Cook: 22 to 28 minutes    Serves: 4*

Tex-Mex and Southwestern food have become a tasty part of the American culinary repertoire. These savory eggs—a great, light, and spicy way to start a Sunday morning—are already an American favorite.

| | |
|---|---|
| 1 large poblano pepper | 4 corn tortillas |
| 2 slices of bacon, cut into ½-inch dice | 4 teaspoons olive oil |
| 1 small red onion, chopped | 8 eggs |
| 1 jalapeño pepper, seeded and minced | ¼ teaspoon freshly ground pepper |
| 2 large ripe tomatoes, peeled, seeded, and coarsely chopped | 2 tablespoons chopped cilantro |
| ¼ teaspoon salt | ½ cup shredded Colby-Jack cheese |
| | 2 scallions, thinly sliced |

**1.** Preheat broiler. Broil poblano as close to heat as possible, turning, until skin is blackened, 8 to 10 minutes. Or char directly over a gas flame. Place in a paper bag, close bag, and let pepper cool. Rub skin from pepper without rinsing under water. Remove stem and seeds. Cut into ½-inch dice.

**2.** In a medium skillet, cook bacon over medium heat until crisp, about 4 minutes. Remove bacon with a slotted spoon and drain on a paper towel.

**3.** Pour off all but 2 teaspoons drippings from skillet. Add poblano, red onion, and jalapeño pepper. Cook over medium heat until onion softens, 3 to 4 minutes. Add tomatoes and cook until softened, about 2 minutes. Stir in salt. Remove from heat and cover to keep warm.

**4.** In large nonstick skillet over medium-high heat, cook 1 tortilla at a time, turning once, until hot and softened, 30 to 45 seconds per side. Place on a baking sheet.

**5.** Add 2 teaspoons oil to skillet. Crack 4 eggs into skillet and cook until desired doneness, turning if desired. Season fried eggs with ⅛ teaspoon pepper. Place 2 eggs on each tortilla. Repeat with remaining oil, eggs, and ⅛ teaspoon pepper. Stir cilantro and bacon into reserved sauce and spoon over eggs. Sprinkle cheese on top.

**6.** Broil 4 to 5 inches from heat until cheese melts, 1 to 2 minutes. Sprinkle with scallions and serve at once.

# 114    RISE AND SHINE GRANOLA

*Prep: 10 minutes    Cook: 42 to 48 minutes    Makes: 8 cups*

Stored in a tightly closed jar, this tasty breakfast mix will keep for up to a month.

⅓ cup vegetable oil
½ cup honey
1½ teaspoons vanilla extract
4 cups old-fashioned oats
¾ cup sliced almonds
½ cup flaked coconut
½ cup unsalted shelled
    sunflower seeds

2 tablespoons sesame seeds
1 cup golden raisins
¾ cup dried cranberries
½ cup dried blueberries
6 dried peach halves, cut into
    ¼-inch dice

**1.** Preheat oven to 300°F. In a small saucepan, combine oil, honey, and vanilla. Cook over medium heat, stirring, until honey melts, 2 to 3 minutes.

**2.** In a large bowl, toss oats, almonds, coconut, sunflower seeds, and sesame seeds to mix. Pour on honey mixture, stirring to coat evenly. Spread out on a jelly-roll pan.

**3.** Bake 40 to 45 minutes, stirring every 10 minutes, or until golden brown and toasted. Place pan on a wire rack to let cool. Turn into a large bowl. Add raisins and dried cranberries, blueberries, and peaches. Toss to mix. Store in an airtight container.

# 115    EGGS BENEDICT

*Prep: 25 minutes    Cook: 7 to 10 minutes    Serves: 4*

This hollandaise sauce is especially tart and lemony, so a little goes a long way. I like to serve this American classic on lazy Sunday mornings for a special treat.

3 tablespoons fresh lemon
    juice
1 stick (4 ounces) unsalted
    butter
2 egg yolks
½ teaspoon salt

¼ teaspoon hot pepper sauce
8 slices of Canadian bacon
4 English muffins
1 tablespoon vinegar
8 eggs

**1.** In a small nonreactive saucepan, bring lemon juice to a boil. Cook until reduced to 1 tablespoon, 1 to 2 minutes. Pour into a blender. In same pan, melt butter over low heat until very hot. Add egg yolks to blender. With machine on, slowly pour hot butter in a thin stream through hole in blender top. Add salt, hot pepper sauce, and 1 tablespoon hot water. Blend until combined and thickened. Scrape into top of a double boiler set over hot—not boiling—water. Keep hollandaise sauce warm over low heat.

**2.** Coat a large skillet with cooking spray. Add Canadian bacon and cook over medium-low heat, turning once, until lightly browned, 3 to 5 minutes. Keep warm. Split and toast English muffins. Butter if desired. Keep warm.

**3.** Bring a large skillet of water to a boil; add vinegar. Crack eggs and gently slip into water. Poach 3 minutes, or until desired degree of doneness.

**4.** Place 2 English muffin halves cut sides up on each of 4 plates. Top each with a slice of bacon and then a poached egg. Whisk hollandaise sauce and spoon over eggs. Serve at once.

---

## 116 POTATO AND PEPPER FRITTATA
*Prep: 15 minutes    Cook: 51 to 60 minutes    Serves: 6 to 8*

5 tablespoons olive oil
2 medium onions, thinly
    sliced
1 medium red bell pepper, cut
    into ½-inch dice
2 garlic cloves, minced
¼ pound baked ham, cut into
    thin strips
4 medium baking potatoes,
    peeled, halved length-
    wise, and sliced ¼ inch
    thick

¾ teaspoon salt
8 large eggs
½ teaspoon freshly ground
    pepper
2 tablespoons chopped
    parsley

**1.** In a 10-inch flameproof nonstick or cast-iron skillet, heat 2 tablespoons oil over medium heat. Add onions and cook, stirring occasionally, until soft, 5 to 7 minutes. Stir in bell pepper and garlic. Cook, stirring occasionally, until pepper is soft and onions are golden brown, 6 to 8 minutes. Turn into a large bowl. Add ham.

**2.** Heat 2 more tablespoons oil in skillet. Add potatoes and season with ¼ teaspoon salt. Cook, turning occasionally, until golden brown and cooked through, about 25 minutes. With a slotted spoon, transfer potatoes to onion mixture. In a small bowl, beat eggs with pepper, parsley, and remaining ½ teaspoon salt. Add to potato mixture and stir well.

**3.** Heat remaining 1 tablespoon oil in skillet over medium heat. Pour in potato mixture and spread evenly. Cover, reduce heat to medium-low, and cook until eggs are almost set, about 12 to 15 minutes.

**4.** Preheat broiler. Set skillet about 4 inches from heat and broil frittata until eggs are set and top is golden brown, 3 to 5 minutes. Cut into wedges to serve.

# 117    BERRY-RHUBARB JAM

*Prep: 10 minutes    Cook: 14 to 19 minutes    Makes: 5 (½-pint) jars*

Nothing makes breakfast more special than a pot of homemade preserves. This one is easy and relatively quick. To avoid the fuss of water-bath processing, I make jam in relatively small batches and store the jars in the refrigerator.

2 pints ripe strawberries,
  rinsed, hulled, and dried
1 cup finely chopped fresh or
  frozen rhubarb
3½ cups sugar
2 tablespoons lemon juice

3 tablespoons grenadine
  syrup
2 cups fresh or frozen
  raspberries
2 teaspoons grated orange zest

1. In a large, deep heavy skillet or flameproof casserole, combine strawberries, rhubarb, sugar, lemon juice, and grenadine. Cook over medium heat, stirring occasionally, until sugar begins to melt, about 3 minutes. Mash about half of strawberries with a potato masher. Stir in raspberries.

2. Increase heat to medium-high and bring to a full rolling boil. Cook at a full rolling boil, stirring constantly, until mixture thickens slightly, 10 to 15 minutes. A small spoonful of mixture when frozen on a plate should thicken; the exact length of time will depend on the juiciness of the berries. Stir in orange zest; boil 1 minute.

3. Ladle jam into hot sterilized ½-pint jars. Place lids and bands on jars loosely and let cool. Tighten bands and refrigerate.

# 118    LOW-FAT BREAKFAST SAUSAGE

*Prep: 10 minutes    Cook: 20 minutes    Makes: about 12 patties*

Freeze uncooked patties, individually wrapped, to have on hand for quick breakfasts. They're good on biscuits. If you like your sausage spicy, double the hot pepper flakes.

2 slices of firm-textured white
  bread, torn in quarters
2 slices of bacon, cut into
  1-inch pieces
1½ pounds pork tenderloin,
  trimmed of fat and cut
  into 1-inch cubes
1½ teaspoons crumbled dried
  sage

1¼ teaspoons salt
1 teaspoon freshly ground
  pepper
½ teaspoon dried thyme
½ teaspoon paprika
¼ teaspoon crushed hot red
  pepper
2 egg whites
1 tablespoon vegetable oil

1. In a food processor, grind bread into crumbs. Turn into a large bowl. Add bacon to food processor and finely chop. Add half of pork cubes. Pulse until very finely chopped. Add meats to bread crumbs. Repeat with remaining pork.

**2.** Add sage, salt, pepper, thyme, paprika, hot pepper, egg whites, and ½ cup water to pork mixture. Stir or mix with your hands until well blended.

**3.** Using wet hands, shape into 12 patties about 3 inches in diameter, using a scant ⅓ cup for each.

**4.** Heat ½ tablespoon oil in a large nonstick skillet over medium heat. Add 6 patties and cook 5 minutes per side, or until well browned and cooked through. Repeat with remaining oil and patties. Serve hot.

---

# 119  GRILLADES AND GRITS
*Prep: 15 minutes   Cook: 28 to 30 minutes   Serves: 4*

This is a Creole dish, usually veal steak that is braised in a rich vegetable sauce. Here it's made with faster-cooking veal cutlets. I like it especially when company's coming for brunch later in the day.

2 tablespoons olive oil
1 medium onion, chopped
1 large celery rib, cut into ½-inch dice
1 small green bell pepper, chopped
4 garlic cloves, minced
1 tablespoon Creole Seasoning (page 152)
1 (14½-ounce) can diced tomatoes in juice
¾ teaspoon salt
¼ teaspoon freshly ground pepper
¾ cup old-fashioned or quick-cooking grits (not instant)
4 veal cutlets (about ½ pound)

**1.** In a medium skillet, heat 1 tablespoon oil over medium heat. Add onion, celery, and bell pepper. Cook, stirring occasionally, until vegetables soften, 4 to 6 minutes. Add 3 garlic cloves and 2 teaspoons Creole seasoning. Cook, stirring, 2 minutes. Add tomatoes, ½ cup water, ¼ teaspoon salt, and ⅛ teaspoon pepper. Bring to a simmer, reduce heat to medium-low, cover, and cook 20 minutes, or until slightly thickened. Remove from heat.

**2.** Cook grits according to package directions, adding remaining garlic clove, ½ teaspoon salt, and ⅛ teaspoon pepper. Set aside.

**3.** Sprinkle veal cutlets on both sides with remaining 1 teaspoon Creole seasoning. Pound lightly with a meat mallet. In a large skillet, heat remaining oil over medium-high heat. Add cutlets to skillet, 2 at a time. Cook quickly to brown lightly on each side, turning once, about 30 seconds per side. Place on a plate.

**4.** Add sauce to skillet and heat through. Add cutlets; turn to coat with sauce and heat cutlets through. Spoon grits onto plates. Top each with a veal cutlet and spoon sauce over all.

## 120 CORNED BEEF HASH

*Prep: 20 minutes    Cook: 34 to 38 minutes    Serves: 6*

If you want to turn this into Red Flannel Hash, add 3 diced cooked beets along with the corned beef in step 3.

5 large red potatoes (about 2 pounds), scrubbed and halved
1 tablespoon butter
2 tablespoons olive oil
1 large onion, chopped
½ medium yellow or green bell pepper, cut into ½-inch dice
½ medium red bell pepper, cut into ½-inch dice

1 carrot, peeled and finely chopped
½ teaspoon salt
½ teaspoon freshly ground pepper
1 pound cooked corned beef, cut into ½-inch dice
2 scallions, thinly sliced

**1.** In a large saucepan, cover potatoes with cold water. Bring to boil and cook until tender but still firm, about 10 minutes; drain. When cool enough to handle, peel and cut into ½-inch dice.

**2.** In a large nonstick skillet, melt butter in oil over medium-high heat. Add onion and cook, stirring occasionally, until softened, about 3 minutes. Stir in potatoes, yellow pepper, red pepper, carrot, salt, and pepper. Cook, pressing and turning with a spatula, 5 minutes. Reduce heat to medium and cook, turning until vegetables are lightly browned, 8 to 10 minutes longer.

**3.** Add corned beef and ¼ cup water. Cook, turning with a spatula, until corned beef is hot, 8 to 10 minutes. Sprinkle scallions on top and serve.

## 121 BUTTERMILK PANCAKES

*Prep: 5 minutes    Cook: 3 minutes per batch    Makes: 8 pancakes*

If you need a bigger batch of these breakfast favorites, then double the recipe.

1 cup flour
1 tablespoon sugar
1 teaspoon baking powder
½ teaspoon baking soda

½ teaspoon salt
1 cup buttermilk
1 egg
2 tablespoons butter, melted

**1.** In a large bowl, combine flour, sugar, baking powder, baking soda, and salt. Stir well to mix. In a small bowl, whisk together buttermilk and egg until blended. Add to dry ingredients. Fold just until blended. Fold in melted butter.

**2.** Coat a large nonstick skillet with cooking spray and heat over medium heat. Ladle batter into skillet by ¼ cupfuls. Cook until bubbles form, about 2 minutes. Turn and cook until browned, about 1 minute. Serve hot.

## 122   BLUEBERRY CORNMEAL FLAPJACKS

*Prep: 12 minutes   Cook: 3 to 4 minutes per batch   Makes: 12*

1 cup flour
⅓ cup cornmeal
2 tablespoons sugar
1 tablespoon baking powder
¼ teaspoon salt
1 egg

1 cup milk
¼ cup sour cream
2 tablespoons butter, melted
1 cup blueberries
Unsalted butter and maple
   syrup as accompaniments

1. In a large bowl, combine flour, cornmeal, sugar, baking powder, and salt. Stir well. In a small bowl, combine egg, milk, and sour cream. Beat with a fork until blended. Add to dry ingredients and stir just until dry ingredients are moistened; there will be some lumps of flour. Add melted butter and stir just until blended.

2. Heat a griddle or large nonstick skillet over medium-high heat. Grease with a little butter. Ladle batter by ¼ cupfuls onto griddle. Sprinkle each pancake with about 1 tablespoon blueberries. Cook until browned on bottom, about 2 minutes, reducing heat if necessary. Turn and cook until browned, 1 to 2 minutes longer. Repeat with more butter and remaining batter and blueberries. Serve hot, with butter and maple syrup.

## 123   BUCKWHEAT CAKES

*Prep: 5 minutes   Cook: 3 minutes per batch*
*Makes: about 10 pancakes*

½ cup buckwheat flour
½ cup whole wheat flour
¼ cup all-purpose flour
1 teaspoon baking powder
½ teaspoon baking soda
½ teaspoon salt

1¼ cups buttermilk
2 tablespoons butter, melted
1 egg
2 tablespoons honey
3 tablespoons wheat germ

1. In a large bowl, combine buckwheat flour, whole wheat flour, all-purpose flour, baking powder, baking soda, and salt. Stir to mix well.

2. In a medium bowl, whisk together buttermilk, melted butter, egg, and honey. Add to dry ingredients and stir just until blended.

3. Heat a nonstick griddle or large skillet over medium heat. Coat with cooking spray. In batches, ladle batter by ¼ cupfuls onto skillet. Cook until browned on bottom and bubbles form on top, about 2 minutes. Sprinkle 1 scant teaspoon wheat germ over each pancake. Turn with spatula and cook until browned on the second side, about 1 minute. Serve hot.

# 124    SOURDOUGH PANCAKES

*Prep: 10 minutes    Cook: 3 minutes per batch    Makes: 12 pancakes*

1¼ cups sourdough starter, at
    room temperature (see
    Note, page 112)
1 egg
1 tablespoon maple syrup
½ cup milk

3 tablespoons butter, melted
1 cup flour
1 teaspoon baking powder
½ teaspoon baking soda
½ teaspoon salt
Butter, for frying

**1.** In a medium bowl, combine sourdough starter, egg, maple syrup, milk, and melted butter. Stir until well blended. In a small bowl, combine flour, baking powder, baking soda, and salt. Stir well. Add to wet ingredients and stir vigorously until blended. Batter will be lumpy.

**2.** Heat a griddle or large nonstick skillet over medium-high heat. Add 1 teaspoon butter and swirl to coat. In batches, ladle batter onto griddle by ¼ cupfuls. Reduce heat to medium and cook until bubbles form and edges are dry, about 2 minutes. Turn and cook until browned on second side, about 1 minute. Serve hot.

# 125    GOSSAMER GRIDDLE CAKES

*Prep: 5 minutes    Cook: 5 minutes per batch*
*Makes: about 12 pancakes*

It might be a bit more trouble to beat egg whites, but in this case it's worth it. Watch out—these are so light they may float off your plate.

1½ cups flour
1 tablespoon baking powder
1 tablespoon sugar
½ teaspoon salt

2 eggs, separated
1¼ cups milk
3 tablespoons butter, melted

**1.** Sift flour, baking powder, sugar, and salt into a medium bowl.

**2.** In a small bowl, beat egg whites with an electric mixer on medium-high speed until stiff but not dry. In another small bowl, beat yolks and milk with a fork. Stir yolk mixture into dry ingredients just until moistened; batter will have lumps. Stir in melted butter. Fold in beaten egg whites.

**3.** Coat a griddle or large skillet with cooking spray. Heat over medium heat until a drop of water sizzles. Pour batter by ⅓ cupfuls onto griddle, spreading batter slightly. Cook until tops have bubbles, about 3 minutes. Turn and cook until cakes are golden brown, about 2 minutes. Reduce heat to low if browning too fast. Serve hot.

# 126  GOLDEN FRENCH TOAST

*Prep: 5 minutes    Cook: 12 to 16 minutes    Serves: 4 to 6*

In French this is called *pain perdu*, or "lost bread," because it's a way of reviving day-old French bread. For a special breakfast, serve with powdered sugar and sliced strawberries.

| | |
|---|---|
| 1 tablespoon sugar | ¾ cup milk |
| ¼ teaspoon cinnamon | 4 tablespoons butter |
| 1 teaspoon vanilla extract | 12 slices (1 inch thick) |
| 2 tablespoons Grand Marnier | diagonally cut stale |
| or other orange liqueur | French bread |
| 5 eggs | |

**1.** In a pie plate, mix together sugar and cinnamon. Stir in vanilla and Grand Marnier. Add eggs and milk. Beat with a fork until blended.

**2.** In a large skillet, melt 2 tablespoons butter over medium heat until hot. Dip 6 slices of bread in egg mixture, letting slices soak but not become too soggy. Place in skillet and cook, turning once, until well browned, 3 to 4 minutes per side. Reduce heat to medium-low if browning too fast. Repeat with remaining butter and bread. Serve hot.

# 127  OVERNIGHT RAISED WAFFLES

*Prep: 10 minutes    Cook: 4 minutes per batch    Stand: overnight*
*Makes: 16 (4-inch) waffles*

| | |
|---|---|
| 1 envelope (¼ ounce) active | 1 tablespoon sugar |
| dry yeast | 2¼ cups flour |
| ⅓ cup warm water (105° to | ½ teaspoon salt |
| 115°F) | ¼ teaspoon baking soda |
| 6 tablespoons butter | 2 eggs, lightly beaten |
| 2 cups milk | 1½ teaspoons vanilla extract |

**1.** In a large bowl, sprinkle yeast over ⅓ cup warm water. Let stand 5 minutes until softened. In a small saucepan, melt butter over low heat, about 1 minute. Add milk and heat, stirring occasionally, until lukewarm, about 3 minutes. Add to yeast mixture. Add sugar, flour, and salt. Whisk until smooth. Cover with plastic wrap and let stand overnight at room temperature.

**2.** When ready to cook waffles, preheat waffle iron. In a small cup, dissolve baking soda in 1 teaspoon water. Add to batter with eggs and vanilla. Stir until blended.

**3.** Cook waffles according to manufacturer's directions until well browned and crisp. Serve hot.

# 128 OATMEAL PECAN BANANA WAFFLES

*Prep: 15 minutes    Cook: about 4 minutes per batch*
*Makes: 16 (4-inch) waffles*

These waffles have lots of flavor on their own and don't really need anything else, but they are good with some warmed honey or spread with butter and sprinkled with cinnamon sugar. Maple syrup overwhelms their delicate flavor.

½ **cup old-fashioned oats**
1 **cup pecans**
¼ **cup packed light brown**
   **sugar**
2 **cups flour**
2 **teaspoons baking powder**
½ **teaspoon baking soda**

¼ **teaspoon salt**
4 **eggs, separated**
4 **tablespoons butter, melted**
   **and cooled**
2 **cups buttermilk**
1 **large ripe banana, cut into**
   **¼-inch dice**

**1.** Preheat oven to 350°F. Spread out oats on a baking sheet. Bake 10 to 12 minutes, stirring once, or until lightly toasted. Set aside. Place pecans on baking sheet and bake 6 to 8 minutes, or until toasted. Let cool. Chop ½ cup pecans and place in a small bowl. Add ¼ cup oats, stir, and set aside.

**2.** In a food processor, combine remaining oats, pecans, and brown sugar. Process until pecans are finely ground. Add flour, baking powder, baking soda, and salt. Process until blended. Turn into a large bowl.

**3.** Preheat waffle iron. In a medium bowl, beat egg whites with an electric mixer on high speed until stiff but not dry. In a medium bowl, whisk together egg yolks and melted butter. Add buttermilk and whisk until blended. Add to dry ingredients. Stir until dry ingredients are moistened. Add banana. Gently fold egg whites into batter.

**4.** Sprinkle waffle iron evenly with some of pecan-oat mixture. Pour in batter. Cook according to manufacturer's directions until well browned and crisp. Repeat with remaining pecan mixture and batter. Serve waffles while hot.

# 129    CRISP SOUR CREAM WAFFLES

*Prep: 10 minutes    Cook: 5 minutes per batch*
*Makes: about 16 (4-inch) waffles*

2 cups flour
1 tablespoon sugar
2 teaspoons baking powder
1 teaspoon baking soda
¼ teaspoon salt

2 eggs, at room temperature
¾ cup sour cream
5 tablespoons butter, melted
1½ cups milk, at room
    temperature

**1.** Preheat waffle iron.

**2.** In a large bowl, combine flour, sugar, baking powder, baking soda, and salt. Stir well. In a medium bowl, whisk eggs, sour cream, butter, and milk until blended. Add to dry ingredients and stir well to combine. Batter will have small lumps of flour.

**3.** Cook waffles in a waffle iron according to manufacturer's directions until iron opens easily and waffles are well browned and crisp, about 5 minutes. Serve while hot.

# 130    HAM AND RED-EYE GRAVY

*Prep: 5 minutes    Cook: 9 minutes    Serves: 4 to 6*

Serve this with eggs over easy, biscuits, and grits for a true Southern breakfast.

1 tablespoon butter
1 fully cooked smoked ham
    steak (about 1 pound)
½ teaspoon cornstarch

½ cup half-and-half
⅓ cup brewed strong coffee
¼ teaspoon freshly ground
    pepper

**1.** In a medium skillet, melt butter over medium-high heat. Add ham slice. Cook, turning once, until browned, about 4 minutes per side. Remove ham to a serving platter. Cover to keep warm.

**2.** Whisk cornstarch into half-and-half. Add coffee and pepper to skillet. Place skillet over medium heat and bring to a boil, scraping up brown bits from bottom of pan, about 1 minute. Stir half-and-half and add to skillet. Bring to a boil, stirring, until slightly thickened, about 1 minute. Pour into a small pitcher and serve gravy with ham.

# 131   DENVER OMELET SANDWICHES
*Prep: 10 minutes    Cook: 8 to 12 minutes    Serves: 4*

Basically a Denver omelet is eggs with ham, onion, and green bell pepper. I like to add lots of pepper and hot sauce for some zip and to serve the omelet on toast. This is a lazy man's way of making an omelet. If available, use a sweet onion, like a Vidalia, Maui, Walla Walla, or Texas sweet.

| | |
|---|---|
| 2  tablespoons butter | ½  teaspoon salt |
| ¾  cup chopped onion | ½  teaspoon freshly ground |
| 1  medium green bell pepper, |    pepper |
|    cut into ½-inch dice | ½  cup shredded Cheddar |
| 6  slices of Canadian bacon, |    cheese |
|    diced | 8  slices of white bread, |
| 8  eggs |    toasted and buttered |
| 1  teaspoon hot pepper sauce | |

**1.** In a large nonstick skillet, melt butter over medium heat. Add onion, bell pepper, and Canadian bacon. Cook, stirring occasionally, until vegetables soften, 4 to 6 minutes.

**2.** Meanwhile, in a medium bowl, beat eggs, hot sauce, salt, pepper, and 2 tablespoons water with a fork. Add egg mixture to skillet. Reduce heat to medium-low and cook, stirring gently, until eggs are set but still moist, 3 to 5 minutes.

**3.** Cut eggs into quarters, turn with a wide spatula, and cook until just set on bottom, about 1 minute. Sprinkle with cheese, cover, and remove from heat. Let stand until cheese melts, about 1 minute.

**4.** Place eggs on buttered toast to make sandwiches. Cut sandwiches in half and serve at once.

# 132   STRAWBERRY-BANANA BREAKFAST SHAKE
*Prep: 5 minutes    Cook: none    Serves: 2*

If you're on the move in the morning, this makes a great breakfast to go.

| | |
|---|---|
| 1  cup nonfat plain yogurt | 1  cup diced mango |
| ½  cup strawberries, hulled | ¼  cup fresh orange juice |
| 1  small ripe banana, cut into | 1  tablespoon honey |
|    chunks | |

In a blender or food processor, combine yogurt, strawberries, banana, mango, orange juice, and honey. Blend on high speed until smooth and serve.

# 133 TRIPLE CHEESE AND TOMATO QUICHE

*Prep: 25 minutes    Chill: 1 hour 10 minutes*
*Cook: 1 hour 12 to 21 minutes    Serves: 6*

1 cup flour
2 tablespoons cornmeal
½ teaspoon salt
¼ cup grated Parmesan cheese
4 tablespoons cold butter, cut into small pieces
4 to 5 tablespoons ice water
2 small tomatoes, cut into 6 wedges each
3 slices of bacon, diced
1 medium red onion, sliced

3 cups packed fresh spinach leaves
1 tablespoon Dijon mustard
½ cup shredded Cheddar cheese
½ cup shredded Swiss cheese
2 whole eggs
2 egg yolks
1 cup half-and-half
¼ teaspoon freshly ground pepper

**1.** In a medium bowl, combine flour, cornmeal, ¼ teaspoon salt, and 3 tablespoons Parmesan cheese. Stir to combine. Add butter and cut in with a pastry blender or 2 knives until texture of meal. Drizzle in ice water, 1 tablespoon at a time, tossing with a fork until dough begins to clump together. Gather into a ball and press into a disk. Wrap in wax paper and refrigerate 1 hour.

**2.** Squeeze tomato wedges gently to remove seeds. Season cut sides lightly with ⅛ teaspoon salt and set aside on paper towels.

**3.** In a medium skillet, cook bacon over medium heat until crisp, 4 to 5 minutes. Remove to paper towels. Drain off all but 2 teaspoons fat from skillet. Add red onion and cook, stirring frequently, until softened and beginning to brown, 6 to 8 minutes. Remove to a plate. Increase heat to medium-high. Add spinach to skillet in 2 or 3 batches, cooking until wilted, about 1 minute per batch. Drain in colander. When cool enough to handle, squeeze to remove as much moisture as possible and coarsely chop.

**4.** On a lightly floured surface with a floured rolling pin, roll out dough to a 12-inch circle. Fit into a 10-inch fluted quiche pan. Press gently against bottom and sides of pan without stretching dough. Run rolling pin over top of pan to remove excess dough. Refrigerate 10 minutes.

**5.** Preheat oven to 425°F. Line pastry shell with foil; fill with dried beans. Bake 15 minutes, or until crust is set. Remove foil and beans and bake until edges are lightly browned and bottom begins to color, about 5 minutes. Let cool on a wire rack. Reduce oven temperature to 325°F.

**6.** Brush tart shell with mustard. Sprinkle with half of Cheddar and Swiss cheese. Top with sautéed red onion and spinach. Arrange tomato wedges in a circle. Sprinkle with bacon and remaining Cheddar and Swiss cheese. In a small bowl, whisk whole eggs, egg yolks, half-and-half, pepper, and remaining ⅛ teaspoon salt until blended. Pour evenly into shell. Sprinkle with remaining 1 tablespoon Parmesan cheese.

**7.** Bake 40 to 45 minutes, or until custard is set. Place on a wire rack and let cool. Serve quiche warm or at room temperature.

# Chapter 6

# The American Bread Basket

Is there anything that smells better than baking bread? Is there anything that tastes better than warm-from-the-oven biscuits, spread with butter? Before the days of grocery stores, housewives had to make bread every week; sometimes even a whole day was set aside just for baking bread. Now we have machines that make bread for us from start to finish, but I think making a loaf of homemade bread by hand is still a satisfying and rewarding thing to do.

Flour varies in moisture content, so when working with yeast breads, the amount of flour needed in a recipe will not always be the same. For best texture, keep doughs on the soft side, adding enough flour to keep the dough from sticking as you knead it. Kneading is an important step for proper texture and the formation of gluten, so don't skip it. Since flours do vary, you may need to add more flour or water to the dough to form a ball.

Bread rises better in a warm environment. Here's what I do: Preheat the oven on warm for 1 minute. Turn the oven off. Fill a pan with boiling water and place it in the oven. Let the bread rise in the oven. This comes close to what professional bakers use, called a proofing box.

A few of the home-style breads offered here are White Bread, Isabel's Jewish Rye Bread, and Cinnamon Raisin Bread. There are also an array of quick biscuits to choose from, such as Southern Buttermilk, Baking Powder, Angel, or Sweet Potato. Any of these can be mixed, baked, and on the table for dinner in no time flat. Remember, light kneading makes for light biscuits with good texture.

Quick mixing breads like Moist and Spicy Pumpkin Bread, Banana Bread, Zucchini Bread, or Cran-Apple Quick Bread make good snack and gift breads and are great to have on hand in the freezer. When mixing quick breads, stir just until the dry ingredients are moistened for the best texture, as overmixing causes breads to be tough.

For weekend mornings, you'll find some wonderful coffee cakes and muffins here—classic Sour Cream Coffee Cake, Apple Crumb Coffee Cake, Bursting with Blueberry Muffins, and Bran Muffins, to name a few. A note on muffin pans: I use muffin pans with cups that measure 2¾ inches across and hold a scant ½ cup. There are smaller muffin pans, which hold only ⅓ cup; if you have one of these, you will need to adjust the number of muffins and the baking time. Use paper liners if you like, although sometimes I prefer the browner sides produced from greased cups.

## 134    BAKING POWDER BISCUITS
*Prep: 10 minutes    Cook: 10 to 12 minutes    Makes: 16*

2 cups flour
1 tablespoon baking powder
½ teaspoon salt
5 tablespoons cold butter, cut
   into small pieces

3 tablespoons solid vegetable
   shortening
⅔ cup milk

**1.** Preheat oven to 450°F. In a food processor, combine flour, baking powder, and salt. Process to mix. Add butter and shortening and process just until mealy in texture; do not overprocess. Turn into a medium bowl. Add milk and stir until a soft dough forms.

**2.** Turn out dough onto a lightly floured surface and knead lightly, about 8 to 10 times. Pat out into an 8-inch square. Cut into 16 square biscuits. Place 1½ inches apart on a large baking sheet.

**3.** Bake 10 to 12 minutes, or until lightly browned. Transfer to a rack. Serve biscuits warm or at room temperature.

## 135    SOUTHERN BUTTERMILK BISCUITS
*Prep: 10 minutes    Cook: 10 to 12 minutes    Makes: 16*

Treat yourself and make a batch of these tender, light biscuits. Serve them hot and watch how quickly they disappear.

2 cups flour
2½ teaspoons baking powder
½ teaspoon baking soda
½ teaspoon salt
⅓ cup solid vegetable
   shortening

3 tablespoons cold butter, cut
   into small pieces
¾ cup buttermilk

**1.** Preheat oven to 425°F. In a large bowl, combine flour, baking powder, baking soda, and salt. Stir until blended. Cut in shortening and butter until mixture is texture of coarse meal. Add buttermilk and stir with a fork until dough clumps together. Turn out onto a lightly floured surface and knead lightly 5 times. Roll with a floured rolling pin to slightly over ½ inch thick. Cut with a floured 2-inch round cutter. Gather scraps and reroll once, cutting remaining biscuits. Place biscuits on an ungreased large baking sheet.

**2.** Bake 10 to 12 minutes, or until biscuits are golden brown. Remove to a rack. Serve hot.

# 136 CORNMEAL CHEDDAR DROP BISCUITS

*Prep: 10 minutes    Cook: 10 to 12 minutes    Makes: 12*

Cooked crumbled bacon, chopped scallions, or corn make great additions to these delightfully cheesy, crunchy biscuits. Add to the batter with the cheese.

2 cups flour
½ cup yellow cornmeal
1 tablespoon baking powder
½ teaspoon cayenne
¼ teaspoon salt
6 tablespoons cold butter, cut
  into small pieces

1 cup shredded sharp
  Cheddar cheese
1 egg, beaten
¾ cup milk

**1.** Preheat oven to 425°F. In a large bowl, combine flour, cornmeal, baking powder, cayenne, and salt. Stir well to mix. Add butter and cut in with a pastry blender or 2 knives until texture of meal. Stir in cheese.

**2.** In a small bowl, beat egg and milk Add to dry ingredients and stir just until moistened. Drop 12 tablespoonfuls 2 inches apart onto a greased large baking sheet.

**3.** Bake 10 to 12 minutes, or until golden brown. Remove to a wire rack to let cool. Serve warm or at room temperature.

# 137 SWEET POTATO BISCUITS

*Prep: 10 minutes    Cook: 12 to 15 minutes    Makes: 16*

Sweet potato adds a lovely golden orange color and extra moisture to these fluffy dinner biscuits. You can use freshly cooked or canned sweet potato or squash. One medium sweet potato yields about ¾ cup mashed.

1 cup heavy cream
¾ cup mashed cooked sweet
  potato, yam, or winter
  squash, cooled

2½ cups flour
1 tablespoon baking powder
¾ teaspoon salt

**1.** Preheat oven to 450°F. In a small bowl, combine cream and sweet potato. Whisk until blended.

**2.** In a large bowl, combine flour, baking powder, and salt. Stir until blended. Add sweet potato mixture. Stir with a fork until dough forms a ball. On a floured surface, knead lightly 5 to 6 times. On a lightly floured surface, with a floured rolling pin, roll out dough to an 8-inch square. Cut into 16 square biscuits. Place on a greased large baking sheet.

**3.** Bake 12 to 15 minutes, or until golden brown. Let cool on wire rack. Serve warm or at room temperature.

# 138    CHERRY HAZELNUT SCONES

*Prep: 10 minutes    Cook: 15 to 18 minutes    Makes: 12*

2 cups flour
¼ cup plus 1 tablespoon sugar
2 teaspoons baking powder
¼ teaspoon salt
6 tablespoons cold butter, cut into small pieces
¼ cup toasted chopped hazelnuts

¾ cup dried tart cherries, coarsely chopped
1 teaspoon grated orange zest
2 eggs
½ cup milk

**1.** Preheat oven to 425°F. In a large bowl, combine flour, ¼ cup sugar, baking powder, and salt. Stir to mix. Add butter and cut in with a pastry blender or 2 knives until mixture resembles coarse meal with some very small pieces of butter. Stir in hazelnuts, dried cherries, and orange zest.

**2.** In a small bowl, beat eggs with a fork. Pour off 1 tablespoon egg for glaze. Add milk to remaining eggs and beat with a fork to blend. Add to dry ingredients and toss with fork just until dry ingredients are moistened.

**3.** Drop dough by 12 heaping spoonfuls 2 inches apart onto a greased large baking sheet. Brush tops with egg glaze and sprinkle with remaining 1 tablespoon sugar.

**4.** Bake 15 to 18 minutes, or until scones are golden brown. Serve warm.

# 139    BUTTERMILK SPICE DOUGHNUTS

*Prep: 15 minutes    Chill: 1½ hours    Cook: 2 minutes per batch Makes: about 16*

3¾ cups flour
1½ tablespoons ground cinnamon
1½ teaspoons ground ginger
1 teaspoon grated nutmeg
2 teaspoons baking powder
1 teaspoon baking soda

½ teaspoon salt
4 tablespoons butter, melted
1¼ cups granulated sugar
2 eggs
1 cup buttermilk
Vegetable oil, for frying
¼ cup powdered sugar

**1.** Sift flour, 1 tablespoon cinnamon, ginger, nutmeg, baking powder, baking soda, and salt into a small bowl. Stir well to make sure spices are evenly mixed.

**2.** In a large bowl, with an electric mixer on low speed, beat butter, ¾ cup granulated sugar, eggs, and buttermilk until combined. Add half of dry ingredients and beat until blended. Stir in remaining dry ingredients. Cover and refrigerate 1½ hours.

3. In a deep fat fryer or heavy, deep skillet, heat 2 inches of vegetable oil to 365°F. Place half of dough on a floured surface and turn dough to coat with flour. Pat out dough to ⅜ inch thick. Cut with a floured 2¾-inch doughnut cutter.

4. Fry 3 to 4 doughnuts and a few holes at a time until browned and cooked through, turning once, about 2 minutes. Drain on a cookie sheet lined with paper towels. Repeat with remaining dough.

5. In a small paper bag, combine powdered sugar with remaining ½ cup granulated sugar and 1½ teaspoons cinnamon. Shake until blended. Shake doughnuts in sugar while warm. These are best served warm or a few hours after frying.

---

# 140 ANGEL BISCUITS
*Prep: 15 minutes    Stand: 35 minutes*
*Cook: 12 to 15 minutes    Makes: about 12*

These biscuits are exceptionally light, due to the triple rising power of baking powder, baking soda, and yeast. The dough can be made ahead and refrigerated for up to 3 days before using. Let the dough come to room temperature before shaping and baking.

1 envelope (¼ ounce) active
   dry yeast
1 tablespoon sugar
¼ cup warm water
   (105° to 115°F)
2½ cups flour
1½ teaspoons baking powder

½ teaspoon baking soda
¾ teaspoon salt
½ cup solid vegetable
   shortening
¾ cup buttermilk
2 tablespoons butter, melted

1. In a glass measuring cup, sprinkle yeast and sugar over ¼ cup warm water. Stir and let stand 5 minutes until yeast is foamy.

2. In a large bowl, combine flour, baking powder, baking soda, and salt. Stir until blended. Add shortening and cut in with a pastry blender until coarse crumbs form. Add yeast mixture and buttermilk and stir until a soft dough forms. Cover and let rest 10 minutes.

3. Preheat oven to 425°F. Turn dough out onto a floured surface. Knead lightly until smooth, about 10 times. With a floured rolling pin, roll out dough ½ inch thick. With a 2½-inch round cutter, cut as many biscuits as possible. Gather and reroll scraps twice, cutting out more biscuits. Place about 2 inches apart on ungreased baking sheets. Cover with a kitchen towel and let rise in a warm place 20 minutes. Remove towel and brush tops lightly with melted butter.

4. Bake 12 to 15 minutes, or until biscuits are browned. Transfer to a wire rack. These are best served warm.

# 141   CINNAMON ROLLS
*Prep: 10 minutes   Rise: about 2 to 2½ hours*
*Cook: 15 to 20 minutes   Makes: 8 to 12*

You can make either 8 jumbo rolls (my preference) or 12 normal-sized rolls.

1   envelope (¼ ounce) active dry yeast
½   cup plus 1 teaspoon granulated sugar
¼   cup warm water (105° to 115°F)
½   cup milk, heated (105° to 115°F)
6   tablespoons butter, softened
1   egg
½   cup unseasoned mashed potatoes
1   teaspoon vanilla extract
½   teaspoon salt
About 3½ cups flour
½   cup currants
1   tablespoon ground cinnamon
Easy Icing (recipe follows)

**1.** In a measuring cup, sprinkle yeast and 1 teaspoon sugar over ¼ cup warm water. Let stand 5 minutes until foamy.

**2.** In a large bowl, combine yeast mixture, ¼ cup sugar, milk, 3 tablespoons butter, egg, potatoes, vanilla, salt, and 2 cups flour. Beat well with a wooden spoon. Stir in enough remaining flour to make a soft dough. Place dough on a floured work surface and knead until smooth and elastic, about 5 minutes, adding additional flour as needed to keep dough from sticking, but keeping dough soft. Place dough in a greased bowl; turn greased side up. Cover and let rise in a warm place until doubled in bulk, 1 to 1½ hours.

**3.** Place currants in a small bowl, cover with hot water, and let stand until soft. In a small bowl, combine remaining ¼ cup sugar and 3 tablespoons butter with cinnamon and 1 tablespoon flour. Stir until well blended.

**4.** Punch down dough. Roll out on a floured surface to a 12 x 14-inch rectangle. Sprinkle dough with cinnamon filling up to ¾ inch from edges. Gently spread with a knife to cover dough. Filling will not cover dough completely. Drain currants and pat dry with a paper towel. Sprinkle over filling. Roll dough up from a short side. Pinch seam to seal. Cut into either 8 or 12 slices with a serrated knife. Place slices, cut sides down, in a large greased 15 x 10-inch jelly-roll pan. Cover and let rise until doubled, about 1 hour.

**5.** Preheat oven to 350°F. Bake rolls 15 to 20 minutes, or until golden brown. Let cool on a wire rack 15 minutes. Drizzle icing over warm rolls. Let rolls cool and serve warm or at room temperature.

## 142 EASY ICING
*Prep: 5 minutes   Cook: none   Makes: about 1 cup*

This simple icing works well for all kinds of sweet rolls, coffee cakes, and doughnuts.

1 cup powdered sugar
¼ teaspoon vanilla extract

4 to 4½ teaspoons milk

In a small bowl, combine powdered sugar, vanilla, and 4 teaspoons milk. Stir to make a smooth, thick glaze. Add remaining milk if necessary to thin enough to drizzle.

## 143 APPLE CRUMB COFFEE CAKE
*Prep: 20 minutes   Cook: 40 to 50 minutes   Serves: 8*

1¾ cups flour
½ cup sugar
1 teaspoon baking powder
½ teaspoon baking soda
½ teaspoon salt
6 tablespoons unsalted butter, melted
2 eggs

¾ cup plain low-fat yogurt
1 teaspoon vanilla extract
Walnut Streusel Topping (recipe follows)
2 McIntosh apples, peeled, cored, and cut into ½-inch dice

**1.** Preheat oven to 350°F. In a large bowl, combine flour, sugar, baking powder, baking soda, and salt. Stir until blended. In a small bowl, combine butter, eggs, yogurt, and vanilla. Whisk to mix. Add to dry ingredients and stir just until batter is blended.

**2.** Spread half of batter in a greased 9-inch round springform pan. It will be a thin layer. Sprinkle half of streusel and half of apples over batter. Drop on remaining batter by teaspoonfuls. Spread evenly; it will not cover apples completely. Sprinkle with remaining apples and then remaining streusel.

**3.** Bake 40 to 50 minutes, or until a toothpick inserted in center comes out clean. Let cool in pan on a wire rack. Serve warm or at room temperature.

### WALNUT STREUSEL TOPPING
*Makes: about 1 cup*

⅓ cup flour
⅓ cup sugar
2 tablespoons unsalted butter, softened

1 teaspoon ground cinnamon
½ cup chopped walnuts

In a small bowl, combine flour, sugar, butter, and cinnamon. Cut with pastry blender or rub with fingers until crumbly. Stir in walnuts.

# 144 STICKY BUNS

*Prep: 30 minutes    Rise: 3 hours    Cook: 27 to 30 minutes    Makes: 9*

Whether you call these sticky buns, honey buns, or sweet rolls, they are an all-time American favorite.

| | |
|---|---|
| 1 **envelope (¼ ounce) active dry yeast** | 9 **tablespoons butter, softened** |
| ¼ **cup warm water (105° to 115°F)** | ½ **teaspoon salt** |
| | ½ **cup plus 2 tablespoons brown sugar** |
| ¼ **cup granulated sugar** | 2 **tablespoons corn syrup** |
| 1 **egg** | 1½ **cups pecan halves** |
| ⅓ **cup milk** | 1 **teaspoon ground cinnamon** |
| 2½ **cups flour** | ¼ **cup raisins** |

**1.** In a measuring cup or small bowl, sprinkle yeast over ¼ cup warm water. Add 1 teaspoon granulated sugar and let stand 5 minutes until foamy. Mix in egg and milk.

**2.** In a food processor, combine remaining granulated sugar, flour, 3 tablespoons butter, and salt. Process until blended. With machine on, pour yeast mixture through feed tube. Process until dough forms a ball. If dough is too wet, add a little more flour 1 tablespoon at a time; if too dry, add water 1 teaspoon at a time until dough forms a ball. Process 45 seconds to knead dough. Remove dough to a greased bowl; turn greased side up. Cover with greased plastic wrap and let rise in a warm place until doubled in bulk, about 1½ hours. Punch dough down, cover, and let rise 30 minutes.

**3.** While dough rises, prepare glaze. In a small saucepan, combine 4 tablespoons butter, ½ cup brown sugar, and corn syrup. Cook over medium heat, stirring, until butter melts and mixture comes to a simmer, about 2 minutes. Pour into a greased 9-inch square baking pan; spread evenly. Sprinkle 1 cup pecan halves over caramel. Chop remaining pecans. In a small bowl, mix remaining 2 tablespoons brown sugar with cinnamon.

**4.** On a lightly floured surface, roll out dough to a 9-inch square. Spread remaining 2 tablespoons butter over dough. Sprinkle with brown sugar mixture, chopped pecans, and raisins. Roll dough up. Pinch long seam to seal. Cut crosswise into 9 slices about 1 inch thick and place cut sides down in pan. Cover with greased plastic wrap and let rise in a warm place until doubled, about 1 hour.

**5.** Preheat oven to 375°F. Bake 25 to 28 minutes, or until buns are well browned. Immediately place a serving plate or cookie sheet over rolls and carefully invert. Leave pan over rolls 5 minutes. Remove pan from rolls; scrape any glaze left in pan onto rolls. Let cool and serve warm.

## 145   CRAN-APPLE QUICK BREAD

*Prep: 10 minutes    Cook: 1 hour 10 to 15 minutes    Makes: 1 loaf*

3 cups flour
1¼ cups sugar
2½ teaspoons baking powder
½ teaspoon baking soda
½ teaspoon salt
1 stick (4 ounces) butter, cut into small pieces
1¼ cups fresh or frozen cranberries, coarsely chopped
1 small Golden Delicious apple, peeled, cored, and finely diced
½ cup chopped walnuts
2 eggs
1 cup fresh orange juice
1½ teaspoons grated orange zest

**1.** Preheat oven to 350°F. In a large bowl, combine flour, sugar, baking powder, baking soda, and salt. Stir well to mix. Add butter and cut in with pastry blender or 2 knives until mixture resembles cornmeal. Stir in cranberries, apple, and walnuts.

**2.** In a small bowl, whisk together eggs, orange juice, and orange zest. Add to flour mixture and stir just until dry ingredients are moistened. Turn into a greased 9 x 5 x 3-inch loaf pan.

**3.** Bake 1 hour 10 to 15 minutes, or until a toothpick inserted in center comes out clean. Cool in pan on wire rack 10 minutes. Run knife around sides and invert onto rack. Turn upright to let cool completely.

## 146   GOLDEN CORN BREAD

*Prep: 10 minutes    Cook: 22 to 25 minutes    Serves: 8*

What part of the country you live in dictates how much sugar to add to corn bread, whether you use buttermilk, and the ratio of cornmeal to flour. Wars could be fought over whose version is best. Here is my favorite. Use stone-ground cornmeal if you can find it.

1½ cups yellow cornmeal
¾ cup flour
2 tablespoons sugar
2 teaspoons baking powder
½ teaspoon baking soda
¾ teaspoon salt
2 eggs
¾ cup buttermilk
¾ cup milk
4 tablespoons butter, melted

**1.** Preheat oven to 425°F. Generously butter a 9-inch square baking pan.

**2.** In a large bowl, combine cornmeal, flour, sugar, baking powder, baking soda, and salt. Stir until well blended. In a small bowl, beat eggs with a fork. Stir in buttermilk and milk. Add to dry ingredients and stir just until dry ingredients are moistened. Add butter and stir quickly, just until blended; batter will not be completely smooth. Pour into pan.

**3.** Bake 22 to 25 minutes, or until golden brown and a toothpick inserted in center comes out clean. Let cool on a rack. Serve warm.

# 147   BANANA BREAD
*Prep: 10 minutes    Cook: 55 to 60 minutes    Makes: 1 loaf*

For best flavor, make sure the bananas are really ripe, which means letting the skins turn brown.

2¼  cups flour
1  teaspoon baking soda
1  teaspoon baking powder
½  teaspoon salt
1  stick (4 ounces) butter, softened
¾  cup sugar

2  eggs
3  ripe bananas, mashed, to yield 1¼ cups
¼  cup sour cream
1½  teaspoons grated orange zest
½  cup chopped pecans

1. Preheat oven to 350°F. Generously grease a 9 x 5 x 3-inch loaf pan.

2. In a medium bowl, combine flour, baking soda, baking powder, and salt. Stir well.

3. In a large bowl, combine butter and sugar. Beat with an electric mixer on medium speed until fluffy, about 1 minute. Beat in eggs one at a time until well blended. Stir in mashed bananas, sour cream, and orange zest. Stir in dry ingredients and pecans until moistened. Pour into pan; spread evenly.

4. Bake 55 to 60 minutes, or until a toothpick inserted in center comes out clean. Let cool on a wire rack 15 minutes. Run a knife around sides and invert onto a rack to unmold. Turn bread rounded side up and let cool completely.

# 148   MOIST AND SPICY PUMPKIN BREAD
*Prep: 10 minutes    Cook: 60 to 65 minutes    Makes: 2 loaves*

3  cups flour
2  teaspoons ground cinnamon
1½  teaspoons baking soda
½  teaspoon baking powder
½  teaspoon salt
½  teaspoon grated nutmeg
2¼  cups packed light brown sugar

¾  cup vegetable oil
3  eggs
1  (16-ounce) can solid-pack pumpkin
1  cup chopped walnuts
1  cup fresh or frozen cranberries, halved
½  cup golden raisins

1. Preheat oven to 350°F. Grease 2 (8 x 4 x 2½-inch) bread pans. Dust with flour; tap out excess.

2. In a medium bowl, combine flour, cinnamon, baking soda, baking powder, salt, and nutmeg. Stir well to mix.

3. In a large bowl, with an electric mixer on low speed, beat brown sugar, oil, and eggs until blended. Beat in half of flour mixture. Beat in half of pumpkin. Repeat with remaining flour and pumpkin. Stir in walnuts, cranberries, and raisins. Spoon batter into prepared pans, dividing evenly.

**4.** Bake 60 to 65 minutes, or until a toothpick inserted in centers comes out clean. Remove to a wire rack and let cool in pans 15 minutes. Run knife around edges and unmold onto rack. Turn top sides up to let cool completely.

---

## 149 SOUR CREAM COFFEE CAKE
*Prep: 15 minutes    Cook: 55 to 60 minutes    Serves: 12*

½  cup packed light brown
    sugar
¾  cup finely chopped pecans
2  teaspoons ground cinnamon
1½  sticks (6 ounces) unsalted
    butter, softened
1⅓  cups granulated sugar
3  large eggs, at room
    temperature

1  tablespoon vanilla extract
3  cups flour
2  teaspoons baking powder
1  teaspoon baking soda
¾  teaspoon salt
1½  cups sour cream

**1.** Preheat oven to 350°F. Grease a 12-cup bundt pan. Dust with flour; tap out excess. In a small bowl, combine brown sugar, pecans, and cinnamon. Stir until topping is mixed.

**2.** In a large bowl, with an electric mixer on medium-high speed, beat butter until fluffy. On medium speed, gradually beat in granulated sugar. Beat 2 minutes. Beat in eggs 1 at a time, mixing well after adding each. Beat in vanilla. Into a small bowl, sift flour, baking powder, baking soda, and salt. With mixer on low speed, alternately beat in flour mixture in thirds and sour cream, beginning and ending with flour mixture and beating just until blended.

**3.** Spread one third of batter (about 2 cups) in pan. Sprinkle with half of topping (¾ cup). Spoon on half of remaining batter. Sprinkle with remaining topping. Top with remaining batter, spreading it evenly.

**4.** Bake 55 to 60 minutes, or until a cake tester inserted in center comes out clean. Let cool in pan on a wire rack 20 minutes. Turn out onto wire rack to let cool completely.

# 150  ZUCCHINI BREAD
*Prep: 15 minutes    Cook: 55 to 60 minutes    Makes: 2 loaves*

This is a bread made by Chuck Page, a Cape Cod friend and bass fishing expert. He learned how to make this bread from his wife Nettie and uses the zucchini from his garden. The joke around town is to keep your car doors locked, so you won't find someone else's surplus on your car seat. If you do, use it up in this recipe.

2⅔ cups flour
1 tablespoon ground
    cinnamon
2 teaspoons baking soda
¼ teaspoon baking powder
1 teaspoon salt

3 eggs
1¾ cups sugar
1 cup vegetable oil
1 tablespoon vanilla extract
2 cups grated zucchini
1 cup walnuts, chopped

**1.** Preheat oven to 350°F. Grease and flour 2 (8 x 4 x 2½-inch) loaf pans.

**2.** Sift flour, cinnamon, baking soda, baking powder, and salt into a medium bowl.

**3.** In a large bowl, beat eggs, sugar, oil, and vanilla with an electric mixer on medium-high speed 2 minutes, or until slightly thickened. Stir in zucchini. Stir in dry ingredients until blended. Stir in nuts. Divide batter evenly between pans.

**4.** Bake 55 to 60 minutes, or until a toothpick inserted in centers comes out clean. Let cool in pans on a wire rack 15 minutes. Run a knife around sides, invert pans over rack, and rap firmly to release. Turn loaves rounded top side up and let cool completely on rack.

# 151  BRAN MUFFINS
*Prep: 10 minutes    Cook: 15 to 18 minutes    Makes: 12*

These are moist, full of raisins and walnuts, and not too sweet.

1 cup milk
¼ cup vegetable oil
3 tablespoons molasses
2 tablespoons light brown
    sugar
2 eggs
¾ cup raisins

1½ cups shredded bran cereal
    (All-Bran)
½ cup all-purpose flour
½ cup whole wheat flour
½ cup walnuts, chopped
1½ teaspoons baking soda
½ teaspoon salt

**1.** In a large bowl, combine milk, vegetable oil, molasses, brown sugar, and eggs. Whisk to blend. Stir in raisins and cereal and let stand 10 minutes, stirring once.

**2.** Preheat oven to 400°F. Line 12 (2¾-inch) muffin cups with paper liners. In a small bowl, combine all-purpose flour, whole wheat flour, walnuts, baking soda, and salt. Stir to mix well.

**3.** Add dry ingredients to bran mixture and stir just until dry ingredients are moistened. Spoon into muffin cups, filling each three-quarters full.

**4.** Bake 15 to 18 minutes, or until muffins spring back when pressed lightly. Let cool in pan 2 minutes. Remove muffins to a wire rack to let cool.

---

# 152    PENNSYLVANIA DUTCH SOFT PRETZELS
*Prep: 15 minutes    Rise: 30 minutes    Cook: 15 to 20 minutes*
*Makes: 8*

If you follow the instructions exactly in step 4, you should have no trouble forming pretzels. If you have any questions, practice with a piece of ribbon.

| | |
|---|---|
| 1 **envelope (¼ ounce) active dry yeast** | 3 **cups flour** |
| ¼ **cup warm water (105° to 115°F)** | ½ **teaspoon salt** |
| | 2 **tablespoons baking soda** |
| | **Coarse kosher salt** |

**1.** In a small bowl, sprinkle yeast over ¼ cup warm water and let stand 5 minutes until softened. Stir in ¾ cup cold water.

**2.** In a food processor, combine flour and salt; process to mix. With machine on, pour yeast mixture through feed tube. Process until dough cleans sides of bowl and forms a ball. Add additional flour or water 1 teaspoon at a time, if needed, if dough is too moist or dry. Process 45 seconds to knead. Place dough in a floured 1-gallon food storage bag, seal bag, and let dough rise in a warm place 30 minutes.

**3.** Preheat oven to 400°F. In a pie plate, whisk ½ cup cold water and baking soda. Punch down dough and divide into 8 equal pieces. Roll each piece into a 20-inch rope.

**4.** To form each into a pretzel shape: Lift ends of dough rope and cross one over other to form a large loop. Twist, switching ends from one hand to the other, and lay ends straight down over loop, extending beyond by about ½ inch. Press lightly to help adhere. Dip pretzels in dissolved baking soda and place on a greased baking sheet 2 inches apart. Sprinkle coarse salt over pretzels.

**5.** Bake 15 to 20 minutes, until browned. Let cool slightly on a wire rack. Serve warm.

# 153  BURSTING WITH BLUEBERRY MUFFINS
*Prep: 12 minutes    Cook: 20 to 25 minutes    Makes: 12*

These are best served warm from the oven. Try them with tiny wild Maine blueberries if you see them at your market.

1¼ cups fresh blueberries,
  rinsed
½ cup sugar
1¾ cups flour
1 tablespoon baking powder
¼ teaspoon salt

1 teaspoon grated lemon zest
1 egg, at room temperature,
  lightly beaten
1 cup milk, at room
  temperature
⅓ cup unsalted butter, melted

**1.** Preheat oven to 400°F. Line 12 (2¾-inch) muffin cups with paper liners. Place blueberries on paper towels and pat gently with paper towels to dry.

**2.** Set aside 1 tablespoon sugar. In a large bowl, combine remaining sugar, flour, baking powder, and salt. Mix well. Stir in blueberries. In a small bowl, combine lemon zest, egg, milk, and melted butter. Beat with a fork until blended. Add to dry ingredients and stir just until dry ingredients are moistened. Spoon into muffin cups, filling each three-quarters full. Sprinkle ¼ teaspoon reserved sugar over top of each.

**3.** Bake 20 to 25 minutes, or until tops spring back when pressed lightly. Let cool in pan 5 minutes. Remove muffins to wire rack to cool. Serve warm.

# 154  DOUBLE CORN MUFFINS
*Prep: 12 minutes    Cook: 15 minutes    Makes: 12*

Corn and Cheddar cheese make these tender muffins irresistible for snacking as well to accompany a meal. Do not use paper liners here, or the muffins will stick to them.

1½ cups yellow cornmeal
¾ cup flour
2 tablespoons sugar
2 teaspoons baking powder
½ teaspoon baking soda
¾ teaspoon salt
½ teaspoon freshly ground
  pepper
2 eggs

¾ cup buttermilk
¾ cup milk
½ cup fresh or frozen corn
  kernels
½ cup shredded sharp
  Cheddar cheese
1 fresh jalapeño pepper,
  seeded and minced
4 tablespoons butter, melted

**1.** Preheat oven to 425°F. In a large bowl, combine cornmeal, flour, sugar, baking powder, baking soda, salt, and pepper. Stir or whisk gently to mix well.

**2.** In a small bowl, beat eggs with a fork. Stir in buttermilk and milk. Add to dry ingredients along with corn, cheese, and jalapeño pepper. Stir just until dry ingredients are moistened. Add butter and stir quickly, just until blended. Spoon batter into 12 well-greased muffin cups, filling each three-quarters full.

**3.** Bake muffins 15 minutes, or until tops spring back when pressed. Let cool in pan 2 minutes. Remove to a wire rack to cool slightly. Serve warm.

---

# 155    CHEWY HOMEMADE BAGELS

*Prep: 20 minutes    Rise: 1 hour 20 minutes    Cook: 21 minutes*
*Makes: 12*

2 envelopes (¼ ounce each)
  active dry yeast
3 tablespoons sugar
1½ cups warm water (105° to
  115°F)

4 cups bread flour
2 tablespoons coarse kosher
  salt
1 egg
  Sesame or poppy seeds

**1.** In 2-cup glass measure, sprinkle yeast and 1 tablespoon sugar over 1½ cups warm water. Stir and let stand 5 minutes until foamy.

**2.** In a food processor, combine flour and 1 tablespoon salt. Process briefly to mix. With machine on, add yeast mixture through feed tube. Process until dough forms a ball. Process another 45 seconds to knead. Place in a bowl, cover with greased plastic wrap, and let rise until doubled, about 1 hour.

**3.** Punch down dough. Divide into 12 pieces. Roll each piece into a 10-inch rope and join ends, pressing firmly. Place 2 inches apart on generously floured cookie sheets and cover with towels. Let rise in a warm place until almost doubled, about 20 minutes.

**4.** Preheat oven to 450°F. Adjust oven rack to upper third. Fill a large deep skillet with water. Bring to a boil. Add remaining sugar and salt to water. Reduce heat so water is at a gentle simmer. Add 3 bagels at a time. Simmer 1 minute, turn, and simmer 30 seconds longer. Remove with a slotted spoon to a towel. Repeat with remaining bagels. Place on greased baking sheets.

**5.** In a small cup, beat egg and 2 teaspoons water with a fork. Brush lightly over bagels. Sprinkle with sesame or poppy seeds. Bake 15 minutes, or until browned. Remove to wire racks to let cool.

# 156 PEPPER PARMESAN POPOVERS
*Prep: 5 minutes    Cook: 55 minutes    Makes: 6*

These got this name because when baked the batter pops up over the cups. They won't be quite as high as plain popovers, but the great taste of Parmesan cheese makes up for it.

2 **eggs**
¾ **cup milk**
1 **cup flour**
½ **teaspoon salt**

½ **teaspoon coarsely ground pepper**
½ **cup grated Parmesan cheese**

**1.** Preheat oven to 375°F. Adjust oven rack to bottom. Generously butter a 6-cup popover pan or 6 (6-ounce) ovenproof glass custard cups.

**2.** In a large bowl, whisk together eggs, milk, and ¼ cup water. Add flour, salt, and pepper. Whisk until blended but still with lumps of flour.

**3.** Pour half of batter into cups, dividing evenly. Sprinkle half of cheese over batter in cups. Repeat with remaining batter and cheese.

**4.** Bake on bottom oven rack 45 minutes. Make a ½-inch slit in each popover with a sharp paring knife. Bake 10 minutes. Remove popovers from cups immediately and serve while hot and crisp.

# 157 GARLIC LOVER'S GARLIC BREAD
*Prep: 10 minutes    Cook: 55 to 60 minutes    Serves: 8*

8 **garlic cloves, peel left on**
   **7 cloves**
3 **tablespoons butter, softened**
2 **tablespoons garlic-flavored oil**
3 **tablespoons grated Parmesan cheese**

2 **tablespoons chopped flat-leaf parsley**
1 **large loaf of Italian bread (about 16 inches long)**

**1.** Preheat oven to 400°F. Wrap garlic cloves with peel in foil and bake 30 minutes, or until soft. Let cool.

**2.** Squeeze pulp from garlic cloves into a small bowl. Mash with a fork. Add butter, oil, cheese, and parsley. Stir well with a fork to blend. Crush remaining clove of raw garlic through a press into butter mixture. Stir well.

**3.** Reduce oven temperature to 350°F. Cut bread into 1-inch-thick slices without cutting completely through loaf, so slices remain attached. Spread garlic mixture on cut sides of slices. Wrap loaf loosely in foil.

**4.** Bake 20 minutes. Unwrap to expose top and bake 5 to 10 minutes, or until crusty and hot. Serve hot.

# 158 OVERNIGHT POTATO ROLLS

*Prep: 10 minutes    Stand: overnight plus 1½ to 2 hours*
*Cook: 15 minutes    Makes: 15*

Yeast seems to thrive on potatoes, which add lightness and moisture to these rolls. It's best to use freshly mashed potatoes, but instant will do. These freeze well.

1 envelope (¼ ounce) active dry yeast
2 tablespoons sugar
¼ cup warm water (105° to 115°)
½ cup milk
5 tablespoons butter
¾ cup unseasoned mashed potatoes

1 egg
1¼ teaspoons salt
3 to 3½ cups flour
1 egg beaten with 1 teaspoon water
Sesame and poppy seeds

**1.** In a small bowl, sprinkle yeast and 1 teaspoon sugar over ¼ cup warm water. Stir, then let stand 5 minutes until foamy. In a small saucepan, heat milk and butter until warm (105° to 115°F); butter does not have to melt completely.

**2.** In a large bowl, combine yeast mixture, remaining sugar, warm milk mixture, and potatoes. Beat well with an electric mixer on low speed. Add egg, salt, and 2½ cups flour. Beat well. Stir in ½ cup flour to make a soft dough. Turn dough out onto a floured surface and knead until smooth, about 8 minutes, kneading in remaining flour as needed to keep dough from sticking. Place dough in a large greased bowl; turn greased side up. Cover with greased plastic wrap. Refrigerate overnight.

**3.** Punch down dough. Divide into 15 pieces. Roll each into a ball. Place in a greased 13 x 9 x 2-inch baking pan. Cover with greased plastic wrap and let rise in a warm place until doubled, 1½ to 2 hours.

**4.** Preheat oven to 375°F. Brush rolls lightly with egg glaze. Sprinkle with seeds, alternating kinds. Bake 15 minutes, or until golden brown. Let cool on a wire rack. Serve warm or at room temperature.

# 159 ISABEL'S JEWISH RYE BREAD

*Prep: 30 minutes    Stand: 2 days    Rise: 1 hour*
*Cook: 30 to 35 minutes    Makes: 2 loaves*

This recipe comes from special friend and expert baker Isabel Tannenbaum, who ran a bakery for 30 years in my hometown of Racine, Wisconsin. Her parents brought this recipe from Russia, and Isabel's customers couldn't wait for this bread to cool before buying as many loaves as she could bake. This recipe gets its old world flavor from a starter that needs a day to develop.

| | |
|---|---|
| 1½ cups medium rye flour | 3 cups all-purpose flour |
| 1¾ cups warm water (105° to 115°F) | 1 tablespoon caraway seeds |
| 1 envelope (¼ ounce) active dry yeast | 2 teaspoons salt |
| | 1 large egg |
| | Cornmeal |

**1.** In a large bowl, combine rye flour and 1½ cups warm water. Whisk until smooth. Cover with a kitchen towel. Let stand in a warm place for 2 days.

**2.** In a small bowl, sprinkle yeast over remaining ¼ cup warm water. Stir into rye starter. In a food processor, combine all-purpose flour, caraway seeds, and salt. Process until blended. With machine on, gradually pour rye starter through feed tube. Process until dough forms a ball. Add water 1 teaspoon at a time if too dry, or flour 1 tablespoon at a time if too wet, until dough forms a ball. Process 30 seconds to knead. Place dough in a lightly oiled bowl; turn over to oil both sides. Cover with oiled plastic wrap and let rest 30 minutes.

**3.** Divide dough in half. Shape each half into an 8-inch-long loaf, tapering ends. Place loaves on a large baking sheet greased and dusted with cornmeal with space in between for rising. Cover with oiled plastic wrap and let rise in warm place until almost doubled, about 1 hour.

**4.** Preheat oven to 450°F. Place a roasting pan on bottom oven rack and fill with boiling water. Beat egg with a pinch of salt. Brush loaves with egg glaze. Make 4 diagonal slashes ½ inch deep in top of each loaf with a sharp knife.

**5.** Bake 15 minutes. Reduce oven temperature to 375°F and bake 15 to 20 minutes, or until well browned. Remove to a wire rack and let cool completely.

# 160    CINNAMON RAISIN BREAD

*Prep: 20 minutes    Rise: about 2¼ to 2¾ hours    Cook: 35 minutes*
*Makes: 1 loaf*

This is a recipe from baker Isabel Tannenbaum. Thanks, Isabel.

1 envelope (¼ ounce) active
   dry yeast
¼ cup granulated sugar
¼ cup warm water (105° to
   115°F)
½ cup evaporated milk
¼ cup corn oil
1 large egg

2¾ cups flour
1 teaspoon salt
¾ cup raisins
2 tablespoons light brown
   sugar
1½ teaspoons ground cinnamon
1 tablespoon butter, at room
   temperature

**1.** In a small bowl, sprinkle yeast and a pinch of granulated sugar over
¼ cup warm water and let stand 5 minutes until foamy.

**2.** In a large bowl, combine yeast mixture, remaining granulated sugar,
evaporated milk, oil, egg, 1½ cups flour, and salt. Beat well with a wooden
spoon. Stir in raisins. Add enough remaining flour to make a soft dough.

**3.** On a lightly floured surface, knead dough until it forms a smooth ball,
adding enough flour to keep dough from sticking but keeping dough soft.
Place in a greased bowl; turn to grease top. Cover with oiled plastic wrap
and let rise in a warm place until doubled, 1½ to 2 hours.

**4.** In a small bowl, combine brown sugar and cinnamon. Punch down
dough. Roll out on a lightly floured surface to a 12 x 7-inch rectangle.
Spread butter over dough and sprinkle cinnamon-brown sugar mixture to
within ¾ inch from edges. Roll up from a short end and pinch seam and
ends to seal. Place seam side down in a well-greased 8 x 4-inch loaf pan.
Cover with oiled plastic wrap and let rise in warm place until almost doubled, about 45 minutes.

**5.** Preheat oven to 350°F. Bake 35 minutes, or until well browned, covering
loosely with foil last 5 minutes if browning too quickly. Remove bread from
pan and let cool completely on a wire rack.

# 161    SAN FRANCISCO–STYLE SOURDOUGH BREAD

*Prep: 25 minutes    Stand: 12 to 24 hours    Rise: 5 to 7 hours*
*Cook: 25 minutes    Makes: 2 loaves*

Warning: This will not taste exactly like San Francisco sourdough bread, so don't be disappointed. People swear there are unique spores in the salt air that make San Francisco sourdough bread so special, and I think it's true. But this is good, and it comes close. Sourdough bread requires some time commitment, but it's stretched out over two days and really is not much work. This recipe has been adapted from King Arthur's version.

| | |
|---|---|
| 1  cup sourdough starter (see Note) | 5  to 6 cups unbleached flour |
| 1½  cups warm water (105° to 115°F) | 1  tablespoon salt |
| | 1  teaspoon baking soda |
| | Cornmeal |

**1.** In a large glass or ceramic bowl, combine sourdough starter, 1½ cups warm water, and 3 cups flour. Beat well with a wooden spoon. Cover with plastic wrap and let rest overnight or up to 24 hours. Mixture will bubble up.

**2.** Remove plastic wrap. In a small bowl, combine 1¾ cups flour, salt, and baking soda; stir well. Add this to the sponge and mix until a soft dough forms. Turn out onto a lightly floured surface. Knead 4 minutes, adding enough remaining flour to keep dough from sticking. Cover dough with a kitchen towel and let rest 5 minutes.

**3.** Clean and grease large bowl. Knead dough until smooth and elastic, 3 to 4 minutes. Place in bowl and turn greased side up. Cover and let rise 3 to 4 hours, or until doubled.

**4.** Punch down dough. Divide in half. Grease a large cookie sheet and sprinkle with cornmeal. Shape each piece into a smooth ball on a lightly floured surface. Place smooth side up on a baking sheet, spacing loaves apart to allow room for rising. Cover with greased plastic wrap and let rise until doubled, 2 to 3 hours.

**5.** Preheat oven to 450°F. Fill a baking pan with boiling water and place on bottom oven rack. Uncover bread. Slash tops ½ inch deep in a tic-tac-toe pattern with a sharp knife.

**6.** Bake 25 minutes, or until well browned. Remove loaves to a wire rack to let cool completely.

**NOTE:**  *To begin making sourdough bread, you need a starter. Rather than relying on chance and the sometimes difficult task of capturing natural yeast spores in the air, I use a proven starter. My favorite is the "Classic Sourdough Starter" from King Arthur, the New England flour producers: The King Arthur Flour Baker's Catalog, P.O. Box 876, Norwich, VT 05055-0876; (800) 827-6836. Specialty food shops and some health food stores also sell starter. If your water is chlorinated, let it sit out uncovered overnight so the chlorine will dissipate, or use bottled water. For additional information, see instructions included with starter.*

# 162     WHITE BREAD

*Prep: 15 minutes     Rise: 1 hour 50 minutes     Cook: 25 to 30 minutes*
*Makes: 2 loaves*

This recipe is based on a recipe from Brother Samuel Pipher, who bakes 25 loaves of this bread every Saturday for his fellow brothers in a religious community in Orleans, Massachusetts. This bread is a great seller at their Christmas fair every year.

| | |
|---|---|
| 6 to 6½ cups bread flour | 2½ teaspoons salt |
| 2 envelopes (¼ ounce each) active dry yeast | ⅓ cup canola oil |
| | 2 cups milk |
| 3 tablespoons sugar | 2 large eggs |

**1.** In a large bowl, combine 2½ cups flour, yeast, sugar, and salt. Stir until well blended.

**2.** In a small saucepan, heat oil and milk over low heat until very warm (120° to 130°F). Add milk mixture to dry ingredients. Beat with an electric mixer on medium speed 2 minutes. Add eggs and ½ cup flour and beat on high speed 2 minutes. Stir in enough remaining flour to make a soft dough. Turn dough out onto a lightly floured surface and knead until smooth and elastic, about 6 minutes

**3.** Place dough in a greased bowl; turn greased side up. Cover with oiled plastic wrap and a kitchen towel and let rise in a warm place until doubled, about 1 hour.

**4.** Punch down dough and divide in half. Roll each half out to a 9 x 7-inch rectangle. Roll up from a short side; pinch seam to seal. Place each loaf seam side down in 2 greased 8 x 4-inch loaf pans. Cover with oiled plastic wrap and a towel and let rise in a warm place until almost doubled, about 50 minutes.

**5.** Preheat oven to 375°F. Bake loaves 25 to 30 minutes, or until well browned. Remove from pans and let cool on a wire rack.

# 163    PARKER HOUSE ROLLS

*Prep: 10 minutes    Rise: about 2 hours 15 minutes*
*Cook: 12 minutes per batch    Makes: about 20*

These buttery rolls, from Boston's Parker House Hotel, have a distinctive shape with a fold in the middle that makes them easy to tear in half.

| | |
|---|---|
| 3  **cups flour** | 1  **teaspoon salt** |
| 1  **envelope (¼ ounce) active** | ¾  **cup milk** |
|      **dry yeast** | 6  **tablespoons butter** |
| 1  **tablespoon sugar** | 1  **large egg** |

**1.** In a food processor, combine flour, yeast, sugar, and salt.

**2.** In a medium saucepan, heat milk over low heat until very warm (120° to 130°F). Add 4 tablespoons butter to milk. Turn on processor and pour warm milk mixture and egg through feed tube. Process until dough forms a ball. If dough is too dry to form a ball, add water by 1 teaspoon at a time; if too wet, add flour 1 tablespoon at a time. Process 45 seconds to knead dough.

**3.** Remove dough to a large greased bowl; turn over to grease top. Cover with plastic wrap and let rise in a warm place until doubled, about 1½ hours.

**4.** Punch down dough. On a floured surface, roll out half of dough to ½ inch thick. Cut out rounds with a floured 2½-inch cookie cutter. Fold rounds over so edges meet in a half-moon shape; press lightly. Place 1 inch apart on greased baking sheets. Repeat with remaining dough. Melt remaining butter. Brush rolls lightly with butter. Cover with oiled plastic wrap and let rise in a warm place until almost doubled in size, about 45 minutes.

**5.** Preheat oven to 375°F. Bake 1 sheet at a time 12 minutes, or until rolls are browned. Remove to wire racks to let cool. Serve warm.

*Chapter 7*

# The Main Event

One of the daily dilemmas most of us face is what to make for dinner. In this chapter you will find over 40 ideas for main-dish chicken, turkey, beef, lamb, and pork, plus a few pizzas and pastas. The following two chapters cover fish and shellfish and barbecued meats and seafood—for a total of over 7 dozen ways to feed your family and guests.

Many of us don't eat meat every night of the week, which was customary in years gone by. We have more variety now than ever before, with products like ground turkey and chicken, and meat counters in the grocery store filled with partially prepared products, such as chicken cut up for stir-fry or trimmed, beef already cubed for stew, to help us get dinner on the table faster. A few home-style dinner classics you'll find here are All-American Beef Stew, Meat Loaf, Down-Home Chicken Pot Pie, Cider and Onion Smothered Pork Chops, and New England Boiled Dinner. There are chilis and stews, skillet dishes and roasts.

One of the most popular foods these days is pasta. All kinds of fresh and dried pastas are available in supermarkets along with lots of good prepared sauces that are a real convenience. Try my Spaghetti and Meatballs, Vegetable Lasagna, Turkey Tetrazzini, or Macaroni and Cheese. I've given each of these favorites my own special twist.

## 164   SUNDAY BEST ROAST CHICKEN
*Prep: 10 minutes    Cook: 1½ hours    Serves: 6 to 8*

1   large roasting chicken (5 to
   5½ pounds)
2   tablespoons olive oil
2   garlic cloves, minced
2   teaspoons minced fresh
   rosemary or ¾ teaspoon
   dried

¾   teaspoon salt
¾   teaspoon freshly ground
   pepper
2   tablespoons flour (optional)

**1.** Preheat oven to 425°F. Rinse chicken and pat dry. In a small bowl, combine oil, garlic, rosemary, and all but ⅛ teaspoon salt and ⅛ teaspoon pepper. Stir to mix.

**2.** Rub about one-third of the garlic oil in cavity of chicken. Loosen skin covering breast with fingers without tearing skin. Rub all but 1½ teaspoons garlic oil under skin on chicken breasts and as much of thighs and drumsticks as possible. Rub outside skin with remaining 1½ teaspoons oil. Season with reserved salt and pepper. Tie drumsticks together. Tuck wings under.

**3.** Place chicken on a rack in a shallow roasting pan. Roast 30 minutes. Reduce oven temperature to 375°F. Roast 1 hour longer, or until an instant-reading thermometer registers 180°F when inserted in thickest part of thigh without touching bone and thigh juices run clear when pierced with tip of a sharp knife.

**4.** If you want to make gravy, spoon off all but 2 tablespoons fat from roasting pan. Add ¾ cup water to roasting pan and bring to a boil over high heat, scraping up brown bits from bottom of pan. In a small jar, shake ¼ cup cold water and 2 tablespoons flour until smooth. Gradually whisk into juices in roasting pan until blended and smooth. Reduce heat and simmer 3 minutes. Season with additional salt and pepper to taste.

## 165   BUTTERMILK FRIED CHICKEN
*Prep: 15 minutes    Chill: 2 hours    Cook: 20 minutes    Serves: 4*

1   small chicken (2¾ to
   3 pounds)
2   cups buttermilk
1½   teaspoons salt
1½   teaspoons freshly ground
   pepper

½   teaspoon cayenne
1½   cups flour
2   tablespoons cornmeal
¼   teaspoon paprika
   Solid vegetable shortening,
   for frying

**1.** Cut chicken into 8 pieces. In a large bowl, stir buttermilk, ¼ teaspoon salt, ¼ teaspoon pepper, and ¼ teaspoon cayenne until blended. Add chicken pieces and turn to coat. Cover and refrigerate chicken 2 hours.

**2.** In a large sturdy paper bag, combine flour, cornmeal, paprika, and remaining 1¼ teaspoons each salt and pepper and ¼ teaspoon cayenne. Shake to mix. Drain chicken in a colander. Remove chicken 1 piece at a time, letting excess buttermilk drip off; add to seasoned flour mixture and shake to coat. Place on a rack, skin side up. Repeat until all chicken is coated.

**3.** In 2 large heavy skillets, melt enough shortening to measure ½ inch deep. Heat over medium-high heat until shortening reaches 360°F. Shake chicken pieces in flour mixture again. Place skin side down in skillets. Cook, turning frequently and maintaining heat at 320°F, until well browned and cooked through, about 20 minutes. Drain on paper towels. Serve hot or at room temperature.

## 166   COUNTRY CAPTAIN
*Prep: 20 minutes    Cook: 25 to 30 minutes    Serves: 4*

2  tablespoons flour
½  teaspoon paprika
4  skinless, boneless chicken
    breast halves, each cut
    crosswise in half
¾  teaspoon salt
¼  teaspoon freshly ground
    pepper
2  tablespoons olive oil
1  medium onion, chopped
1  medium yellow bell pepper,
    cut into ½-inch dice
½  medium green bell pepper,
    cut into ½-inch dice

½  medium red bell pepper, cut
    into ½-inch dice
2  garlic cloves, crushed
    through a press
2  teaspoons curry powder
¼  teaspoon dried thyme
1  (16-ounce) can diced
    tomatoes in juice
¼  cup dry red wine
3  tablespoons dried currants
⅓  cup sliced almonds, toasted
    Hot cooked rice and
    mango chutney, as
    accompaniments

**1.** On a plate, mix flour and paprika. Season chicken pieces with ¼ teaspoon salt and ⅛ teaspoon pepper. Dredge in seasoned flour to coat; shake off excess. Heat oil in a large flameproof casserole over medium-high heat. Add chicken and cook 2 minutes on each side, or until lightly browned.

**2.** Reduce heat to medium. Add onion and bell peppers to casserole. Cook, stirring frequently, 5 minutes, or until softened. Stir in garlic, curry powder, and thyme and cook, stirring, 1 minute. Add tomatoes with their juice, wine, and remaining ½ teaspoon salt and ⅛ teaspoon pepper. Bring to a boil. Reduce heat and simmer 5 minutes. Stir in currants.

**3.** Return chicken to casserole. Partially cover and simmer until chicken is tender and white in center, 10 to 15 minutes. Sprinkle with almonds. Serve over rice with chutney.

## 167    OVEN-FRIED CHICKEN
*Prep: 10 minutes    Chill: 1 hour    Cook: 1 hour    Serves: 4*

An easy way to remove the skin from chicken since it's so slippery is to hold it with a piece of paper towel and pull.

| | |
|---|---|
| 1 (3½-pound) chicken, cut into 8 pieces | 3 tablespoons flour |
| 1 cup buttermilk | 3 tablespoons cornmeal |
| 1 garlic clove, crushed through a press | 1 teaspoon salt |
| ½ cup plain dry bread crumbs | ½ teaspoon freshly ground pepper |
| | ¼ teaspoon cayenne |

**1.** Remove as much skin as possible from chicken. In a medium bowl, combine buttermilk and garlic. Add chicken and turn to coat. Cover and refrigerate 1 hour or overnight.

**2.** In a paper bag, combine bread crumbs, flour, cornmeal, salt, pepper, and cayenne. Shake to combine. Drain chicken in a colander. Pick up chicken 1 piece at a time, letting excess buttermilk drip off. Add to bag and shake in crumb mixture until coated.

**3.** Preheat oven to 400°F. Place chicken bone side down on a jelly-roll pan coated with olive oil cooking spray. Spray chicken lightly with cooking spray.

**4.** Bake chicken 1 hour, or until browned outside with no trace of pink near bone.

## 168    CHICKEN AND DUMPLINGS
*Prep: 25 minutes    Cook: 56 to 64 minutes    Serves: 4*

| | |
|---|---|
| ½ cup plus 1⅓ cups flour | 4 large carrots, peeled and sliced |
| 1 teaspoon salt | 2 medium celery ribs, cut into ½-inch dice |
| ½ teaspoon freshly ground pepper | 1 bay leaf |
| 1 (3½-pound) chicken, cut into 8 pieces | ½ teaspoon dried thyme |
| 2 tablespoons olive oil | ¼ teaspoon crumbled dried sage |
| 1 tablespoon butter | ½ cup frozen peas |
| 2 large leeks (white part only), sliced, rinsed, and drained | 2 teaspoons baking powder |
| 1 small onion, chopped | 2 tablespoons chopped parsley |
| 2½ cups chicken broth | ¾ cup half-and-half |

**1.** In a pie plate, combine ½ cup flour, ½ teaspoon salt, and pepper. Stir to mix. Dredge chicken in seasoned flour to coat. Shake off excess.

**2.** In a large Dutch oven, heat oil and butter over medium-high heat. Add chicken in 2 batches and cook, turning, until browned, 6 to 7 minutes per batch. Drain on paper towels. Pour off all but 2 tablespoons drippings from pan. Add leeks and onion to Dutch oven. Cook over medium heat, stirring occasionally, until softened, 2 to 3 minutes. Add broth, carrots, celery, bay leaf, thyme, and sage. Bring to a boil, add chicken, and reduce heat to medium-low. Simmer 30 to 35 minutes, partially covered, stirring occasionally, until chicken is tender and cooked. Remove and discard bay leaf. Add peas.

**3.** Make dumplings: Sift 1⅓ cups flour, baking powder, and remaining ½ teaspoon salt into a medium bowl. Stir in parsley. Add half-and-half and stir just until blended. Spoon rounded tablespoons of the dough over chicken mixture, making 8 dumplings. Cover and simmer over medium-low heat 12 minutes, or until a toothpick inserted into dumplings comes out clean.

---

# 169   CHICKEN AND RICE CASSEROLE
*Prep: 20 minutes   Cook: 62 to 67 minutes   Serves: 6*

1¼ cups long-grain white rice
1 (3½-pound) chicken, cut into 8 pieces, skin removed
½ teaspoon salt
¼ teaspoon freshly ground pepper
2 teaspoons olive oil
1 medium onion, chopped
1 medium red bell pepper, cut into ½-inch dice
1 medium green bell pepper, cut into ½-inch dice

3 garlic cloves, crushed through a press
¼ teaspoon crushed hot red pepper
1 (14.5-ounce) can Italian-style stewed tomatoes
2 cups chicken broth
⅓ cup sliced pimiento-stuffed green olives
2 tablespoons chopped cilantro

**1.** Preheat oven to 350°F. Spread rice over bottom of a 13 x 9 x 2-inch baking dish.

**2.** Sprinkle chicken with ¼ teaspoon salt and ⅛ teaspoon pepper. In a large nonstick skillet, heat oil over medium-high heat. Cook chicken in batches, about 3 minutes on each side, or until browned. Remove to a plate.

**3.** Reduce heat to medium. Add onion, red pepper, and green pepper to skillet. Cook 5 minutes, stirring frequently, until softened. Stir in garlic, crushed hot pepper, tomatoes, chicken broth, and remaining salt and pepper. Bring to a boil. Pour half over rice. Add chicken and pour remaining tomato mixture over chicken. Cover dish tightly with foil.

**4.** Bake 45 to 50 minutes, or until chicken and rice are tender. Uncover and sprinkle with olives and cilantro.

# 170 DOWN-HOME CHICKEN POT PIE
*Prep: 30 minutes    Chill: 1 hour    Cook: 35 to 41 minutes    Serves: 4*

Baking the pastry separately from the filling here and sliding it on top just before serving ensures a crisp crust. Luckily, they both cook at the same time and temperature.

1¼ cups flour
¼ teaspoon dried thyme
⅜ teaspoon salt
9 tablespoons plus 1 teaspoon cold butter
1 tablespoon chopped parsley
2 to 3 tablespoons ice water
1¾ cups chicken broth
1 large all-purpose potato, peeled and cut into ½-inch dice
1 medium sweet potato, peeled and cut into ½-inch dice

1 large carrot, peeled and cut into ½-inch dice
1 medium celery rib, cut into ½-inch dice
1¾ cups milk
¼ teaspoon pepper
⅛ teaspoon poultry seasoning
2 cups cubed cooked chicken (about 8 ounces)
½ cup corn kernels
½ cup frozen peas

**1.** In a medium bowl, combine 1 cup flour, thyme, and ⅛ teaspoon salt. Stir to mix. Cut up 5 tablespoons and 1 teaspoon butter into small pieces and add to seasoned flour. Cut in with a pastry blender or 2 knives until crumbly with some pieces of butter size of a split pea. Stir in parsley. Drizzle in ice water 1 tablespoon at a time, tossing with a fork, until dough begins to clump together. Gather dough into a ball, wrap in plastic wrap, and refrigerate 1 hour.

**2.** In a large skillet, combine 1 cup chicken broth, all-purpose potato, sweet potato, carrot, and celery. Bring to a boil. Cover, reduce heat to medium-low, and simmer until vegetables are tender, 12 to 15 minutes. Pour vegetables and broth into a large bowl.

**3.** In same skillet, melt remaining butter over medium heat. Stir in remaining flour until smooth. Cook, stirring, 1 minute. Remove from heat. Gradually whisk in remaining ¾ cup broth until smooth. Whisk in milk, pepper, poultry seasoning, and remaining ¼ teaspoon salt. Bring to a boil over medium heat, stirring frequently, until thick, 1 to 2 minutes. Reduce heat and simmer, stirring occasionally, 3 minutes. Add sauce, chicken, corn, and peas to vegetables in bowl. Stir until combined.

**4.** Preheat oven to 400°F. Pour filling into a 2½-quart shallow round baking dish. On a lightly floured surface, roll out dough ¼ inch thick. Trim to fit just inside baking dish. Place pastry on a small cookie sheet. Crimp edge if desired.

**5.** Bake pastry and filling separately until pastry is browned and filling is bubbly, 18 to 20 minutes. Slide pastry onto filling and serve.

# 171    CHICKEN ENCHILADAS
*Prep: 20 minutes    Cook: 57 to 69 minutes    Serves: 6*

3 poblano peppers
2 tablespoons olive oil
1 large sweet onion, thinly
   sliced
2 cups shredded cooked
   chicken (about 8 ounces)
1 (10-ounce) can mild
   enchilada sauce
1¼ cups thick and chunky salsa

12 corn tortillas
2 cups shredded Monterey
   Jack cheese
2 tablespoons chopped
   cilantro
2 scallions, finely chopped
⅓ cup sour cream
3 tablespoons milk

**1.** Roast peppers directly over gas burners or under a broiler as close to heat as possible, turning, until skins are blackened, 8 to 10 minutes. Place in a paper bag, seal bag, and let stand until cool. Rub skins from peppers. Remove stems and seeds. Cut peppers into thin strips.

**2.** In a large nonstick skillet, heat oil over medium heat. Add onion and cook, stirring occasionally, until soft and golden brown, 10 to 15 minutes. Stir in poblano pepper strips and cook 2 minutes. Stir in chicken. Remove skillet from heat. In a small bowl, blend enchilada sauce and salsa. Stir ½ cup sauce into skillet; transfer filling to a medium bowl.

**3.** Wipe out skillet. Place over medium-high heat. Add tortillas 1 at a time, cooking until hot and softened, about 30 seconds per side. Place on a plate.

**4.** Preheat oven to 375°F. Grease a 13 x 9-inch baking dish. Spread ¼ cup sauce in bottom of baking dish. Lay tortillas on work surface. Place about ¼ cup chicken and pepper filling along bottom third of each tortilla. Sprinkle 1¼ cups cheese over filling, dividing it evenly. Roll up and place seam side down in baking dish. Pour remaining sauce over enchiladas and sprinkle remaining ¾ cup cheese on top.

**5.** Bake 25 to 30 minutes, or until hot and bubbly. In a small bowl, combine cilantro, scallions, sour cream, and milk. Stir until blended. Serve on the side to drizzle over enchiladas.

# 172 ROAST TURKEY WITH MAPLE PEPPER GLAZE

*Prep: 15 minutes    Cook: 3½ to 4 hours    Serves: 12 to 16*

Here's a holiday bird with a difference.

1 **(14-pound) fresh turkey**
1 **teaspoon salt**
  **Corn Bread and Wild Rice Stuffing (page 201) or Sage and Onion Stuffing (page 203)**
6 **tablespoons butter**
1 **(13¾-ounce) can chicken broth**

1 **large onion, cut up**
1 **medium celery rib, cut up**
¾ **cup cranberry juice**
½ **cup maple syrup**
1 **tablespoon lemon juice**
1 **teaspoon freshly ground pepper**
⅓ **cup flour**

**1.** Preheat oven to 325°F. Remove turkey giblets and neck and set aside. Discard liver. Remove excess fat from turkey. Rinse with cold water and pat dry. Season inside and out with ½ teaspoon salt. Stuff cavities loosely; close with poultry pins and string. Tuck wings under and tie legs together. Place turkey breast side up on a rack in a large shallow roasting pan about 2 inches deep. Insert a meat thermometer in thickest part of thigh without touching bone. Melt 1 tablespoon butter and brush over turkey breast. Roast turkey 2½ hours.

**2.** While turkey roasts, make giblet broth and glaze. In a medium saucepan, combine chicken broth, turkey neck, giblets, onion, celery, and 3 cups water. Bring to a boil. Reduce heat and simmer, partially covered, 2 hours. Strain broth and reserve for gravy. In a small nonreactive saucepan, combine cranberry juice, maple syrup, lemon juice, pepper, and remaining 5 tablespoons butter. Bring to a boil, reduce heat, and simmer until reduced to ¾ cup, about 20 minutes. Set glaze aside.

**3.** After turkey has roasted 2½ hours, reheat glaze, whisking until smooth. Brush turkey with one fourth of glaze. Roast turkey, brushing with glaze 3 more times, until thermometer registers 180°F, 1 to 1½ hours longer. Add enough water to cover bottom of roasting pan when dry. When turkey is done, remove to a platter, cover loosely with foil, and let rest 15 to 20 minutes before carving.

**4.** Meanwhile, pour juices from roasting pan into a 4-cup glass measure. Spoon off fat and reserve ⅓ cup. Discard remaining fat. Add reserved giblet broth and enough water if necessary to pan juices to equal 4 cups. Place roasting pan over 2 burners; add reserved fat. Whisk in flour and cook over medium heat until smooth and bubbly, about 1 minute. Whisk in 4 cups pan juices and bring to a boil, scraping up brown bits from bottom of pan. Boil, whisking, until thickened and smooth, about 5 minutes. Add any juices on turkey plattter and remaining salt.

**5.** Remove pins and string from turkey. Spoon stuffing into a serving bowl. Carve turkey and pass with stuffing and hot gravy.

# 173   KENTUCKY BURGOO
*Prep: 20 minutes    Cook: 4 hours    Serves: 10 to 12*

This is what's served on Derby Day in Kentucky, and it's simmered in big caldrons, the thicker the better. Some say if it's not cooked for 6 hours, it isn't burgoo. Recipes and ingredients are a matter of debate, but a few different meats and lots of vegetables are always agreed upon.

1 (3½-pound) chicken
2 pounds lean beef short ribs
1 pound lamb shoulder chops
2 bay leaves
1 teaspoon dried thyme
2 medium onions, sliced
3 large carrots, peeled and coarsely chopped
2 large all-purpose potatoes, peeled and cut into 1-inch chunks
2 medium celery ribs, coarsely chopped
3 large garlic cloves, crushed through a press

¼ teaspoon crushed hot red pepper
1 (16-ounce) can diced tomatoes in juice
2 cups sliced fresh or frozen okra
2 cups fresh or frozen corn kernels
1 (10-ounce) box frozen lima beans
1 teaspoon salt
¼ teaspoon freshly ground black pepper

**1.** In a large pot or Dutch oven, combine chicken, beef, lamb, bay leaves, thyme, and 2½ quarts water. Bring to a boil. Reduce heat, cover, and simmer 1 hour 45 minutes. Remove chicken and lamb to a plate. Cook beef 15 minutes longer, or until tender. Let meats cool, then refrigerate.

**2.** Remove all fat from broth. To broth, add onions, carrots, potatoes, celery, garlic, hot pepper, and tomatoes with their juices. Bring to a boil, reduce heat, and simmer 1 hour. Add okra, corn, lima beans, ¾ teaspoon salt, and black pepper. Simmer 30 minutes.

**3.** Meanwhile, remove all skin, fat, and bones from chicken, beef, and lamb. Cut meats into 1-inch pieces. Add to pot and simmer about 30 minutes longer, stirring occasionally, or until thickened. Taste and add remaining salt if necessary. Remove and discard bay leaves before serving.

# 174    CHILI CON CARNE
*Prep: 15 minutes    Cook: 1 hour 23 to 26 minutes    Serves: 8*

This chili gets better if allowed to mellow overnight.

2  tablespoons chili powder
1  tablespoon ground cumin
1  teaspoon dried oregano
2  pounds lean ground beef
1  tablespoon vegetable oil
2  medium onions, chopped
8  garlic cloves, minced
1  teaspoon salt
¼  teaspoon pepper

⅛  teaspoon ground cinnamon
1  (28-ounce) can diced
   tomatoes in juice
1  (12-ounce) bottle beer
2  chipotle chiles in adobo
   sauce, minced (optional)
1  (15-ounce) can pinto beans,
   rinsed and drained

**1.** In a small skillet, combine chili powder, cumin, and oregano. Cook over medium heat, stirring, until fragrant and lightly toasted, 1 to 2 minutes. Immediately transfer to a small bowl.

**2.** Place beef in a large nonreactive Dutch oven. Cook over high heat, stirring to break up beef, until no longer pink, about 8 minutes. Drain in a colander.

**3.** Add oil and onions to Dutch oven and cook over medium heat, stirring, until softened, 3 to 5 minutes. Add garlic and cook 1 minute. Add toasted spices, beef, salt, pepper, cinnamon, tomatoes with their juices, beer, and chipotle chiles. Bring to a boil, reduce heat to medium-low, cover, and simmer 30 minutes, stirring occasionally.

**4.** Uncover and simmer 30 minutes longer, stirring frequently, until thickened. Skim off any excess fat. Stir in beans and simmer 10 minutes. Let cool, then cover and refrigerate overnight if you have time. Reheat over low heat.

# 175    TURKEY TETRAZZINI
*Prep: 10 minutes    Cook: 44 to 49 minutes    Serves: 6*

½  pound spaghetti
4  tablespoons butter
10  ounces mushrooms, sliced
1  medium celery rib, finely
   chopped
3  tablespoons flour
2  cups chicken broth
1½  cups half-and-half or milk

2  tablespoons dry sherry
¼  teaspoon salt
¼  teaspoon freshly ground
   pepper
3  cups cubed cooked turkey
½  cup freshly grated Parmesan
   cheese
¼  cup fresh bread crumbs

**1.** In a large pot of boiling salted water, cook spaghetti until tender but still firm, about 10 minutes. Drain, rinse under cold running water, and drain well.

**2.** In a large skillet, melt 1 tablespoon butter over medium-high heat. Add mushrooms and cook, stirring, until pan is dry, about 5 minutes. Set mushrooms aside on a plate.

**3.** Add remaining 3 tablespoons butter and celery to skillet. Cook over medium-low heat, stirring occasionally, until celery softens, about 3 minutes. Whisk in flour and cook, stirring, 1 minute. Whisk in broth. Increase heat to medium-high and bring to a boil, stirring frequently. Whisk in half-and-half and simmer 3 minutes. Stir in sherry and simmer 2 minutes longer. Stir in salt and pepper. Remove sauce from heat.

**4.** Preheat oven to 425°F. Grease a 13 x 9 x 2-inch baking dish. Place spaghetti in dish. Pour half of sauce over spaghetti. Add mushrooms and turkey; stir to mix. Pour remaining sauce over all. In a small bowl, mix Parmesan cheese and bread crumbs. Sprinkle over top.

**5.** Bake 20 to 25 minutes, until browned and bubbly.

---

# 176  UNCLE BILL'S YANKEE POT ROAST
*Prep: 20 minutes    Cook: 3 hours 50 minutes    Serves: 8*

This down-home pot roast is even better if made ahead and refrigerated for a day. For best flavor, brown the roast well, just short of burning it. Serve with mashed potatoes.

| | |
|---|---|
| 1  **(4- to 4½-pound) bottom round beef roast for pot roast** | 2  **tablespoons vegetable oil** |
| | 3  **medium onions, chopped** |
| | 1  **cup finely chopped carrot** |
| 1  **teaspoon salt** | 2  **bay leaves** |
| ½  **teaspoon freshly ground pepper** | 8  **gingersnaps, crumbled** |

**1.** Preheat oven to 350°F. Pat roast dry with paper towels and season with ¼ teaspoon each salt and pepper. In a large Dutch oven, heat oil over medium-high heat. Add roast and cook, turning, until well browned all over, about 10 minutes. Remove to a plate.

**2.** Add onions and carrot to pot. Reduce heat to medium and cook, stirring frequently, until onions are browned and bottom of pot is clean, about 10 minutes. Stir in bay leaves and 1½ cups water. Return roast to pan. Bring to a boil and cover pot.

**3.** Bake 2½ hours, turning roast twice. Remove roast to a carving board and let cool.

**4.** Remove and discard bay leaves from pan juices. Skim off any fat. Add gingersnaps and stir until dissolved. Puree pan juices in batches in a blender until smooth. Pour back into pot. Stir in remaining salt and pepper.

**5.** Cut roast lengthwise in half. Cut across the grain into thin slices about ¼ inch thick. Return slices to gravy in pot and turn to coat. Bring to a simmer. Cover and simmer gently 1 hour, or until meat is tender, stirring occasionally without breaking up meat.

# 177    TEXAS ALL-BEEF CHILI

*Prep: 25 minutes    Cook: 3 hours 4 to 34 minutes    Serves: 6*

This meaty chili contains no beans. I like to serve it with chopped red onion and shredded Cheddar cheese.

4  slices of bacon, chopped
2  pounds trimmed beef
    brisket, cut into ½-inch
    cubes
2  medium onions, chopped
2  teaspoons ground cumin
3  garlic cloves, crushed
    through a press
2  tablespoons chili powder
1  teaspoon paprika

¾  teaspoon freshly ground
    pepper
½  teaspoon dried oregano
½  teaspoon salt
¼  teaspoon dried thyme
    Pinch of ground cinnamon
1  cup beef broth
1  (14½-ounce) can diced
    tomatoes in juice
2  dried chipotle chiles

**1.** In a large nonreactive Dutch oven, cook bacon over medium heat until crisp, about 5 minutes. Remove with a slotted spoon and set aside. Remove and reserve drippings. Return 1 tablespoon bacon fat to pan, increase heat to high, and add one fourth of beef. Cook, stirring occasionally, until meat is well browned and juices evaporate, about 4 minutes. Repeat in 3 more batches with remaining beef, adding more bacon fat as needed. Place beef in a bowl.

**2.** Add 2 tablespoons bacon fat to pan, reduce heat to medium, and add onions. Cook, stirring occasionally, 10 minutes, or until lightly browned. Add cumin and cook, stirring, until fragrant and toasted, about 2 minutes. Stir in garlic, chili powder, paprika, pepper, oregano, salt, thyme, and cinnamon. Cook, stirring, 1 minute. Stir in reserved bacon, beef broth, tomatoes with their juices, chiles, ½ cup water, and beef with any juices that have collected in bowl.

**3.** Bring to a boil, scraping up any brown bits from bottom of pan. Reduce heat, cover partially, and simmer gently 2½ to 3 hours, or until beef is tender. Stir frequently toward end of cooking time to prevent sticking. Add ½ cup water if chili becomes too thick.

# 178    ALL-AMERICAN BEEF STEW

*Prep: 25 minutes    Cook: 2 hours 58 minutes to 3 hours 38 minutes*
*Serves: 6*

This savory beef stew tastes even better if it's refrigerated overnight to mellow and then is reheated the next day.

3 pounds lean chuck stew
   meat (cut into 1½-inch
   cubes)
½ teaspoon salt
½ teaspoon freshly ground
   pepper
3 tablespoons olive oil
2 slices of bacon, cut
   crosswise into ½-inch
   pieces
1 large onion, chopped
¾ teaspoon dried thyme
¼ teaspoon dried rosemary
2 bay leaves

2 cups dry red wine
3 tablespoons tomato paste
4 cups beef broth
½ pound small white button
   mushrooms
1 cup frozen pearl onions
5 medium carrots, peeled and
   cut into ¾-inch diagonal
   slices
2 large Yukon Gold potatoes,
   peeled and cut into 1-inch
   chunks
¼ cup flour

**1.** Pat meat dry with paper towels. Season with ¼ teaspoon salt and ¼ teaspoon pepper. In a large heavy Dutch oven, heat 2 tablespoons oil over medium-high heat. Add beef in 3 or 4 batches and cook, turning, until well browned, 5 to 7 minutes per batch. Remove to a plate. Pour off any fat in pot.

**2.** Reduce heat to medium. Add bacon and chopped onion to pot. Cook, stirring occasionally, until onion is golden, about 8 minutes. Add thyme, rosemary, bay leaves, wine, and tomato paste to pot. Whisk to combine and scrape up brown bits from bottom of pot. Add 3 cups beef broth and beef along with any juices that have collected on plate. Bring to a boil. Reduce heat to medium-low, cover, and simmer until beef is tender but not falling apart, 2 to 2½ hours.

**3.** Meanwhile, in a medium skillet, heat remaining 1 tablespoon oil over medium-high heat. Add mushrooms and pearl onions and cook, stirring frequently, until browned, about 5 minutes.

**4.** Gently stir mushroom mixture, carrots, and potatoes into stew. Bring back to a simmer. Simmer 15 minutes.

**5.** Whisk flour into remaining 1 cup cold beef broth; stir into pot. Season with remaining ¼ teaspoon each salt and pepper. Simmer 15 minutes, stirring occasionally, until vegetables are tender. Remove and discard the bay leaves before serving.

# 179    PAN-FRIED PEPPER STEAK

*Prep: 5 minutes    Stand: 30 minutes    Cook: 12 to 14 minutes*
*Serves: 2 to 4*

This will serve 2 steak lovers with big appetites or 4 daintier eaters.

| | |
|---|---|
| 2 **New York strip steaks, cut 1 inch thick (about 9 ounces each)** | 2 **teaspoons olive oil** |
| | ¼ **teaspoon salt** |
| | 1 **large shallot, minced** |
| 2 **tablespoons assorted whole peppercorns (black, white, pink, green)** | 1 **garlic clove, crushed through a press** |
| | ½ **cup beef broth** |
| 1 **tablespoon plus 1 teaspoon unsalted butter** | 3 **tablespoons brandy** |
| | ⅓ **cup heavy cream** |

**1.** Trim steaks and pat dry with paper towels. Place peppercorns in a small plastic food storage bag. Seal bag. Coarsely crush with a rolling pin. Place on a plate. Coat steaks with peppercorns, pressing into meat to stick. Let steaks stand at room temperature 30 minutes.

**2.** In a large skillet, melt 1 teaspoon butter in oil over medium-high heat. When butter is golden, add steaks. Cook, turning once, 3 to 4 minutes per side for medium-rare or longer to desired doneness. Remove steaks to a plate. Season with ⅛ teaspoon salt and cover loosely with foil to keep warm.

**3.** Pour off drippings from skillet Add remaining 1 tablespoon butter to skillet and melt over medium heat. Add shallot and garlic. Cook until softened, about 2 minutes. Add broth and bring to a boil over high heat. Boil 2 minutes, stirring up browned bits from bottom of pan. Add brandy and cook 1 minute. Stir in heavy cream. Cook, stirring, 1 minute, or until sauce thickens. Stir in remaining ⅛ teaspoon salt. Pour over steaks and serve at once.

---

# 180    CHICKEN-FRIED STEAK WITH CREAMY PEPPER GRAVY

*Prep: 15 minutes    Cook: 13 to 17 minutes    Serves: 4*

This is a truck-stop classic, which absolutely *has* to be served with mashed potatoes. See page 190 for Mom's Mashed Potatoes.

| | |
|---|---|
| 4 **cube steaks (1 to 1¼ pounds)** | 2 **teaspoons freshly ground pepper** |
| 2 **eggs** | |
| 1 **(5-ounce) can evaporated milk** | **Shortening or vegetable oil, for frying** |
| 1 **cup flour** | ½ **cup beef broth** |
| 1 **teaspoon salt** | |

**1.** Pound steaks with a meat pounder until ¼ inch thick.

**2.** In a pie plate, beat eggs and 2 tablespoons evaporated milk. In another pie plate, mix flour with salt and pepper.

**3.** Dredge steaks in seasoned flour. Dip in egg to coat, letting excess drip off. Dredge in flour until coated on both sides. Set on a piece of wax paper. Let stand for 2 minutes. Coat in flour again. Reserve 2 tablespoons flour for gravy.

**4.** In a large skillet, preferably cast-iron, heat enough shortening or oil to measure ½ inch over medium heat until it reaches 360°F. Add steaks 2 at a time. Cook until golden brown on bottom, 2 to 4 minutes. Turn and cook until golden brown on second side, about 3 minutes. Place on a cookie sheet lined with paper towels. Cover with foil to keep warm.

**5.** Carefully pour off all but 2 tablespoons drippings from skillet. Whisk in reserved flour and cook over medium heat, whisking 1 minute. Gradually whisk in remaining evaporated milk, beef broth, and ⅓ cup water. Bring to a boil, reduce heat, and simmer 2 minutes, stirring occasionally, until thickened. Transfer steaks to plates, pour gravy over steaks, and serve at once.

---

## 181 LIVER AND CARAMELIZED ONIONS WITH CRISP SAGE LEAVES

*Prep: 12 minutes    Cook: 28 minutes    Serves: 4*

4  slices of bacon, cut crosswise into ½-inch pieces
2  large onions, thinly sliced
2  tablespoons balsamic vinegar
½  teaspoon salt

½  teaspoon freshly ground pepper
4  slices of calves liver, cut ½ inch thick (about 1 pound)
1  tablespoon olive oil
12  fresh sage leaves

**1.** In a medium skillet, cook bacon over medium heat until crisp, about 5 minutes. Remove bacon to paper towels. Pour off all but 1 tablespoon fat from pan. Add onions to pan and cook, stirring, until onions begin to soften, about 3 minutes. Cover and cook until soft, about 3 minutes. Uncover and cook until browned, about 8 minutes. Stir in vinegar, ¼ teaspoon salt, and ¼ teaspoon pepper. Remove from heat and cover to keep warm. Season liver with remaining salt and pepper.

**2.** In a large nonstick skillet, heat oil over medium-high heat. Add sage and cook, turning once, until crisp, about 1 minute. Remove sage to a plate.

**3.** Add liver to skillet 2 pieces at a time. Cook until browned but still slightly pink inside, about 2 minutes per side. To serve, place liver on plates and top with onions and bacon. Crumble sage over top.

# 182    SWISS STEAK

*Prep: 15 minutes    Cook: 1 hour 51 minutes to 1 hour 55 minutes*
*Serves: 6*

This is a classic that has gone by the wayside, and it's really good. Serve it on a cold fall night with some mashed potatoes or noodles and see if everyone isn't practically licking their plates clean.

2 pounds boneless round steak, cut ½ inch thick
¼ cup flour
¾ teaspoon salt
½ teaspoon freshly ground pepper
3 tablespoons olive oil
3 medium onions, thinly sliced

1 medium red bell pepper, thinly sliced
2 garlic cloves, crushed through a press
1 (16-ounce) can diced tomatoes in juice
½ cup dry red wine
½ teaspoon dried thyme

**1.** Cut steak into 8 pieces. In a small bowl, mix flour, ½ teaspoon salt, and pepper. Sprinkle flour on both sides of meat and pound into steak with a meat mallet or side of a heavy saucer.

**2.** In a large skillet, heat 2 tablespoons oil over medium-high heat. Cook steak pieces in 2 batches, turning and adding remaining oil as necessary, until steak is browned, 4 to 5 minutes per side. Reduce heat to medium if flour begins to burn. Remove steak to a plate as it browns.

**3.** Add onions, bell pepper, and garlic to skillet. Reduce heat to medium-low and cook, stirring, until softened, about 5 minutes. Stir in remaining ¼ teaspoon salt, tomatoes with their juices, wine, thyme, and ¼ cup water. Bring to a simmer. Return meat to skillet, pushing it down into liquid.

**4.** Simmer gently, covered, over very low heat, until meat is fork-tender, about 1½ hours. Stir occasionally to prevent sticking. Stir in ¼ cup water as meat cooks if sauce is too thick.

# 183 NEW ENGLAND BOILED DINNER

*Prep: 20 minutes    Cook: 3 hours 20 minutes    Serves: 6*

1 corned beef (4 to 5 pounds)
1 medium onion, halved
2 bay leaves
3 medium beets
½ medium rutabaga, peeled
   and cut into 1-inch
   chunks
4 large red potatoes, scrubbed
   and cut into quarters
4 large carrots, peeled and cut
   diagonally into 1-inch
   pieces

2 parsnips, peeled, halved
   lengthwise and crosswise
1 small head of green cabbage
   (2¼ pounds)
   Coarse grainy mustard and
   horseradish, as
   accompaniments

**1.** In a large Dutch oven, cover corned beef with cold water. Add onion and bay leaves. Bring to a boil, reduce heat to medium-low, cover, and simmer until tender, about 3 hours.

**2.** Place beets in a medium saucepan, cover with cold water, and bring to a boil. Simmer until tender, about 35 minutes; drain. When cool, peel, cut into quarters, and return to pan.

**3.** About 10 minutes before corned beef is done, add rutabaga to same pot. When beef is tender, remove to a platter and cover with foil to keep hot.

**4.** Add potatoes, carrots, and parsnips to pot with rutabaga. Simmer 15 minutes. Leaving core intact, cut cabbage into 6 wedges. Add to pot, cover, and simmer 5 minutes, until cabbage is tender but still slightly crisp. Add ½ cup broth from pot to beets and place over medium heat to heat through.

**5.** Thinly slice corned beef across grain and arrange in center of a large platter. Surround with vegetables. Spoon some hot broth over meat and vegetables. Remove and discard bay leaves before serving. Pass mustard and horseradish.

# 184    MEAT LOAF

*Prep: 10 minutes    Cook: 1 hour 23 minutes    Serves: 6*

This is the all-American diner, truck-stop, and Mom classic that has come back into vogue. There are many recipes for meat loaf, with all kinds of exotic ingredients, but this is a basic, simple version, topped with another classic—ketchup. If you prefer an all-beef meat loaf, use 2 pounds ground beef and omit the pork.

| | |
|---|---|
| 1 large onion, minced | 1 teaspoon salt |
| 2 teaspoons vegetable oil | ½ teaspoon freshly ground |
| 1½ pounds lean ground beef |    pepper |
| ½ pound ground pork | ½ cup ketchup |
| 2 eggs | 1 tablespoon Dijon mustard |
| ½ cup dried bread crumbs | 1 tablespoon brown sugar |
| ½ cup milk | 1 tablespoon cider vinegar |

**1.** Preheat oven to 350°F. In a nonstick medium skillet, cook onion in oil over medium-low heat, stirring occasionally, until softened, about 8 minutes. Place all but 2 tablespoons onions in a large bowl and let cool slightly.

**2.** Add beef, pork, eggs, bread crumbs, milk, salt, pepper, 2 tablespoons ketchup, and 2 teaspoons mustard to bowl with onion. With hands or a spoon, mix well to thoroughly combine. Place meat loaf mixture in center of a greased 13 x 9 x 2-inch baking pan. Shape into a 9 x 5-inch oval football-shaped loaf.

**3.** Bake 1 hour. Meanwhile, add remaining ketchup and mustard, brown sugar, and vinegar to skillet with reserved onion. Bring to a simmer over medium heat. Reduce heat to low and cook, stirring occasionally, until thickened, about 5 minutes.

**4.** Spread glaze over meat loaf and bake 15 minutes. Let stand about 10 minutes before slicing.

# 185    SHEPHERD'S PIE

*Prep: 25 minutes    Cook: 1 hour 4 to 5 minutes    Serves: 6*

1½ pounds lean ground beef or
    lamb
2 medium onions, chopped
4 medium carrots, peeled and
    thinly sliced
½ pound shiitake mushrooms,
    stems removed, caps
    sliced
1 teaspoon salt
¾ teaspoon dried rosemary
½ teaspoon dried thyme
½ teaspoon freshly ground
    pepper

1 (13¾-ounce) can beef broth
½ cup dry white wine
2 tablespoons tomato paste
2 tablespoons cornstarch
2 teaspoons Worcestershire
    sauce
2 pounds Idaho potatoes,
    peeled and quartered
8 garlic cloves, thinly sliced
½ cup hot milk
1 cup frozen peas
2 tablespoons grated
    Parmesan cheese

**1.** In a large skillet, cook beef over high heat, stirring frequently, until no longer pink, about 5 minutes. Spoon off and reserve 1 tablespoon drippings. Drain beef in a colander. Return reserved drippings to skillet.

**2.** Add onions and carrots to skillet. Reduce heat to medium-high and cook, stirring, until onion is golden, about 5 minutes. Add mushrooms, ½ teaspoon salt, ½ teaspoon rosemary, ¼ teaspoon thyme, and ¼ teaspoon pepper. Reduce heat to medium and cook until mushrooms soften, about 2 minutes. Scrape into a large bowl. Stir in beef.

**3.** In same skillet, combine broth, wine, tomato paste, cornstarch, and Worcestershire. Whisk until smooth and cornstarch dissolves. Bring to a boil over medium heat, stirring until thickened, 1 to 2 minutes. Add to beef mixture and stir to mix.

**4.** In a medium saucepan, combine potatoes, garlic, and remaining ¼ teaspoon each rosemary and thyme. Cover with water and bring to a boil. Reduce heat to medium-low, cover, and simmer until tender, about 20 minutes; drain. Return potatoes to saucepan. Cook over low heat, shaking pan, to dry potatoes, about 1 minute. Remove from heat and mash with a potato masher. Add milk and season with remaining ½ teaspoon salt and ¼ teaspoon pepper. Mash well.

**5.** Preheat oven to 400°F. Stir peas into beef mixture. Pour into a 3-quart shallow baking dish. Spread evenly. Spoon mashed potatoes over beef, leaving a 1-inch margin uncovered around edges. Spread potatoes to cover beef. Sprinkle cheese on top.

**6.** Bake 30 minutes, or until browned and bubbly. Let stand 5 minutes before serving.

# 186 LAMB STEW WITH SQUASH AND PEAS

*Prep: 25 minutes    Cook: 1 hour 47 minutes    Serves: 6*

3 tablespoons olive oil
2½ pounds lean boneless lamb
    shoulder, trimmed, cut
    into 1½-inch cubes
2 medium onions, chopped
2 garlic cloves, crushed
    through a press
1 teaspoon salt
1 teaspoon paprika
1 teaspoon ground cumin
½ teaspoon ground coriander

½ teaspoon ground ginger
½ teaspoon freshly ground
    pepper
¼ teaspoon cayenne
1½ pounds Hubbard or
    butternut squash, peeled,
    seeded, and cut into
    1-inch cubes
1 large ripe tomato, peeled,
    seeded, and chopped
1 cup frozen peas

**1.** In a large Dutch oven, heat 2 tablespoons oil over medium-high heat. Brown lamb in batches, cooking about 3 minutes per batch. Place lamb on a plate.

**2.** Add remaining oil and onions to pot, reduce heat to medium, and stir to scrape up brown bits. Add garlic, salt, paprika, cumin, coriander, ginger, pepper, and cayenne. Stir well and cook until onion softens, about 3 minutes. Add lamb and 2 cups water; bring to a boil. Cover, reduce heat, and simmer until lamb is just tender, about 1 hour.

**3.** Add squash and tomato. Cover and simmer until squash and lamb are tender, about 30 minutes, adding additional water if necessary. Stir in peas and cook 2 minutes. Skim fat off surface before serving.

# 187 SAUSAGE-STUFFED PEPPERS

*Prep: 25 minutes    Cook: 60 to 69 minutes    Serves: 4*

1 large red bell pepper
1 large yellow bell pepper
2 tablespoons olive oil
½ pound turkey sausage,
    removed from casing
1 medium onion, chopped
2 garlic cloves, minced
1 (4-ounce) can diced green
    chiles, rinsed and drained
4 cups shredded spinach
½ teaspoon salt

¼ teaspoon freshly ground
    pepper
1 cup cooked rice
1 cup shredded hot pepper
    Monterey Jack cheese
2 ripe medium tomatoes,
    peeled, seeded, and diced
1 serrano pepper, seeded and
    minced
½ teaspoon ground cumin

**1.** Bring a large pot of water to a boil. Halve bell peppers lengthwise. Add bell peppers to boiling water and cook 3 minutes; drain.

**2.** In a medium skillet, heat 1 tablespoon oil over medium heat. Add sausage and cook, stirring frequently to crumble, until cooked through, 5 to 6 minutes. Remove with a slotted spoon to a large bowl. Heat 2 teaspoons oil in skillet. Add onion and cook, stirring occasionally, until golden, 6 to 8 minutes. Add garlic, green chiles, spinach, ¼ teaspoon salt, and pepper. Cook, stirring occasionally, until spinach wilts, about 5 minutes. Add to sausage. Add rice and stir well to combine. Add ½ cup cheese and mix well.

**3.** Preheat oven to 350°F. Fill pepper halves with rice mixture. Place in a shallow baking dish.

**4.** In medium skillet, heat remaining oil over medium-low heat. Add tomatoes and serrano pepper. Cook, stirring, until softened, 1 to 2 minutes. Remove from heat and stir in cumin and remaining ¼ teaspoon salt. Spoon tomato mixture over rice stuffing. Sprinkle remaining ½ cup cheese on top. Cover dish loosely with foil.

**5.** Bake 30 minutes. Uncover and bake 10 to 15 minutes, or until hot.

---

# 188 COUNTRY PORK ROAST
*Prep: 10 minutes    Stand: 45 minutes    Cook: 1 hour 37 minutes*
*Serves: 6*

Be sure to ask your butcher to cut through the chin bone for you so the roast can be carved easily.

| | |
|---|---|
| **3  garlic cloves, minced** | **1  teaspoon kosher salt** |
| **2  tablespoons Dijon mustard** | **½  teaspoon freshly ground** |
| **1  tablespoon olive oil** | **pepper** |
| **2  tablespoons fresh rosemary, minced, or 1 tablespoon dried** | **1  (4-pound) bone-in center-cut pork loin roast, chin bone cut through** |
| **1  teaspoon fresh thyme leaves, minced, or ½ teaspoon dried** | |

**1.** Preheat oven to 400°F. In a small bowl, combine garlic, 1 tablespoon mustard, oil, rosemary, thyme, salt, and pepper. Stir well.

**2.** Place roast fat side up in a shallow roasting pan. Rub fat side with mustard mixture. Let stand at room temperature 30 minutes.

**3.** Bake 20 minutes. Reduce oven temperature to 325°F. Bake 1 hour 15 minutes, or until internal temperature of roast reaches 160°F on an instant-reading thermometer. Remove roast to a platter and let stand 15 minutes before slicing.

**4.** While meat rests, skim fat from pan juices. Add remaining 1 tablespoon mustard and ½ cup water to juices in roasting pan. Bring to a boil over medium-high heat. Boil, scraping up brown bits from pan, until slightly thickened, about 2 minutes. Serve roast with pan juices.

## 189    SAVORY BEEF STROGANOFF
*Prep: 15 minutes    Cook: 9 minutes    Serves: 4*

Serve this saucy classic over hot cooked egg noodles. To reduce the fat, use low-fat or nonfat sour cream.

2 tablespoons olive oil
1 pound trimmed sirloin
   steak, thinly sliced across
   grain
2 shallots, thinly sliced
½ pound Italian brown
   cremini mushrooms,
   sliced
1 garlic clove, crushed
   through a press

½ cup beef broth
1 tablespoon sun-dried
   tomato paste
2 teaspoons Worcestershire
   sauce
2 teaspoons cornstarch
¼ teaspoon salt
¼ teaspoon freshly ground
   pepper
⅓ cup sour cream

**1.** In a large nonstick skillet, heat 1½ teaspoons oil over medium-high heat. Add half of beef and stir-fry quickly until lightly browned, about 1 minute. Remove to a plate and repeat with 1½ teaspoons oil and remaining beef.

**2.** Heat remaining 1 tablespoon oil in skillet. Add shallots and mushrooms. Cook, stirring, until soft and beginning to brown, about 4 minutes. Stir in garlic. Reduce heat to medium and cook 1 minute, stirring constantly. Remove skillet from heat.

**3.** In a small bowl, whisk beef broth, tomato paste, Worcestershire, and cornstarch until smooth. Add any juices from beef that have collected on plate.

**4.** Pour broth mixture into skillet. Cook over medium heat, stirring constantly, until sauce boils and thickens, about 1 minute. Add beef and cook, stirring, to heat through, about 1 minute longer. Remove from heat and season with salt and pepper. Stir in sour cream and serve.

## 190    CIDER AND ONION SMOTHERED PORK CHOPS
*Prep: 10 minutes    Cook: 1 hour 29 minutes    Serves: 4*

4 (1-inch-thick) center-cut loin
   pork chops
½ teaspoon salt
¼ teaspoon pepper
1 tablespoon vegetable oil

1 pound onions, sliced
2 cups apple cider
2 tablespoons coarse grainy
   mustard

**1.** Trim excess fat from chops. Season with ¼ teaspoon salt and ⅛ teaspoon pepper. In a large skillet, heat oil over medium-high heat. Add pork chops and cook, turning, until well browned, about 4 minutes per side. Remove to a plate.

**2.** Reduce heat to medium-low and add onions to skillet. Cook, stirring occasionally, until softened and browned, about 12 minutes.

**3.** Add cider, increase heat to medium-high, and boil until cider is reduced by half, about 8 minutes. Stir in mustard and remaining salt and pepper.

**4.** Return chops with any juices that have accumulated on plate to skillet and push down into onions, covering with onions. Reduce heat to low, cover, and simmer, turning once, until chops are fork-tender, about 1 hour.

---

# 191   CINCINNATI FIVE-WAY CHILI
*Prep: 20 minutes    Cook: 1 hour 15 minutes    Serves: 6*

This unique way Cincinnati has of serving chili is called five-way because of the different accompaniments that are added. It is traditional to serve it over spaghetti.

| | |
|---|---|
| 1½ **pounds lean ground chuck** | ¾ **teaspoon ground cinnamon** |
| 1 **medium onion, chopped** | ½ **teaspoon salt** |
| 2 **garlic cloves, crushed** | ¼ **teaspoon freshly ground** |
| **through a press** | **pepper** |
| 1 **(15-ounce) can tomato sauce** | **Pinch of ground cloves** |
| 1 **cup beef broth** | ½ **ounce unsweetened** |
| 2 **tablespoons red wine** | **chocolate, finely chopped** |
| **vinegar** | ½ **pound spaghetti** |
| 2 **tablespoons Worcestershire** | 1 **cup cooked kidney beans** |
| **sauce** | ¼ **cup chopped red onion** |
| 2 **tablespoons chili powder** | 1 **cup shredded Cheddar** |
| 1 **teaspoon dried oregano** | **cheese** |
| 1 **teaspoon ground cumin** | **Oyster crackers** |

**1.** In a large nonreactive Dutch oven, cook chuck, onion, and garlic over medium heat until meat is no longer red and vegetables are tender, about 15 minutes. Stir occasionally to break up meat. Spoon off any fat.

**2.** Stir in tomato sauce, beef broth, vinegar, and Worcestershire sauce. Bring to a simmer. Stir in chili powder, oregano, cumin, cinnamon, salt, pepper, cloves, and chocolate. Simmer, stirring frequently, 1 hour, or until thick.

**3.** In a large pot of boiling salted water, cook spaghetti until tender but still firm, 10 to 12 minutes; drain.

**4.** To serve, divide spaghetti among 6 plates. Ladle chili over spaghetti and sprinkle beans, onion, cheese, and crackers on top.

# 192    BEEF AND BEAN TAMALE PIE

*Prep: 15 minutes    Cook: 47 to 54 minutes    Serves: 6*

1 tablespoon vegetable oil
1 pound lean ground beef
1 medium red onion, finely
  chopped
1 small red bell pepper, cut
  into ½-inch dice
1 garlic clove, crushed
  through a press
2 tablespoons plus ½ teaspoon
  chili powder
1½ teaspoons ground cumin
1 teaspoon salt

1 (14½-ounce) can diced
  tomatoes in juice
1 (15-ounce) can kidney or
  black beans, rinsed and
  drained
2½ cups milk
¾ cup cornmeal
1 cup fresh or frozen corn
  kernels
1 cup shredded Cheddar
  cheese
1 egg

**1.** In a large skillet, heat oil over medium-high heat. Add beef, red onion, and bell pepper. Cook, stirring occasionally to break up meat, until beef is no longer pink and vegetables are tender, 6 to 8 minutes. Pour off any fat. Stir in garlic, 2 tablespoons chili powder, cumin, and ½ teaspoon salt. Cook, stirring, 1 minute. Stir in tomatoes with their juice and beans. Cover and simmer 5 minutes. Set aside.

**2.** Preheat oven to 375°F. In a medium saucepan, bring milk just to a boil. Reduce heat to low. Gradually whisk in cornmeal. Cook, stirring, until thickened, about 5 minutes. Remove from heat. Stir in corn, remaining ½ teaspoon salt, remaining ½ teaspoon chili powder, and ½ cup cheese. In a small bowl, beat egg. Add 1 cup cornmeal mixture and blend well. Stir into cornmeal in saucepan. Spoon beef mixture evenly into a 3-quart shallow baking dish. Spoon cornmeal mixture over beef, spreading evenly. Sprinkle remaining ½ cup cheese over top.

**3.** Bake 30 to 35 minutes, or until hot and bubbly around edges.

# 193   STUFFED PORK CHOPS

*Prep: 15 minutes    Cook: 46 to 54 minutes    Serves: 4*

2 slices of firm-textured white bread, cut into ½-inch cubes
2 tablespoons pine nuts
2 tablespoons golden raisins
2 tablespoons balsamic vinegar
2 tablespoons olive oil
1 small onion, finely chopped
1 garlic clove, crushed through a press
2 tablespoons minced oil-packed sun-dried tomatoes

2 tablespoons chopped flat-leaf parsley
½ teaspoon grated lemon zest
¼ teaspoon salt
¼ teaspoon freshly ground pepper
1 cup reduced-sodium chicken broth
4 center-cut pork chops, about 1¼ inches thick

**1.** Preheat oven to 350°F. Place bread cubes in a single layer on a jelly-roll pan. Bake 8 to 10 minutes, or until dry and lightly toasted. Transfer to a medium bowl. Place pine nuts in pan and bake until lightly toasted, 6 to 8 minutes. Add to bowl. Meanwhile, in a small bowl, combine raisins and vinegar. Let soak 15 minutes.

**2.** In a small skillet, heat 1 tablespoon oil over medium heat. Add onion and cook, stirring occasionally, until golden and soft, about 6 minutes. Stir in garlic and cook until softened and fragrant, 1 to 2 minutes. Remove 2 table-spoons to a small bowl and set aside. Scrape remaining onions from skillet into bowl with bread.

**3.** Drain raisins, reserving vinegar. Add raisins, 1 tablespoon sun-dried tomatoes, parsley, lemon zest, ⅛ teaspoon salt, and ⅛ teaspoon pepper to bread mixture. Mix well. Stir in 2 to 3 tablespoons chicken broth to moisten. Cut a pocket in each pork chop and fill with stuffing. Close openings with a toothpick. Season both sides of chops with remaining salt and pepper.

**4.** In a large nonstick skillet, heat remaining 1 tablespoon oil over medium-high heat. Add pork chops and cook, turning, until nicely browned, 3 to 4 minutes per side. Add remaining chicken broth to skillet and bring to a boil. Reduce heat, cover, and simmer, turning once, until chops are cooked through, about 15 minutes. Remove chops from skillet to a plate.

**5.** Add reserved vinegar, onions, and remaining sun-dried tomatoes to skil-let. Bring to a boil over high heat. Boil until sauce is reduced and thickens slightly, 3 to 4 minutes. Add pork chops and any juices on plate. Turn chops to coat with sauce and heat through, about 1 minute. Place pork chops on plates and pour sauce over chops.

# 194    PORK AND HOMINY POSOLE

*Prep: 20 minutes    Cook: 2 hours 17 minutes    Serves: 6*

Posole is a Southwestern stew traditionally eaten on Christmas or New Year's Eve. It's a great dish to make ahead and reheat.

2 tablespoons olive oil
2 pounds lean boneless pork shoulder, cut into 1½-inch cubes
2 medium onions, chopped
4 garlic cloves, minced
3 tablespoons pure ground chile powder
1½ teaspoons dried oregano
1 teaspoon ground cumin
1 (13¾-ounce) can reduced-sodium chicken broth

1 large ripe tomato, chopped
2 (15½-ounce) cans hominy, rinsed and drained
1 large zucchini, halved lengthwise and sliced
1 teaspoon salt
Shredded iceberg lettuce, thinly sliced radishes, diced avocado, and lime wedges, as accompaniment

**1.** In a heavy soup pot, heat oil over medium-high heat. Add pork cubes in 3 batches and cook, turning, until browned, about 4 minutes per batch. Remove pork to a plate.

**2.** Add onions to pot, reduce heat to medium, and cook, stirring occasionally, until softened, about 5 minutes. Stir in garlic, chile powder, oregano, and cumin.

**3.** Return pork to pot. Add chicken broth. Bring to a boil. Reduce heat to low, cover, and simmer, stirring occasionally, 1½ hours.

**4.** Add tomato, hominy, zucchini, salt, and ¾ cup water. Simmer, covered, 30 minutes longer, or until pork and vegetables are tender. Skim off any fat from surface of stew. Serve in bowls, with lettuce, radishes, avocado, and lime wedges on the side.

# 195    BAKED BOURBON-GLAZED HAM

*Prep: 15 minutes    Cook: 2½ hours    Serves: 12*

1 (12-pound) bone-in fully cooked smoked ham
1 cup packed light brown sugar
¾ cup bourbon

1 cup apple juice
1 tablespoon freshly ground pepper
⅓ cup Dijon mustard

**1.** Preheat oven to 350°F. Trim excess fat from ham, leaving a ¼-inch-thick layer. Score fat in a diamond pattern. Place ham in a shallow roasting pan fat side up. In a small bowl, blend brown sugar and bourbon. Spoon about one third over ham. Pour apple juice into pan.

**2.** Bake ham 1½ hours, basting with remaining bourbon mixture 2 more times.

3. In a small bowl, mix pepper and mustard. Brush ham with some of drippings in pan. Spread mustard mixture over ham. Bake 1 hour longer. Let ham stand for 15 minutes before slicing.

---

## 196   STUFFED CABBAGE
*Prep: 40 minutes    Cook: 1 hour 42 to 44 minutes    Serves: 8*

1 head of savoy cabbage
  (2½ pounds)
1 tablespoon olive oil
1 pound sweet Italian
  sausage, casing removed
2 medium onions, chopped
½ pound mushrooms,
  chopped
3 garlic cloves, minced
½ cup dry white wine
1 teaspoon dried thyme

1 (10-ounce) package frozen
  chopped spinach, thawed
  and squeezed dry
2 cups cooked white rice
2 eggs, lightly beaten
¾ teaspoon salt
¼ teaspoon freshly ground
  pepper
1 cup chicken broth
3 cups marinara sauce

1. Bring a large pot of water to a boil. Remove 12 outer leaves from cabbage. Add to boiling water, pushing leaves down into water. Cook 2 minutes, or until wilted. Remove to a colander, rinse under cold running water, and let drain. Cut remaining cabbage in half and add to boiling water. Cook until tender, about 5 minutes. Drain in colander and rinse with cold water. Place cabbage on paper towels and blot dry.

2. In a large skillet, heat oil over medium-high heat. Add sausage and cook, stirring to break up meat, until sausage begins to brown, 8 to 10 minutes. With a slotted spoon, remove sausage to a large bowl. Pour off all but 1 tablespoon fat from pan. Add onions, reduce heat to medium-low, and cook until softened, about 4 minutes. Stir in mushrooms and garlic and cook until tender, about 4 minutes. Add wine and thyme, increase heat to high, and cook until the wine evaporates, about 3 minutes. Stir in spinach and cook, stirring, 1 minute. Add to sausage.

3. Preheat oven to 350°F. Core cooked cabbage halves and chop finely. Add to sausage mixture. Add rice, eggs, salt, and pepper. Stir to mix well. Line a 2½-quart ovenproof glass bowl with cabbage leaves, reserving 2 leaves for top. Overlap leaves with bottom of leaves (rib end) up. Fill with rice mixture. Pack down firmly. Fold ends of cabbage leaves over filling and place reserved leaves over filling to cover. Pour chicken broth around edge of dish between cabbage and bowl. Cover with a piece of greased aluminum foil.

4. Bake 1 hour 15 minutes. Let stand 10 minutes. Meanwhile, heat marinara sauce. Pour off broth from bowl. Place a serving platter over cabbage and invert. Remove bowl and cut stuffed cabbage into wedges. Serve with marinara sauce on the side.

# 197  LEMONY LAMB AND VEGETABLE KEBABS
*Prep: 15 minutes    Marinate: 1 hour    Cook: 8 to 12 minutes*
*Serves: 6*

While I give broiling instructions here, these kebabs are perfect for grilling, too. Try tossing fresh herbs on the hot coals for extra flavor. Rice Pilaf (page 198) makes a great accompaniment.

¼ cup fresh lemon juice
⅓ cup olive oil
2 large garlic cloves, minced
2 tablespoons chopped fresh
  oregano or 2 teaspoons
  dried
¾ teaspoon salt
½ teaspoon freshly ground
  pepper
2 pounds well-trimmed
  boneless leg of lamb, cut
  into 1½-inch cubes

2 small zucchini, cut into
  ¾-inch slices
1 large red onion, cut into
  12 wedges
1 large red bell pepper, cut
  into 1½-inch cubes
1 lemon, thinly sliced

**1.** In a small bowl, combine lemon juice, oil, garlic, oregano, ¼ teaspoon salt, and pepper. Whisk until blended. Pour into a 2-gallon food storage bag; add lamb. Seal bag and turn to coat lamb. Place on a plate and refrigerate to marinate 1 hour or up to 6 hours. Return to room temperature before cooking.

**2.** Preheat broiler. Remove lamb from marinade and thread on metal skewers alternately with zucchini, onion, bell pepper, and lemon slices folded in half. Sprinkle with remaining salt.

**3.** Place skewers on a broiling pan with rack. Broil 4 inches from heat, turning a few times and brushing with marinade, until lamb is browned on the outside and pink on the inside, 8 to 12 minutes.

# 198  MACARONI AND CHEESE
*Prep: 10 minutes    Cook: 32 minutes    Serves: 4*

In this classic favorite, I've reduced the fat by omitting butter and using low-fat milk. It still has lots of cheesy flavor from three kinds of cheese.

½ pound elbow macaroni
2½ cups low-fat milk
2 tablespoons cornstarch
½ teaspoon salt
¼ teaspoon pepper
4 slices of sharp American
  cheese, chopped

1½ cups shredded sharp
  Cheddar cheese
¼ cup grated Parmesan cheese
¼ cup fresh bread crumbs

**1.** Preheat oven to 400°F. In a large pot of boiling salted water, cook macaroni until tender but still firm, about 6 minutes; drain.

**2.** In a small saucepan, heat 2 cups milk until hot but not boiling. In a medium saucepan, whisk remaining ½ cup milk and cornstarch until smooth. Stir in hot milk. Bring to a boil over medium heat, whisking constantly. Reduce heat, simmer 1 minute, whisking until smooth. Remove from heat. Stir in salt, pepper, and American cheese, which may not melt completely.

**3.** Spread half of macaroni in a greased 2-quart shallow baking dish. Sprinkle with half of Cheddar cheese and half of grated Parmesan cheese. Pour on half of sauce. Top with remaining macaroni, Cheddar cheese, and sauce. In a small bowl, stir remaining 2 tablespoons Parmesan cheese and bread crumbs. Sprinkle over top.

**4.** Bake 25 minutes, or until hot and bubbly.

---

## 199 CHICAGO-STYLE DEEP-DISH VEGETABLE PIZZA

*Prep: 25 minutes    Cook: 53 to 60 minutes    Serves: 6*

2 tablespoons olive oil
1 large onion, sliced
3 garlic cloves, minced
1 medium eggplant, cut into ¾-inch cubes
2 small zucchini, halved lengthwise and sliced
1 large red bell pepper, thinly sliced
2 tablespoons tomato paste
2 tablespoons balsamic vinegar
1 (2¼-ounce) can sliced black olives, drained

¼ teaspoon salt
¼ teaspoon crushed hot red pepper
¼ cup chopped fresh basil
Easy Processor Pizza Dough (page 73) or 1¼ pounds frozen, thawed
2 cups shredded mozzarella cheese
¼ cup grated Parmesan cheese
3 large plum tomatoes, thinly sliced

**1.** In a large skillet, heat 1 tablespoon oil over medium heat. Add onion and cook, stirring frequently, until softened and golden brown, 8 to 10 minutes. Add remaining oil, garlic, eggplant, zucchini, and bell pepper. Cook, stirring occasionally, until eggplant softens, about 10 minutes. Stir in tomato paste, vinegar, olives, salt, and hot pepper. Increase heat to medium-high and cook, stirring frequently, until vegetables are tender and any liquid evaporates, 5 to 10 minutes. Stir in basil. Set aside on a plate to cool.

**2.** On a lightly floured surface, roll out dough to a 14-inch circle. Fit into a greased 10-inch cast-iron skillet. Press dough up sides of skillet.

**3.** Preheat oven to 450°F. Sprinkle 1½ cups mozzarella cheese over dough. Sprinkle with 2 tablespoons grated Parmesan cheese. Top with vegetable mixture, spreading evenly. Top with tomato slices.

**4.** Bake on bottom oven rack 20 minutes. Sprinkle remaining mozzarella and Parmesan cheese over pizza. Transfer skillet to top oven rack and bake 10 minutes, or until cheese melts. Let stand 5 minutes before serving.

## 200   SPAGHETTI AND MEATBALLS

*Prep: 25 minutes    Cook: 2 hours 12 minutes    Serves: 6*

3 tablespoons olive oil
¾ pound country pork ribs
1 medium onion, finely
   chopped
1 large carrot, peeled and
   grated
3 garlic cloves, crushed
   through a press
2 (28-ounce) cans peeled plum
   tomatoes, juices reserved

1 (6-ounce) can tomato paste
½ cup dry red wine
1 teaspoon dried basil
¾ teaspoon dried oregano
½ to ¾ teaspoon salt
¼ teaspoon freshly ground
   pepper
Meatballs (recipe follows),
   prepared through step 2
1½ pounds spaghetti

**1.** Heat oil in a heavy nonreactive 6-quart pot over medium-high heat. Add ribs and cook, turning occasionally, until well browned, about 6 minutes. Remove ribs to a plate.

**2.** Reduce heat to low. Add onion and carrot to pot. Cook, stirring occasionally, until softened, about 5 minutes. Add garlic and cook 1 minute longer. Remove from heat. Add tomatoes with their juices to pot, crushing or breaking them up with your hands. Add tomato paste, wine, basil, oregano, ½ teaspoon salt, pepper, and ½ cup water. Return browned ribs to pot. Bring to a boil, reduce heat, and simmer, covered, 30 minutes.

**3.** Add meatballs to sauce. Continue to simmer, partially covered and stirring frequently, until sauce thickens, about 1½ hours. Taste and add remaining salt if necessary. Remove ribs from sauce (they're the cook's bonus).

**4.** In a large pot of boiling salted water, cook spaghetti until tender but still firm, 10 to 12 minutes; drain. To serve, ladle meatballs and sauce over spaghetti.

## 201   MEATBALLS

*Prep: 20 minutes    Cook: 5 to 6 minutes per batch    Serves: 6*

1½ pounds lean ground beef
2 eggs
½ cup milk
⅓ cup fine dry bread crumbs
¼ cup grated Parmesan cheese

¼ cup chopped parsley
1 teaspoon salt
½ teaspoon freshly ground
   pepper
2 tablespoons olive oil

**1.** In a medium bowl, combine beef, eggs, milk, bread crumbs, Parmesan cheese, parsley, salt, and pepper. Mix well with your hands to blend. Wet hands to prevent sticking and using heaping tablespoons, shape into about 24 meatballs.

**2.** Heat a large skillet over medium-high heat. Add oil. Add meatballs, in batches, and cook until browned, turning occasionally, about 5 to 6 minutes per batch, reducing heat if necessary. Remove to paper towels.

# 202    PASTA PRIMAVERA

*Prep: 20 minutes    Cook: 10 to 12 minutes    Serves: 4*

Sirio Maccioni at Le Cirque, a chic New York restaurant, is credited for this lush, all-vegetable pasta. Mine is a slimmed-down version.

| | |
|---|---|
| ⅓ **cup part-skim ricotta cheese** | ½ **pound fettuccine** |
| ⅓ **cup chicken broth** | 1 **tablespoon olive oil** |
| 2 **tablespoons butter** | ¼ **pound mushrooms, sliced** |
| ¾ **teaspoon salt** | 1 **shallot, minced** |
| ¼ **teaspoon freshly ground** | ½ **pound plum tomatoes,** |
| **pepper** | **seeded and diced** |
| 2 **cups small broccoli florets** | 1 **garlic clove, minced** |
| **(about ½ pound)** | ⅓ **cup packed basil leaves,** |
| 2 **medium carrots, peeled and** | **shredded** |
| **cut into thin strips** | ½ **cup frozen peas** |
| ¼ **pound asparagus, cut into** | ⅓ **cup grated Parmesan cheese** |
| **1-inch pieces** | |

**1.** In a food processor, puree ricotta until smooth. With machine on, pour in chicken broth. Add 1 tablespoon butter, ¼ teaspoon salt, and ⅛ teaspoon pepper; process until well blended.

**2.** In a large pot of boiling salted water, cook broccoli, carrots, and asparagus together 2 minutes, or until tender-crisp. Remove with a slotted spoon to a colander. Rinse with cold water until cool.

**3.** Return water to a boil and add fettuccine. Cook, stirring occasionally, until tender but still firm, 8 to 10 minutes.

**4.** While pasta cooks, heat oil in a large nonstick skillet over medium-high heat. Add mushrooms and shallot. Cook, stirring constantly, until mushrooms begin to brown, about 3 minutes. Reduce heat to medium. Stir in tomatoes, garlic, and remaining ½ teaspoon salt and ⅛ teaspoon pepper. Cook until tomatoes are hot, about 2 minutes. Stir in cooked vegetables and basil. Reduce heat to low and cover to keep warm.

**5.** When pasta is just done, add peas to pot. Drain pasta and peas into a colander. Shake to release excess water. Immediately transfer to a large serving bowl. Add remaining 1 tablespoon butter, ricotta mixture, and tomato-vegetable mixture. Toss well. Serve sprinkled with Parmesan cheese.

# 203    JOE'S PARTY LASAGNA

*Prep: 25 minutes    Cook: 3 hours    Serves: 8 to 10*

This is friend and chef Joe Costanzo's recipe for lasagna. It's delicious. Definitely make the meat sauce ahead to save time, and also because it gets better after sitting a day or two.

1    medium celery rib, cut into 1-inch pieces
1    medium carrot, peeled and sliced
1    medium onion, cut into 6 wedges
¼    pound salt pork or pancetta, finely diced
2    tablespoons olive oil
½    pound lean ground beef
½    pound lean ground pork
½    pound ground veal
1    (28-ounce) can crushed tomatoes

1    (6-ounce) can tomato paste
1    cup dry white or red wine
½    teaspoon salt
½    teaspoon freshly ground pepper
12    lasagna noodles
3    cups shredded part-skim mozzarella cheese
1    cup freshly grated Parmesan cheese
      White Sauce (recipe follows)

**1.** In a food processor, in batches if necessary, combine celery, carrot, onion, and salt pork. Pulse until very finely chopped. In a nonreactive Dutch oven, heat oil over medium heat. Add chopped vegetables and cook, stirring occasionally, until soft, about 10 minutes. Add ground beef, pork, and veal. Stir well to break up meat. Add crushed tomatoes, tomato paste, ¾ cup water, wine, salt, and pepper. Bring to a simmer, cover, and cook, stirring occasionally, 2 hours, or until meat sauce is thick.

**2.** Meanwhile, in a large pot of boiling salted water, cook noodles until tender but still firm, about 12 minutes. Drain, rinse with cold water until cool, and drain well.

**3.** Preheat oven to 350°F. Spread ¾ cup meat sauce in bottom of a 13 x 9 x 2-inch baking dish. Arrange 3 noodles in dish. Spread ¾ cup meat sauce over noodles. Sprinkle on 1 cup mozzarella cheese, then ¼ cup Parmesan cheese. Spoon ½ cup white sauce over cheeses. Repeat layering 2 more times, starting with 3 noodles. Top with remaining 3 noodles. Spread with remaining meat sauce and then remaining white sauce. Sprinkle with remaining Parmesan cheese. Cover loosely with foil.

**4.** Bake 40 minutes. Remove foil and bake 10 minutes, or until bubbly. Let stand 10 minutes before serving.

## WHITE SAUCE
*Makes: about 2½ cups*

5  tablespoons butter
5  tablespoons flour
3  cups hot milk

½  teaspoon salt
¼  teaspoon pepper

In a medium saucepan, melt butter over medium-low heat. Add flour; stir until smooth. Cook, stirring, 2 minutes. Remove from heat. Gradually whisk in hot milk. Return to heat. Bring to a simmer, stirring constantly. Simmer 5 minutes, stirring occasionally. Stir in salt and pepper.

---

## 204  ALMOST INSTANT LASAGNA
*Prep: 10 minutes    Cook: 55 minutes    Serves: 8*

Almost instant to prepare, that is. You can pop this family favorite in the oven in about 10 minutes.

½  pound lean ground beef
½  pound bulk hot Italian
    sausage
1  (26-ounce) jar pasta sauce
1  (5.2-ounce) package garlic-
    herb soft cheese
1  egg

1  (15-ounce) container part-
    skim ricotta cheese
½  cup grated Parmesan cheese
12  no-boil lasagna noodles
3  cups shredded part-skim
    mozzarella cheese

1. Preheat oven to 375°F. In a large nonstick skillet, combine beef and sausage. Cook over high heat, stirring to crumble meats, until browned, about 5 minutes. Drain off fat. Stir in pasta sauce and ½ cup water.

2. Crumble herb cheese into a medium bowl. Add egg, ricotta, and Parmesan cheese. Stir until blended.

3. Spread ¾ cup sauce in a 13 x 9 x 2-inch baking dish. Top with 4 noodles, overlapping slightly to fit. Spoon on half of ricotta mixture and spread to cover pasta. Sprinkle with 1 cup mozzarella cheese. Spoon on 1 cup sauce. Repeat layering starting with 4 noodles. Top with remaining 4 noodles. Spoon on remaining sauce, covering noodles. Cover dish loosely with foil.

4. Bake 30 minutes. Uncover, sprinkle remaining mozzarella cheese over top, and bake 20 minutes, or until hot and bubbly. Let stand 15 minutes before serving.

# 205    VEGETABLE LASAGNA

*Prep: 30 minutes    Cook: 1 hour 10 to 20 minutes    Serves: 8*

- 3 medium zucchini, cut lengthwise into ¼-inch-thick slices
- 2 medium red bell peppers, cut into 1-inch-wide strips
- 2 tablespoons garlic-flavored olive oil
- ¼ teaspoon salt
- ½ pound fresh shiitake mushrooms, stems removed, caps sliced
- 3 medium carrots, peeled and shredded
- 1 (10-ounce) package frozen chopped spinach, thawed and squeezed dry
- 1 (15-ounce) container part-skim ricotta cheese
- ½ cup grated Parmesan cheese
- ½ cup crumbled feta cheese
- 1 egg
- 1 (26-ounce) jar sun-dried tomato pasta sauce
- 12 no-boil lasagna noodles
- 2 cups shredded part-skim mozzarella cheese

**1.** Preheat oven to 450°F. Place zucchini and bell peppers in single layers on 2 lightly oiled jelly-roll pans. Brush with 1 tablespoon garlic oil. Sprinkle with salt. Roast 15 to 20 minutes, or until tender, reversing pans on oven racks once for even cooking. Reduce oven temperature to 350°F.

**2.** In a large nonstick skillet, heat remaining oil over medium-high heat. Add mushrooms and cook, stirring, until lightly browned, about 4 minutes. Stir in carrots and cook, stirring, 1 minute longer. Remove from heat.

**3.** In a medium bowl, combine spinach, ricotta cheese, Parmesan cheese, feta cheese, and egg. Mix to blend well.

**4.** Spread ½ cup pasta sauce over bottom of a 13 x 9 x 2-inch glass baking dish. Top with 4 noodles, overlapping slightly. Spoon on half of spinach-ricotta mixture, spreading to cover noodles. Top with half of roasted vegetables and mushrooms and carrots. Drizzle ½ cup sauce over vegetables and sprinkle on ¾ cup mozzarella cheese. Repeat layering starting with noodles. Top with remaining 4 noodles and spread remaining sauce over noodles to cover completely. Cover dish with foil.

**5.** Bake 30 minutes. Uncover, sprinkle remaining ½ cup mozzarella cheese over top of lasagna, and bake 20 to 25 minutes longer, or until hot and bubbly. Let stand 15 minutes before serving.

# 206 SAUSAGE PIZZA WITH ONIONS, PEPPERS, AND BROCCOLI

*Prep: 5 minutes    Cook: 25 to 30 minutes    Serves: 4 to 6*

This pizza can be on the table in the time that it takes for a take-out pizza to be ordered and delivered.

½ pound hot Italian sausage,
  casing removed
1 medium red bell pepper,
  thinly sliced
1 medium red onion, sliced
2 cups small (1-inch) broccoli
  florets (about 6 ounces)

1 (12-inch) baked pizza shell,
  such as Boboli
½ cup pizza sauce
2 cups shredded part-skim
  mozzarella cheese

**1.** Preheat oven to 450°F. Crumble sausage into a large nonstick skillet; add bell pepper and red onion. Cook over medium-high heat, stirring frequently, 5 minutes. Reduce heat to medium and cook until sausage is browned and vegetables soften, 6 to 8 minutes. Drain off any fat. Stir in broccoli, cover, and cook about 2 minutes, until broccoli is crisp-tender.

**2.** Place pizza shell on a baking sheet. Spread sauce over shell, leaving a ¾-inch margin around edge. Sprinkle on ½ cup cheese. Top evenly with sausage mixture. Sprinkle remaining cheese on top.

**3.** Bake on bottom rack of oven 12 to 15 minutes, or until cheese melts and crust is browned and crisp on bottom.

# Chapter 8

# Catch of the Day

Travel around our beautiful countryside and shorelines and survey the bounty of our waters. Start in Alaska with salmon; the Pacific coast with Dungeness crab, squid, abalone, sole, and sand dabs; Washington and Oregon with razor and geoduck clams, Olympia oysters, and mussels. Inland lakes and streams offer trout, perch, smelt, pike, and whitefish. The Gulf Coast teems with catfish, mahimahi, grouper, pompano, snapper, tuna, shrimp, stone crabs, redfish, oysters, and crawfish. Along the Atlantic Coast are crabs, bluefish, cod, clams, haddock, halibut, scallops, lobster, shad, and swordfish. Whew! And these are certainly not all of the kinds of seafood, fish, and shellfish available in this bountiful country. We are fortunate in that many of these varieties are now available to everyone in grocery stores.

Fish lends itself to many methods of cooking. It is good broiled, fried, poached, baked, grilled, and steamed. One thing to remember is not to overcook it, as it becomes dry and not too appealing. A general rule of thumb is to cook fish 7 to 10 minutes per inch, with times varying for different kinds of fish. One of the tests for fresh fish is to smell it, and don't be shy about asking to do this. I'm lucky enough to have access to some great New England fish and fish markets, and when you walk in the door all you smell is a faint, fresh clean scent of the sea. Supermarkets carry fresh fish these days, too, and ideally it should not be prewrapped, so you can smell it too. Fish fillets and steaks should be firm, moist, and translucent.

Some of our favorite American fish recipes are Maryland Shore Crab Cakes, Boiled Maine Lobster, San Francisco Cioppino, Louisiana Shrimp Boil, and Mississippi Fried Catfish. I've included all of these plus some more contemporary American recipes that take advantage of the best of our local seafood. In general, fish is quick to prepare and cook so get one of these recipes on the table in a flash and your family will fall for them hook, line, and sinker.

# 207  MISSISSIPPI FRIED CATFISH
*Prep: 5 minutes    Cook: 8 to 12 minutes    Serves: 4*

Catfish is a moist and wonderful fish. It's great fried with a crunchy and slightly spicy cornmeal coating. While you're at it make up a batch of hush puppies and some coleslaw and really feel like you've been transported below the Mason-Dixon line. Serve with Tartar Sauce (page 153) and lemon wedges.

¼ cup flour
⅓ cup yellow cornmeal
2½ teaspoons Creole
    Seasoning, store-bought
    or homemade (page 152)

4 catfish fillets (5 to 6 ounces
    each)
¼ cup milk
    Vegetable oil, for frying

**1.** In a pie plate, mix flour, cornmeal, and 1¼ teaspoons Creole seasoning. Pat catfish fillets dry and sprinkle on both sides with remaining seasoning. Place milk in a pie plate.

**2.** In a large skillet, heat ½ inch vegetable oil until hot over medium-high heat. While oil heats, dredge fillets in cornmeal mixture. Dip quickly in milk just to moisten and dip again in cornmeal to coat both sides.

**3.** Add 2 fillets to skillet, reduce heat to medium, and cook until coating is golden brown and crisp and fish is cooked through, about 2 to 3 minutes per side. Drain on paper towels and repeat with remaining fillets. Serve immediately while hot and crisp.

# 208  CREOLE SEASONING
*Prep: 3 minutes    Cook: none    Makes: ⅔ cup*

A batch of this seasoning will keep on your pantry shelf for up to 3 months.

2½ tablespoons paprika
2 tablespoons salt
1½ tablespoons garlic powder
1 tablespoon cayenne
1 tablespoon freshly ground
    black pepper
1 tablespoon onion powder

2 teaspoons ground white
    pepper
2 teaspoons dried thyme,
    crumbled
2 teaspoons dried oregano,
    crumbled

In a small bowl, combine paprika, salt, garlic powder, cayenne, black pepper, onion powder, white pepper, thyme, and oregano. Stir to mix well. Store in a tightly covered container. Stir before using.

## 209    TARTAR SAUCE

*Prep: 5 minutes    Cook: none    Makes: 1⅓ cups*

1 cup mayonnaise
2 tablespoons sweet pickle
  relish
2 tablespoons finely chopped
  dill pickle
1½ tablespoons spicy brown
  mustard

1 tablespoon chopped parsley
1 teaspoon lemon juice
½ teaspoon grated lemon zest
¼ teaspoon Tabasco sauce

In small bowl, combine all ingredients. Stir well. Cover and refrigerate for up to 2 days before using.

## 210    CAPE COD FISH CAKES

*Prep: 15 minutes    Cook: 55 to 59 minutes    Serves: 4*

My Yankee grandmother, Mimi, made her codfish cakes the traditional way—with salt cod. Although not absolutely authentic, I'm sure she would approve of these.

1¼ pounds all-purpose
  potatoes, peeled and
  quartered
1¼ teaspoons salt
1 pound cod fillets
4 tablespoons butter

1 cup finely chopped onion
¼ teaspoon pepper
1 egg, beaten
¼ cup cornmeal
2 tablespoons vegetable oil

1. In a medium saucepan, cover potatoes with water and add ½ teaspoon salt. Bring to a boil, cover, and cook 20 minutes, or until tender; drain. While potatoes are still hot, place in a large bowl and mash.

2. Place fish in saucepan and cover with water. Bring to a simmer. Cover and simmer 5 minutes, or until opaque throughout. Remove with a slotted spoon to a plate. Discard cooking water. Add 2 tablespoons butter to pan and heat over medium heat. Add onion and cook, stirring occasionally, until golden, about 10 minutes.

3. Mix onion into potatoes. Add fish, breaking it up into large chunks. Add pepper, egg, and remaining salt. Stir until well blended. Place cornmeal on a plate. Shape mixture into 8 cakes 3 inches in diameter, using about ½ cup for each. Coat both sides lightly with cornmeal, handling cakes carefully as they are somewhat soft.

4. In a large skillet, melt 1 tablespoon butter in 1 tablespoon oil over medium heat. Add 4 fish cakes. Cook, turning with a wide spatula and reducing heat slightly if necessary, 5 to 6 minutes per side, or until well browned. Wipe out skillet and repeat with remaining oil, butter, and fish cakes. Serve hot.

# 211    CRAB-STUFFED FLOUNDER
*Prep: 15 minutes    Cook: 23 to 28 minutes    Serves: 6*

2 tablespoons butter
1 small onion, finely chopped
½ cup fresh bread crumbs
¼ cup mayonnaise
½ pound fresh crabmeat
2 tablespoons chopped
parsley

1 teaspoon grated lemon zest
4 large flounder fillets (1½
pounds)
¼ cup dry white wine
⅛ teaspoon salt
⅛ teaspoon pepper

**1.** Preheat oven to 400°F. In a medium skillet, melt 1 tablespoon butter over medium heat. Add onion and cook, stirring occasionally, until soft and golden, about 5 minutes. Add bread crumbs and cook, stirring, until crumbs are golden brown, about 3 minutes. Let cool slightly.

**2.** In a medium bowl, combine onion mixture, mayonnaise, crabmeat, parsley, and lemon zest. Stir gently to mix.

**3.** Cut each flounder fillet in half lengthwise along natural separation. Lay skinned side up (the side with some brown on it) on work surface. Place filling on each piece of flounder, dividing it evenly. Roll up starting at wide end. Place seam side down in a buttered 13 x 9 x 2-inch baking dish. Pour wine over fish and sprinkle with salt and pepper. Dot with remaining butter.

**4.** Bake 15 to 20 minutes, or until fish is opaque throughout. Serve with any juices in pan spooned over fish.

# 212    BAKED BOSTON SCROD
*Prep: 5 minutes    Cook: 10 to 12 minutes    Serves: 4*

1½ pounds scrod fillets, cut
1 inch thick
3 tablespoons butter, melted
¼ teaspoon salt
1 cup coarse fresh bread
crumbs

¼ teaspoon paprika
2 teaspoons Dijon mustard
2 teaspoons lemon juice
½ teaspoon grated lemon zest
¼ teaspoon pepper
⅛ teaspoon dried thyme

**1.** Preheat oven to 400°F. Cut fish into 4 equal-sized pieces. Tuck thin ends under and place in a generously buttered 9 x 13-inch baking dish. Brush a little melted butter over fish. Season fish with salt. Stir bread crumbs and paprika into remaining melted butter.

**2.** In a small dish, stir mustard, lemon juice, lemon zest, pepper, and thyme until blended. Spread over fish. Sprinkle bread crumbs over fish, pressing to stick.

**3.** Bake 10 to 12 minutes, or until fish is opaque throughout and crumbs are browned.

# 213     MAHIMAHI WITH PINEAPPLE-MACADAMIA SALSA

*Prep: 15 minutes     Chill: 1 hour     Cook: 14 to 17 minutes     Serves: 4*

Mahimahi is a meaty fish that has long been a mainstay of the Hawaiian diet. It is also found off the California coast and in recent years has taken the mainland by storm.

¼  cup soy sauce
2  teaspoons grated fresh ginger
1  tablespoon dry sherry
1  garlic clove, crushed through a press
1½  pounds mahimahi fillet, in 1 piece, cut 1¼ inches thick
¼  cup flaked coconut
1  cup fresh or canned unsweetened chopped pineapple, drained

1  small ripe mango, peeled, pitted, and cut into ½-inch dice
1  scallion, thinly sliced
⅛  teaspoon crushed hot red pepper
2  teaspoons Asian sesame oil
¼  cup chopped macadamia nuts

1. In a small bowl, whisk together soy sauce, ginger, sherry, and garlic. Place fish in a large food storage bag. Pour in soy mixture, seal bag, and turn to coat. Refrigerate 1 hour.

2. Preheat oven to 350°F. Spread coconut on a cookie sheet. Bake 4 to 5 minutes, stirring once, or until lightly browned. Set aside to cool.

3. In a medium bowl, combine pineapple, mango, scallion, and hot pepper. Toss gently to mix. Set salsa aside.

4. Prepare a hot fire in a barbecue grill or preheat broiler. Remove fish from marinade, reserving marinade. Brush both sides with sesame oil. On a well-oiled grill rack over a medium-hot fire, or on a lightly oiled broiling pan about 4 inches from heat, grill or broil fish 5 to 6 minutes per side, brushing with reserved marinade a few times, or until opaque in center. Stir coconut and macadamia nuts into salsa and serve with fish.

## 214   MUSTARD-GLAZED SALMON STEAKS

*Prep: 10 minutes    Cook: 8 to 9 minutes    Serves: 4*

If you're not a caper fan, simply omit them. This quick-to-fix glaze will still have lots of flavor.

3 tablespoons mayonnaise
2 tablespoons Dijon mustard
1 tablespoon chopped fresh dill
1 tablespoon capers, rinsed and chopped
1 teaspoon grated lemon zest
1 garlic clove, crushed through a press

1 teaspoon balsamic vinegar
4 salmon steaks (8 ounces each)
½ teaspoon freshly ground pepper
Lemon wedges

**1.** Preheat broiler. In a small bowl, combine mayonnaise, mustard, dill, capers, lemon zest, garlic, and vinegar. Stir until blended.

**2.** Spray rack of broiling pan with vegetable cooking spray. Place salmon steaks on rack and season both sides with pepper.

**3.** Broil salmon 4 to 5 inches from heat 4 minutes. Turn steaks over and broil 3 minutes. Spread with glaze and broil 1 to 2 minutes, or until glaze is bubbly and browned in spots and salmon is opaque in center but still moist. Serve with lemon wedges.

## 215   MARYLAND SHORE CRAB CAKES

*Prep: 20 minutes    Chill: 1 hour    Cook: 10 minutes    Serves: 4*

Crab cakes are a popular Maryland specialty, and there are countless versions. This is a basic version, kept simple, so crab is the star. Make sure to pick over the crabmeat, breaking up the lumps as little as possible, because there is always some shell remaining.

1 egg
2 scallions, minced
1 tablespoon chopped parsley
½ teaspoon grated lemon zest
⅓ cup mayonnaise
1½ teaspoons Old Bay seasoning
⅛ teaspoon salt

¼ teaspoon freshly ground pepper
1 pound lump crabmeat, preferably jumbo, picked over
½ cup dry bread crumbs
¼ cup vegetable oil

**1.** In a medium bowl, beat egg lightly. Stir in scallions, parsley, lemon zest, mayonnaise, seasoning, salt, and pepper. Add crabmeat and ¼ cup bread crumbs. Stir until well blended, breaking up crabmeat as little as possible. Shape mixture into 4 cakes about 3½ inches in diameter. Place on a plate in a single layer, cover, and refrigerate 1 hour.

**2.** Place remaining bread crumbs on a plate and turn crab cakes in crumbs until coated, handling cakes gently so they don't fall apart. In a large heavy skillet, heat oil over medium heat. Add crab cakes to skillet and cook, turning once, until browned outside and hot throughout, about 5 minutes per side.

## 216 TUNA NOODLE CASSEROLE
*Prep: 25 minutes    Cook: 21 to 24 minutes    Serves: 6*

Here is one of those classics that we grew up with, updated in a made-from-scratch version.

| | |
|---|---|
| 10 ounces medium egg noodles | 2 tablespoons flour |
| 6 tablespoons butter | 3 cups hot milk |
| ½ cup grated Parmesan cheese | ¾ teaspoon salt |
| ½ pound mushrooms, sliced | ½ teaspoon freshly ground |
| 2 small celery ribs, finely | pepper |
| chopped | 1 (12-ounce) can solid white |
| 1 small red bell pepper, finely | tuna in water, drained |
| chopped | and flaked |
| 3 shallots, minced | ½ cup fresh bread crumbs |

**1.** In a large pot of boiling salted water, cook noodles until tender but firm, 4 to 5 minutes; drain. While noodles are hot, place in a flameproof 13 x 9 x 2-inch baking or gratin dish. Add 1 tablespoon butter and stir until melted. Sprinkle ¼ cup Parmesan cheese over noodles.

**2.** In a large skillet, melt 2 tablespoons butter over medium heat. Add mushrooms, celery, bell pepper, and shallots to skillet. Cook, stirring frequently, until liquid evaporates and vegetables soften, about 8 minutes. Add to noodles. Cover with foil to keep warm.

**3.** Melt 2 tablespoons butter in skillet over medium heat. Add flour and cook, stirring, 1 minute. Gradually whisk in hot milk, salt, and pepper. Bring to a simmer and cook 2 minutes, whisking occasionally. Add tuna to noodles. Pour hot sauce over tuna and stir to combine.

**4.** Preheat broiler. Broil casserole 4 to 5 inches from heat until hot and bubbly, 5 to 6 minutes. Combine remaining Parmesan cheese with bread crumbs and sprinkle over casserole. Dot with remaining 1 tablespoon butter. Broil until browned, 1 to 2 minutes.

## 217 MONTANA PAN-FRIED TROUT

*Prep: 10 minutes    Stand: 30 minutes    Cook: 18 to 20 minutes*
*Serves: 4*

3 tablespoons olive oil
1 tablespoon lemon juice
1 shallot, minced
2 tablespoons chopped
 parsley
¾ teaspoon salt
¼ teaspoon freshly ground
 pepper

4 rainbow trout (10 to
 12 ounces each), cleaned,
 with head and tails left on
½ cup cornmeal
2 tablespoons flour
4 tablespoons butter
 Lemon wedges, as
 accompaniment

**1.** In a small bowl, combine 1 tablespoon of oil, lemon juice, shallot, parsley, ¼ teaspoon salt, and ⅛ teaspoon pepper. Stir until blended. Rinse and pat trout dry. Place in a shallow nonreactive baking dish. Spoon parsley mixture into cavities, spreading with a spoon. Let stand for 30 minutes, turning once.

**2.** On a piece of wax paper, stir remaining salt and pepper, cornmeal, and flour. Coat both sides of trout with seasoned cornmeal.

**3.** In a large cast-iron skillet, melt 2 tablespoons butter in 1 tablespoon oil over medium-high heat. When sizzling, add 2 trout. Cook 5 minutes, turn, and cook 4 to 5 minutes, or until cooked through, reducing heat if browning too fast. Remove to a plate. Wipe out skillet and repeat with remaining butter, oil, and trout. Serve hot, with lemon wedges.

## 218 BLACKENED SNAPPER

*Prep: 3 minutes    Cook: 4 to 6 minutes    Serves: 4*

Chef Paul Prudhomme of New Orleans gets the credit for popularizing this method of cooking fish. Make sure to have your vent on high when cooking this, so you don't get smoked out of the kitchen.

4 skinless snapper fillets
 (about 6 ounces each)
4 tablespoons butter, melted

1½ tablespoons Creole
 Seasoning (page 152)

**1.** Heat a large cast-iron skillet over medium-high heat until very hot.

**2.** While skillet heats, dip fish fillets in butter and sprinkle on both sides with Creole seasoning.

**3.** Add fillets to skillet. Cook, turning once with a wide spatula, until blackened and cooked through but still moist, 2 to 3 minutes per side.

# 219    SAN FRANCISCO CIOPPINO
*Prep: 25 minutes    Cook: 37 to 43 minutes    Serves: 8*

16  littleneck clams, scrubbed
16  mussels, scrubbed and
     debearded
 2  cups dry white or red wine
½  cup clam juice or water
 1  pound medium shrimp,
     shelled and deveined,
     shells reserved
 1  (28-ounce) can whole
     tomatoes in juice
¼  cup olive oil
 4  garlic cloves, minced
 1  large onion, chopped
 1  medium red bell pepper, cut
     into ½-inch dice

 1  teaspoon dried thyme
¼  teaspoon crushed hot red
     pepper
 1  teaspoon salt
½  teaspoon freshly ground
     pepper
¼  cup chopped fresh basil
 1  pound sea bass, snapper, or
     cod fillets, cut into 2-inch
     pieces
½  pound sea scallops, halved
¼  pound lump crabmeat
 2  tablespoons chopped
     parsley

**1.** In a large nonreactive soup pot or kettle, combine clams, mussels, and ½ cup wine. Bring to a boil over high heat, cover, and cook until clams and mussels open, 4 to 6 minutes. Remove to a bowl as they open. Discard any that do not open. Cover bowl to keep warm.

**2.** Add shrimp shells to pot along with remaining wine and clam juice. Bring to a boil. Cover and cook 10 minutes. Strain liquid through a sieve lined with cheesecloth, pressing on shells to extract all juice. Discard shells and reserve liquid. Rinse out pot.

**3.** In a food processor, process tomatoes with juices until tomatoes are finely chopped but not smooth. In pot, heat oil over medium heat. Add garlic and cook, stirring, just until golden but not brown, about 2 minutes. Add onion, bell pepper, thyme, and hot pepper. Cook, stirring occasionally, until onion and pepper are softened, 3 to 5 minutes. Add reserved liquid, tomatoes, salt, and pepper. Bring to a boil, reduce heat, cover, and simmer 15 minutes.

**4.** Stir in basil and fish; bring to a simmer. Add shrimp and scallops. Cover and simmer until seafood is just cooked through and opaque in center, 3 to 5 minutes. Divide crab among individual serving bowls. Ladle cioppino over crab. Garnish each bowl with clams and mussels. Sprinkle parsley on top and serve at once.

## 220   CLAMBAKE IN A POT
*Prep: 10 minutes   Cook: 15 minutes   Serves: 4*

This doesn't taste quite the same as a clambake dug on a beach and cooked over a wood fire, layered with seaweed and covered with a tarp, but it's the next best thing.

12  small red potatoes (about 2 pounds), scrubbed
8  small boiling onions, peeled
4  (1½-pound) live lobsters
4  ears of corn, husked
1  pound mussels, scrubbed and debearded

1  pound soft-shell or littleneck clams, scrubbed
1  stick (4 ounces) butter, melted

**1.** Fill 2 (6-quart) pots with 2 inches water. Add half of potatoes and onions to each pot. Bring to a boil. Add 2 lobsters to each pot. Cover and bring back to a boil. Boil 10 minutes.

**2.** Add 2 ears of corn and half of mussels and clams to each pot. Return to a boil, cover, and cook 5 minutes, or until mussels and clams have opened. Discard any that do not open.

**3.** Remove clams, mussels, corn, lobsters, onions, and potatoes to a large serving platter. Place hot cooking broth and butter in individual small bowls for dipping.

## 221   PAN-FRIED SOFT-SHELLED CRABS AMANDINE
*Prep: 10 minutes   Cook: 13 to 14 minutes   Serves: 4*

Soft-shelled crabs are hard-shelled crabs that have shed their old shells and are caught before they grow new ones. Like lobsters, they should be alive and cleaned shortly before cooking. Have your fish market do this for you.

8  soft-shelled crabs, cleaned
¼  teaspoon cayenne
½  cup flour
5  tablespoons unsalted butter
2  tablespoons vegetable oil

½  cup fresh orange juice
2  tablespoons chopped toasted almonds
2  tablespoons minced fresh chives

**1.** Preheat oven to 250°F. Rinse crabs and pat dry with paper towels. Season with cayenne. Place flour on a sheet of wax paper and dredge crabs in flour to coat, shaking off excess.

**2.** In a large skillet, melt 2 tablespoons butter in 1 tablespoon oil over medium-high heat. Add 4 crabs, reduce heat to medium, and cook 3 minutes per side, until browned. Remove crabs to paper towel–lined cookie sheet. Keep warm in low oven. Wipe out skillet and repeat with same amounts of butter, oil, and crabs.

CATCH OF THE DAY   161

3. Pour off any fat from skillet. Add orange juice and remaining 1 table-spoon butter to skillet. Increase heat to medium-high and cook until juice reduces slightly and becomes syrupy, 1 to 2 minutes. Remove from heat and stir in almonds and chives. Spoon over crabs and serve at once.

---

## 222   BAKED STUFFED CLAMS
*Prep: 15 minutes   Cook: 51 minutes   Serves: 4 to 6*

Quahogs are the largest of common hard-shelled clams, often used for chowder. Because of their size, they are usually tough and must be chopped up, but their big flavor makes mighty good eating.

6 medium-sized quahog
  clams (3 inches wide),
  scrubbed
3 slices of bacon, chopped
1 small onion, finely chopped
3 garlic cloves, minced
2 tablespoons olive oil
3 cups fresh coarse bread
  crumbs

2 tablespoons chopped
  parsley
¼ teaspoon freshly ground
  pepper
⅛ teaspoon cayenne
2 tablespoons butter
  Lemon wedges, as
  accompaniment

1. Fill a large pot or Dutch oven with 1 inch water. Add clams. Bring to a boil over high heat, cover, reduce heat slightly, and cook just until clams start to open, about 5 minutes. Discard any that do not open. Remove clams to a plate. Strain broth through a sieve lined with dampened cheese-cloth and reserve.

2. When clams are cool enough to handle, pry them open. Loosen the meat and finely chop. Place in a large bowl. Reserve the shells.

3. In a medium skillet, cook bacon over medium heat until crisp, about 5 minutes. Remove bacon to bowl with clams. Pour off all but 1 tablespoon drippings from pan. Add onion and cook over medium heat, stirring occa-sionally, until onion is golden, about 5 minutes. Add garlic and cook, stir-ring, 1 minute. Add to clams.

4. Add oil to skillet and stir in bread crumbs. Cook over medium-low heat, stirring constantly, until crumbs are lightly toasted, about 5 minutes. Add to bowl. Add parsley, pepper, and cayenne. Stir until blended. Drizzle in enough reserved clam broth (about ½ cup), tossing to moisten crumbs. Mound mixture in reserved clam shells. Place clams on a jelly-roll pan. Dot with butter. (The clams can be prepared to this point and refrigerated up to 3 hours.)

5. Preheat oven to 375°F. Bake in upper third of oven 30 minutes, or until crumbs are lightly browned and stuffed clams are heated through. Serve hot, with lemon wedges.

## 223    BOILED MAINE LOBSTER

*Prep: 2 minutes    Cook: 12 minutes    Serves: 4*

Make sure to have bibs and lots of napkins handy to enjoy one of the best seafood feasts there is. A trick for reducing some of the water that lobsters give off before you crack them is, after cooking, to snip ½ inch off the tips of the claws and hold the lobsters up by the tail to let the water drain off.

| | |
|---|---|
| 4  live lobsters, 1½ pounds each | Lemon wedges, as accompaniment |
| 1  stick (4 ounces) butter, melted | |

**1.** Bring 2 large pots, at least 6-quart size, filled two-thirds full with salted water to a boil. Plunge 2 lobsters into each pot, head first. Cover pots and return to a boil. Uncover and boil 10 to 12 minutes, until lobsters are bright red and curled. Remove lobsters with tongs and place on plates.

**2.** Reheat butter if necessary and pour into small bowls. Serve with lobster along with lemon wedges.

---

## 224    STEAMED MUSSELS WITH GARLIC AND LEMON

*Prep: 15 minutes    Cook: 8 to 12 minutes    Serves: 4*

You'll end up with lots of tasty juices here, so be sure to serve plenty of French or Italian bread for dunking.

| | |
|---|---|
| 3  tablespoons olive oil | 2  pounds mussels, scrubbed and debearded |
| 4  garlic cloves, minced | 1  cup dry white wine |
| 3  shallots, finely chopped | 1  teaspoon grated lemon zest |
| 1  small onion, sliced | 2  tablespoons chopped parsley |
| ¼  teaspoon crushed hot red pepper | |

**1.** In a large soup pot or kettle, heat oil over medium heat. Add garlic, shallots, onion, and hot pepper. Cook, stirring occasionally, until softened but not browned, 3 to 5 minutes.

**2.** Add mussels and wine. Bring to a boil over high heat, cover, reduce heat slightly, and cook until mussels open, 5 to 7 minutes. Discard any mussels that do not open.

**3.** With a strainer or large slotted spoon, remove mussels to bowls. Stir lemon zest into juices in pot. Pour over mussels. Sprinkle with parsley and serve at once.

# 225    SCALLOPED SCALLOPS
*Prep: 10 minutes    Cook: 11 minutes    Serves: 6*

This is an indulgent but delicious way to prepare scallops. Make sure not to overcook the delicate shellfish, or they will turn rubbery. I think the best way to cook them is over high heat, quickly, so they remain juicy and don't steam in their own juices. They should be just translucent in the center.

1 tablespoon plus 1 teaspoon
  olive oil
½ cup fresh bread crumbs
2 oil-packed sun-dried tomato
  halves, minced (about
  1 tablespoon)
2 tablespoons grated
  Parmesan cheese
1 tablespoon chopped parsley

1 teaspoon grated lemon zest
1½ pounds bay scallops
⅛ teaspoon salt
⅛ teaspoon freshly ground
  pepper
1 cup heavy cream
1 garlic clove, crushed
  through a press

**1.** In a large nonstick skillet, heat 1 teaspoon oil over medium-high heat. Add bread crumbs, reduce heat to medium, and cook, stirring constantly, until crisp and lightly toasted, about 2 minutes. Turn into a small bowl. Add minced sun-dried tomatoes, Parmesan cheese, parsley, and lemon zest to crumbs. Stir to mix.

**2.** Wipe out skillet. Rinse scallops and pat dry. Season with salt and pepper. Add ½ tablespoon olive oil to skillet and heat over medium-high heat. Add half of scallops. Cook, turning once, until still slightly translucent in center, about 2 minutes. Remove to a plate and repeat with remaining oil and scallops.

**3.** Preheat broiler. Place scallops in a shallow baking dish in a single layer. Add cream and garlic to skillet. Boil over medium-high heat until thickened and reduced to ¾ cup, about 3 minutes. Pour over scallops. Sprinkle seasoned crumbs on top.

**4.** Broil 4 to 5 inches from heat until crumbs are golden and cream is bubbly around edges, watching so crumbs don't burn, about 2 minutes.

# 226   SEAFOOD GUMBO

*Prep: 25 minutes    Cook: 1 hour 2 to 7 minutes    Serves: 8*

*Gumbo* is a translation of an African word for okra. Gumbo is also a thick, rich Louisiana stew, which varies depending on the ingredients added. It usually is made with a roux, a mixture of oil and flour cooked to varying shades of brown, to add flavor and thickness. Gumbos are further thickened with either okra or filé powder, but never both.

½ cup vegetable oil
½ pound hot smoked sausage, diced
½ cup flour
2 large onions, chopped
3 large celery ribs, chopped
1 large green bell pepper, chopped
6 garlic cloves, minced
4 teaspoons Creole Seasoning, store-bought or homemade (page 152)

1½ quarts chicken broth
1 (28-ounce) can diced tomatoes in juice
2 bay leaves
½ pound fresh okra, cut into ½-inch slices
1½ pounds medium shrimp, shelled and deveined
½ pound crabmeat
Hot cooked white rice

**1.** In a medium skillet, heat 1 tablespoon oil over medium heat. Add sausage and cook, stirring occasionally, until browned, 6 to 8 minutes. With a slotted spoon, remove sausage to a small bowl.

**2.** Pour any drippings in skillet into a large Dutch oven or heavy pot. Add remaining oil. Place over medium-high heat and whisk in flour. Cook, whisking constantly, until roux turns medium brown in color, the shade of coffee with milk, about 5 to 8 minutes. Immediately remove from heat and stir in onions, celery, and bell pepper. Return to heat, reduce heat to medium, and cook, stirring occasionally, until vegetables soften, about 5 minutes. Stir in garlic and Creole seasoning. Stir in chicken broth. Add tomatoes, bay leaves, okra, and sausage.

**3.** Bring to a boil. Reduce heat to medium-low and simmer, stirring occasionally, 45 minutes.

**4.** Stir in shrimp and crabmeat. Cook 1 minute. Remove pot from heat, cover, and let stand 10 minutes. Discard bay leaves. Serve gumbo in bowls, ladled over a large spoonful of rice in the center of each bowl.

# 227    JAMBALAYA
*Prep: 20 minutes    Cook: 38 minutes    Serves: 6*

A Cajun dish from Louisiana, Jambalaya varies according to the cook, but always contains rice, tomatoes, and what some call the holy trinity of Cajun cooking—onions, celery, and green pepper. This makes a great meal for entertaining, with nothing else needed but a simple green salad.

1 (16-ounce) can whole
  tomatoes in juice
1 tablespoon olive oil
¼ pound smoked ham, cut
  into ½-inch dice
½ pound spicy smoked
  sausage, sliced ½ inch
  thick
1 large onion, chopped
2 medium celery ribs,
  chopped

1 medium green bell pepper,
  chopped
4 garlic cloves, crushed
  through a press
1 tablespoon Creole
  Seasoning, store-bought
  or homemade (page 152)
1 teaspoon dried thyme
1½ cups long-grain rice
1 pound medium shrimp,
  shelled and deveined

**1.** Pour tomatoes into a colander set over a bowl. Cut tomatoes into small pieces and let drain. Measure juice into a bowl and add enough water to equal 3 cups.

**2.** In a large Dutch oven, heat oil over medium-high heat. Add ham and sausage and cook, stirring, until browned, about 6 minutes. Remove with a slotted spoon to a plate. Add onion, celery, and bell pepper to drippings in pan. Cook, stirring occasionally, until softened, about 5 minutes.

**3.** Reduce heat to medium. Stir in garlic, Creole seasoning, and thyme. Cook, stirring, 1 minute. Add rice and cook, stirring, 1 minute longer. Add tomatoes, reserved liquid, sausage, and ham. Bring to a boil, stirring occasionally. Cover, reduce heat to low, and simmer, stirring once, 20 minutes.

**4.** Stir in shrimp. Cover and cook, stirring once, 5 minutes, or until shrimp are pink and curled and rice is tender. Remove from heat and let stand, covered, 5 minutes before serving.

# 228   SPICY CAJUN BARBECUED SHRIMP
*Prep: 10 minutes    Cook: 5 to 7 minutes    Serves: 4*

Be sure to serve this with French bread to sop up every bit of the delicious sauce.

1½ **pounds large shrimp in the shell**
1 **teaspoon paprika**
1 **teaspoon freshly ground black pepper**
¼ **teaspoon cayenne**
¼ **teaspoon crushed hot red pepper**
¼ **teaspoon dried oregano**

⅛ **teaspoon salt**
6 **tablespoons butter**
1 **teaspoon Worcestershire sauce**
1 **teaspoon Tabasco sauce**
2 **garlic cloves, crushed through a press**
½ **cup chicken broth**
½ **cup dry white wine**

**1.** With kitchen scissors, cut through curved outside shell of each shrimp; remove the black veins, leaving shells intact and attached. Place shrimp in a large bowl. Add paprika, black pepper, cayenne, hot pepper, oregano, and salt. Toss gently to mix. Let stand at room temperature 15 minutes.

**2.** In a large skillet, melt 3 tablespoons butter over medium-high heat. Add seasoned shrimp, Worcestershire sauce, Tabasco, and garlic. Cook, stirring constantly, until shells turn pink, about 2 minutes. Add remaining butter, chicken broth, and wine. Increase heat to high. Cook, stirring occasionally, 2 to 3 minutes, or until shrimp are curled and opaque in center.

**3.** With a slotted spoon, remove shrimp to a large deep platter. Boil liquid in skillet, stirring constantly, until slightly thickened, 1 to 2 minutes. Pour over shrimp and serve.

# 229   LOUISIANA SHRIMP BOIL
*Prep: 10 minutes    Cook : 20 to 21 minutes    Serves: 4*

This one-pot meal would work well with crabs or crawfish if you're lucky enough to get them. Serve this with lots of napkins and ice cold beer.

2 **tablespoons Old Bay seasoning spice**
¼ **teaspoon cayenne**
2 **tablespoons coarse kosher salt**
8 **small white boiling onions, peeled**
8 **small red potatoes, scrubbed and halved**

½ **pound hot smoked sausage, cut into 1½-inch lengths**
4 **ears of corn, husked and broken in half**
1 **pound medium shrimp**
2 **teaspoons Tabasco sauce**
4 **tablespoons melted butter**

**1.** In a stockpot or large kettle, combine seasoning spice, cayenne, salt, and 3 quarts of water. Bring to a boil over high heat; boil 5 minutes. Add onions, potatoes, and sausage. Return to a boil, reduce heat to medium, and simmer 10 minutes.

**2.** Add corn, return to a boil, and cook 3 minutes. Add shrimp and cook until shrimp are pink and curled, 2 to 3 minutes. With a skimmer or slotted spoon, remove shrimp and vegetables to a large platter.

**3.** In a small bowl, stir Tabasco and butter until blended. Serve on the side for drizzling.

---

# 230    LOW-COUNTRY SHRIMP PILAU
*Prep: 15 minutes    Cook: 50 to 56 minutes    Serves: 6*

Low country is the low-lying coastal area of North Carolina, South Carolina, and Georgia. Pilau is another word for pilaf. While some are served as side dishes, this one, full of shrimp and topped with bacon, is a meal unto itself.

- 1 pound medium shrimp, shelled and deveined, shells reserved
- 2½ cups reduced-sodium chicken broth
- 6 slices of bacon, cut into ½-inch dice
- 1 large onion, finely chopped
- 1¼ cups long-grain rice
- ½ teaspoon salt
- ¼ teaspoon cayenne
- 4 ripe medium tomatoes, peeled, seeded, and coarsely chopped
- 1½ teaspoons Worcestershire sauce
- 2 tablespoons chopped parsley

**1.** Place shrimp shells in a medium saucepan, add broth, and bring to a boil. Cover and cook 3 minutes. Strain broth through a sieve set over a bowl, pressing on shells to extract as much liquid as possible. Set broth aside; discard shells.

**2.** Preheat oven to 350°F. In a large ovenproof casserole, cook bacon over medium heat, stirring, until crisp, about 5 minutes. With a slotted spoon, remove bacon to paper towels to drain. Pour off all but 2 tablespoons fat from casserole. Add onion and cook, stirring occasionally, until soft, about 5 minutes. Add rice and cook, stirring, 2 to 3 minutes. Stir in salt, cayenne, tomatoes, Worcestershire sauce, and reserved broth. Bring to a boil and cover.

**3.** Transfer casserole to oven and bake 25 to 30 minutes, or until rice is tender and liquid is absorbed. Stir in shrimp. Cover and bake 10 minutes, or until shrimp are pink and curled. Remove from oven and let stand covered 5 minutes. Sprinkle with bacon and parsley and serve.

# Chapter 9

# Backyard Barbecue

Grilling in warm weather (or even in winter, if you're a fanatic) is a real American tradition. It's a skill that some people take seriously, like the contestants in rib cook-offs or those dedicated people who barbecue the fabulous country fair chicken in a lot of states. There are grillers who build their own special cookers or pits and some who have secret, closely guarded recipes for their barbecue sauce. You could say that in many households, the backyard barbecue is more than a tradition; it has become a passion.

Barbecue means different things to different people. To some it means what you cook on the grill. To others, it signifies a dish—a specific cut of meat, usually either pork shoulder or beef brisket—which is the only real barbecue to them. To others it means the piece of equipment itself or an event centered around food cooked on the grill.

Barbecue was born in Virginia and North Carolina, and it usually meant cooking a whole side of beef or pork over an open pit. There are many towns and states that claim to be "the barbecue capital of the world," each having its own distinctive cooking method, favorite cut of meat, or kind of sauce.

The barbecue recipes in this book were tested in a covered kettle charcoal grill, though all of the recipes will work beautifully on a gas grill. Gas grills have the advantage of being instant starters, though they lack some of the rich smokiness achieved in a charcoal grill. My favorite tool for getting a fire started in a charcoal grill is a chimney starter, which you can find at most hardware stores. It eliminates having to use lighter fluid, which can impart an off-taste to food. Place some crumpled newspapers in the bottom of the chimney. Fill with charcoal. Remove the cooking rack from your grill and place the chimney on the lower rack. Light it and wait about 30 minutes, or until the coals are gray. Carefully turn the coals out, adding more coals if necessary. Place the cooking rack back on the grill. If additional coals have been added, allow them time to heat, and you're ready to go.

A common grilling mistake is to place foods on the grill when the fire is too hot, resulting in foods that are charred on the outside and raw inside. Generally a medium-hot fire, meaning coals are gray with a red underglow, is the right stage to start cooking. Trim meats and poultry of excess fat to prevent flare-ups and keep a spray bottle filled with water handy in case the fire does flare up. Brush on most sauces toward the end of the grilling time, as the sugar in them tends to burn before the foods are cooked. A pair of long-handled tongs, a wide spatula, a basting brush, an instant-reading thermometer, oven mitts, and a stiff wire brush for cleaning the rack are all tools that make grilling easier.

There are two ways to cook in a covered grill. One is by direct heat, which means foods are placed on the cooking rack directly over the coals as described above—by far the most common method for most foods. But for foods that require longer cooking, such as large cuts of meat or a whole bird, indirect heat is the way to go. Coals are placed either on two sides with the center open or to one side of the grill. Then the food is set on the part of the rack that is not over the coals, over a drip pan. A Thanksgiving turkey is great cooked on the grill, and it frees up space in the oven.

Whether you are cooking over charcoal or gas, wood chunks or chips can add great flavor to grilled foods. Soak them in water at least 30 minutes before adding them to the fire; in the case of gas grills, follow the manufacturer's instructions. Hickory, mesquite, oak, apple, cherry, and alder are a few of the hardwoods used.

I have a dream—to travel around the country in search of the best barbecue (whether that means ribs, chicken, pork, lamb, or beef), that hidden-away place that only the locals know about. Think it still exists? I sure hope so.

---

# 231   ALL-AMERICAN BARBECUED CHICKEN
*Prep: 15 minutes    Cook: 40 minutes to 1 hour    Serves: 8*

I like to buy chickens whole and cut them up myself, thereby controlling the size of the parts, but feel free to substitute 4 to 5 pounds of any chicken part. The skin is removed so the rub and sauce permeate the meat. To prevent overbrowning and flare-ups, spread coals out, leaving a few inches around the edge without coals so you can place chicken over this area if it is browning too fast. The secret to this moist flavorful chicken is fairly frequent turning and a covered grill.

2 **whole chickens**
   **(3¼ to 3½ pounds each)**
2 **tablespoons Barbecue Rub**
   **(page 172)**

**Kitchen Sink Barbecue**
**Sauce (page 171)**

**1.** Cut each chicken into 8 pieces. Remove skin from drumsticks, thighs, and breasts. Cut breasts in half. Place chicken pieces on a jelly-roll pan and sprinkle both sides with barbecue rub.

**2.** Prepare a medium-hot fire in a covered charcoal or gas grill. Place chicken on rack. Cover with lid with vents partially closed. Grill chicken 30 to 45 minutes, turning frequently. Brush with sauce. Grill covered, turning and brushing with sauce, until chicken is cooked through with no trace of pink near bone, 10 to 15 minutes more.

## 232    KITCHEN SINK BARBECUE SAUCE

*Prep: 10 minutes    Cook: 30 minutes    Makes: 2 cups*

This is an all-purpose barbecue sauce, fairly tart. It's fun to create your own barbecue sauce. I sometimes feel like a mad chemist adding some of this and that depending on my mood. I think it's worth it to make your own. If you need a big batch, double the recipe.

2 tablespoons olive oil
1 medium onion, finely chopped
2 garlic cloves, crushed through a press
1½ cups ketchup
½ cup cider vinegar
¼ cup fresh lemon juice
¼ cup Worcestershire sauce
¼ cup packed dark brown sugar
¼ cup bourbon
2 tablespoons molasses
2 teaspoons dry mustard
1 teaspoon paprika
1 teaspoon Tabasco sauce
½ teaspoon freshly ground pepper

**1.** In a medium saucepan, heat oil over medium heat. Add onion and cook, stirring, until softened, about 5 minutes.

**2.** Stir in garlic, ketchup, vinegar, lemon juice, Worcestershire, brown sugar, bourbon, molasses, dry mustard, paprika, Tabasco sauce, and pepper. Bring to a boil. Reduce heat and simmer until thickened, stirring occasionally, about 25 minutes.

## 233    CHILI-LIME FLANK STEAK

*Prep: 5 minutes    Marinate: 1 hour    Cook: 8 to 10 minutes*
*Serves: 4*

1 tablespoon olive oil
2 garlic cloves, crushed through a press
1 tablespoon chili powder
1 teaspoon ground cumin
½ teaspoon freshly ground pepper
1 flank steak (1¾ pounds)
¾ teaspoon salt
2 tablespoons fresh lime juice
½ teaspoon hot pepper sauce
1 tablespoon balsamic vinegar
1 tablespoon honey
2 tablespoons finely chopped cilantro

**1.** In a small bowl, combine oil, garlic, chili powder, cumin, and pepper. Place flank steak in a shallow baking dish, pour chili mixture over, and spread to coat steak on both sides. Let steak sit 1 hour or cover and refrigerate overnight.

**2.** Prepare a medium-hot fire in a covered charcoal or gas grill. Sprinkle steak on both sides with ½ teaspoon salt. Grill steak, 4 to 5 minutes on each side for medium-rare. Remove to a cutting board to stand 10 minutes.

**3.** In a small bowl, combine remaining salt, lime juice, hot pepper sauce, vinegar, honey, and cilantro. Whisk until blended. Thinly slice steak diagonally across the grain. Serve with sauce on the side to drizzle over.

## 234    TEXAS T-BONE STEAKS
*Prep: 2 minutes    Cook: 6 to 8 minutes    Serves: 4*

The best steak I've ever had was on a ranch in Texas. It was a T-bone, grilled to perfection, with absolutely nothing on it. This recipe is almost that simple. The steak is seasoned with a dry rub and spread with a little seasoned butter.

| | |
|---|---|
| 4  small T-bone steaks | 1  tablespoon butter, softened |
| 4½  teaspoons Barbecue Rub (page 172) | 1  teaspoon kosher salt |

**1.** Sprinkle steaks with ½ teaspoon barbecue rub on each side and let sit at room temperature while preparing grill. In a small bowl, stir butter and remaining ½ teaspoon barbecue rub until blended.

**2.** Prepare a hot fire in a covered charcoal or gas grill. Grill steaks, 3 to 4 minutes per side for medium-rare. Place on plates, sprinkle with kosher salt, and spread with butter. Let rest 5 minutes before serving.

## 235    BARBECUE RUB
*Prep: 2 minutes    Cook: none    Makes: ⅓ cup*

This is an all-purpose rub that adds extra flavor to grilled foods. It is not overly salty as some rubs can be. Use it on chicken, pork, and beef.

| | |
|---|---|
| 2  tablespoons paprika | 1  tablespoon freshly ground pepper |
| 1  tablespoon salt | 1  teaspoon cayenne |
| 1  tablespoon ground cumin | |
| 1  tablespoon chili powder | |

In a small bowl, stir paprika, salt, cumin, chili powder, pepper, and cayenne until mixed. Store airtight in glass jar. Stir before using. It will last almost indefinitely.

## 236    GRILLED BUTTERFLIED LEG OF LAMB
*Prep: 10 minutes    Chill: 8 hours    Cook: 15 to 25 minutes    Serves: 6 to 8*

| | |
|---|---|
| 1  cup dry red wine | 2  tablespoons olive oil |
| ¼  cup reduced-sodium soy sauce | 2  tablespoons Dijon mustard |
| 4  garlic cloves, thinly sliced | ½  teaspoon freshly ground pepper |
| 2  tablespoons chopped fresh rosemary | 3  to 4 pounds boned, butterflied leg of lamb |

**1.** In a medium bowl, combine wine, soy sauce, garlic, rosemary, olive oil, mustard, and pepper. Whisk until blended.

**2.** Trim lamb of excess fat. Place lamb in a 2-gallon food storage bag. Pour marinade over lamb. Seal bag. Turn bag over a few times to distribute marinade. Place on a jelly-roll pan and refrigerate 8 to 24 hours, turning a few times.

**3.** Remove lamb from refrigerator 30 minutes before grilling to come to room temperature.

**4.** Prepare a medium-hot fire in a covered charcoal or gas grill. Remove lamb from marinade; reserve marinade. Thread 2 skewers through lamb for easier turning.

**5.** Grill lamb, turning and basting with marinade every 10 minutes, until instant-reading thermometer inserted in thickest part reads 145°F for medium-rare, 15 to 25 minutes, depending on your grill. Remove lamb to a carving board to rest 10 minutes before cutting across the grain into thin slices.

---

## 237 PETE'S RIBS
*Prep: 5 minutes    Stand: 1 hour    Cook: 2½ to 3 hours    Serves: 6*

These ribs are the specialty of my brother, the grilling expert in our family. He is serious about ribs, and there are few that meet his standards. According to him, baby back ribs are the only way to go. Use the recipe for Kitchen Sink Barbecue Sauce (page 171) or a sauce of your own choosing.

3  **racks baby back ribs (4½ to 5 pounds)**
3  **tablespoons Barbecue Rub (page 172)**

3  **cups barbecue sauce**

**1.** Pat ribs dry with paper towels. Sprinkle with barbecue rub and rub in with fingers. Let ribs stand at room temperature while preparing grill or 1 to 2 hours.

**2.** Prepare covered kettle grill for indirect cooking according to manufacturer's directions with charcoal on one side. If using a gas grill, cook on low heat. Place rack on grill and place ribs on part of rack with no coals underneath, overlapping racks slightly if necessary to fit. Cover with vents open. Grill 2 to 2½ hours, adding coals every hour or as directed by manufacturer. Turn ribs occasionally.

**3.** Brush ribs with half of sauce. Grill covered, 30 minutes longer, or until glazed and tender when pierced with a sharp knife. Cut in 3-rib portions. Serve with plenty of napkins and pass remaining sauce on the side.

## 238   TEXAS BARBECUED BRISKET

*Prep: 10 minutes    Stand: 1 hour    Cook: 4 to 5 hours    Serves: 8*

This is a recipe for real barbecue fans. It's something to cook while you're spending a day working in the yard or house. It doesn't require much work, just being around to add a few coals every hour. The result is definitely worth it. In Texas, putting sauce on brisket while it cooks is unheard of. Serve the sauce on the side.

1   beef brisket (about
    6 pounds)
¼  cup Barbecue Rub
    (page 172)

3   cups mesquite chunks or
    chips
    Tangy Tomato Barbecue
    Sauce (page 174)

**1.** Trim brisket, leaving a layer of fat about ¼ inch thick. Rub brisket all over with barbecue rub. Let brisket sit to come to room temperature, about 1 hour. Meanwhile, place mesquite chunks in a bowl, cover with cold water, and let soak 1 hour.

**2.** Prepare a covered kettle grill for cooking using indirect heat, following manufacturer's directions, building coals against one wall of grill. Place a disposable foil drip pan with 1 inch water next to coals. When coals are gray, or medium heat, drain wood chips and add a handful to coals. Set rack on grill. Place brisket on side of rack not over coals so no part of brisket is over coals. Cover grill with vents open. Grill 3 hours, adding 5 to 6 pieces of charcoal every hour, to maintain heat at 200°F, turning brisket a few times. Add remaining wood chips halfway through cooking. Wrap brisket in foil, return to rack, and cook 1 to 2 hours longer, or until very tender, again adding 5 to 6 pieces of charcoal every hour.

**3.** Remove brisket to a cutting board. Let stand 15 minutes. Thinly slice brisket across the grain. Serve with barbecue sauce.

## 239   TANGY TOMATO BARBECUE SAUCE

*Prep: 10 minutes    Cook: 30 minutes    Makes: 2 cups*

This is a thinner vinegary sauce best with barbecued pork or beef sandwiches.

1   (8-ounce) can tomato sauce
1   cup cider vinegar
1   small onion, finely chopped
1   large garlic clove, crushed
    through a press
½  cup packed light brown
    sugar

2   tablespoons yellow mustard
2   tablespoons Worcestershire
    sauce
½  teaspoon salt
½  teaspoon cayenne

In a small saucepan, combine all ingredients. Bring to a boil, stirring occasionally. Reduce heat and simmer 30 minutes, stirring occasionally, or until slightly thickened.

# 240    CAROLINA BARBECUED PULLED PORK

*Prep: 10 minutes    Stand: 30 minutes    Cook: 5½ to 6 hours*
*Serves: 6 to 8*

This is true pork barbecue at its best. Depending on where in the Carolinas you come from will determine what kind of sauce you serve with the pork and whether or not it contains tomato. Wars could be fought over what should go into barbecue sauce—it depends on what part of the country you live in. You can also use what's called a picnic arm roast for this; it's a different part of the shoulder.

1  **fresh pork butt (6 pounds)**
3  **tablespoons Barbecue Rub (page 172)**
3  **cups hickory chunks or chips**
1  **cup cider vinegar**
2  **tablespoons sugar**
1  **tablespoon salt**
1½ **teaspoons crushed hot red pepper**

½  **teaspoon freshly ground pepper**
¼  **teaspoon cayenne**
   **Kaiser or other sandwich rolls, split in half**
   **Tangy Tomato Barbecue Sauce (page 174)**

**1.** Rub pork all over with barbecue rub. Let sit at room temperature 30 minutes. Cover hickory with water and let soak 30 minutes.

**2.** Prepare covered kettle grill for indirect cooking with coals on one side of grill against wall. Place disposable foil drip pan next to coals. When coals are gray, or medium heat, add a handful of chips. Place rack on grill, with handle over coals so coals can be added easily. Place pork butt on grill so no part is over the coals. Cover and grill with vents open 5½ to 6 hours, or until very tender and a knife slips out easily when inserted in meat. Add 6 to 8 coals every hour. Add remaining hickory chips halfway through cooking. Turn butt once or twice.

**3.** While pork cooks, in a small saucepan, combine vinegar, sugar, salt, hot pepper, ground pepper, and cayenne. Bring to a boil, reduce heat, and simmer 3 minutes.

**4.** Remove pork from grill. Let sit 15 minutes. Pull meat from bones. Shred or chop meat. Moisten meat with ½ cup vinegar mixture. Serve pork on rolls. Serve with remaining vinegar mixture and Tangy Tomato Barbecue Sauce on the side.

# 241    BEEF FAJITAS

*Prep: 25 minutes    Chill: 1 hour    Cook: 11 to 13 minutes    Serves: 6*

Skirt steak makes the best fajitas. If your store doesn't carry it, ask for it. You can also use flank steak.

2 tablespoons fresh lime juice
3 garlic cloves, crushed
   through a press
2½ tablespoons olive oil
1½ teaspoons ground cumin
1½ pounds skirt steak, trimmed
   and cut into 3 pieces, or
   flank steak
12 (7-inch) flour tortillas
2 poblano or medium green
   bell peppers, thinly sliced
1 large red bell pepper, thinly
   sliced

1 large yellow bell pepper,
   thinly sliced
1 large red onion, thinly
   sliced
2 jalapeño peppers, halved,
   seeded, and thinly sliced
½ teaspoon salt
   Fresh Tomato Salsa
   (page 16)
   Guacamole (page 14)

**1.** In a small bowl, whisk lime juice, 2 garlic cloves, 1 tablespoon olive oil, and cumin. Pour into a large food storage bag, add steak, seal bag, and turn to coat. Refrigerate 1 hour to marinate.

**2.** Prepare charcoal grill or preheat broiler. Remove steak from marinade. Place steak on grill or broiling pan. Grill or broil 4 inches from heat, 3 to 4 minutes per side, or until medium-rare. Place on a carving board and let stand 5 minutes. Wrap tortillas in foil and place on grill or in oven to heat through.

**3.** In a large skillet, heat remaining 1½ tablespoons oil over medium-high heat. Add poblano peppers, bell peppers, red onion, and jalapeños. Cook, stirring frequently, until peppers begin to soften, about 3 minutes. Stir in remaining garlic and ¼ teaspoon salt. Cook, stirring, until tender-crisp, about 2 minutes.

**4.** Sprinkle steak with remaining salt. Thinly slice steak diagonally across the grain. Serve with pepper mixture, salsa, guacamole, and tortillas.

# 242   PORK KEBABS WITH MANGO-PINEAPPLE SALSA

*Prep: 20 minutes    Chill: 1 hour    Cook: 12 to 14 minutes    Serves 6*

If tangerines are not available, use navel oranges.

2   pork tenderloins
(1¾ pounds), trimmed
½   cup fresh tangerine juice
1   tablespoon olive oil
2   tablespoons soy sauce
1   tablespoon honey
2   garlic cloves, crushed
through a press
1   teaspoon grated tangerine
zest
½   teaspoon freshly ground
pepper

1   large red onion, cut into
wedges
1   large red bell pepper, cut
into 1-inch squares
1   medium zucchini, cut into
¾-inch-thick slices
¼   teaspoon salt
Mango-Pineapple Salsa, as
accompaniment (recipe
follows)

**1.** Cut pork into 1-inch chunks. Place in a plastic food storage bag. In a small bowl, whisk tangerine juice, oil, soy sauce, honey, garlic, tangerine zest, and pepper. Whisk until blended. Pour over pork. Seal bag. Turn to coat. Refrigerate 1 hour.

**2.** Prepare a medium-hot fire in a covered charcoal or gas grill. Remove pork from marinade. Thread pork, red onion, bell pepper, and zucchini onto 6 skewers.

**3.** Grill kebabs, turning frequently, brushing with marinade until well browned and pork is cooked through, about 12 to 14 minutes. Sprinkle with salt. Serve with salsa.

# 243   MANGO-PINEAPPLE SALSA

*Prep: 20 minutes    Cook: none    Makes: about 2½ cups*

1   tangerine, peeled, white
pith removed, sectioned,
seeds removed
1   ripe mango, peeled and
diced
1   cup diced fresh or canned
unsweetened pineapple
2   tablespoons minced red
onion

1   chipotle chile in adobo
sauce, minced
1   tablespoon cider vinegar
2   tablespoons chopped fresh
mint
¼   teaspoon salt

In a small bowl, combine tangerine segments, mango, pineapple, red onion, chile, vinegar, mint, and salt. Stir to mix. Set salsa aside at room temperature.

## 244    GRILLED BRATWURST WITH APPLE CRANBERRY RELISH

*Prep: 15 minutes    Cook: 41 to 44 minutes    Serves: 4*

Use the coarsely ground, uncooked bratwurst here, not the precooked variety.

| | |
|---|---|
| 1 **apple, peeled, cored, and cut into ¼-inch dice** | ½ **cup cranberries, coarsely chopped** |
| 1 **small red onion, halved and sliced** | 1 **(12-ounce) bottle beer** |
| 2 **tablespoons sugar** | 4 **bratwurst** |
| 3 **tablespoons red wine vinegar** | 2 **tablespoons grainy mustard** |
| | 1 **tablespoon butter, melted** |
| | 4 **good-quality hot dog buns** |

**1.** In a medium skillet, combine apple, onion, sugar, vinegar, and cranberries. Bring to a boil, reduce heat, and simmer, stirring occasionally, until onions are soft, about 20 minutes. Set aside.

**2.** In a medium saucepan, bring beer and bratwurst to a boil. Reduce heat and simmer 15 minutes, or until cooked through.

**3.** Prepare a charcoal or gas grill. Grill bratwurst over medium-hot coals, turning frequently until browned, about 5 to 8 minutes.

**4.** Stir together mustard and butter. Spread lightly on cut sides of rolls. Place rolls cut sides down on rack and grill until toasted, about 1 minute. Place bratwurst in rolls and top with apple cranberry relish.

## 245    PROVINCETOWN GRILLED SWORDFISH

*Prep: 10 minutes    Cook: 8 to 10 minutes    Serves: 4 to 6*

There is nothing like fresh swordfish, prepared simply and grilled. During summers spent on Cape Cod we did nothing more than grill it and serve it with lemon wedges. This is just about that easy.

| | |
|---|---|
| 2 **large swordfish steaks, 1 inch thick (2 pounds)** | 1 **tablespoon chopped flat-leaf parsley** |
| ¼ **cup olive oil** | ½ **teaspoon grated lemon zest** |
| ¼ **cup fresh lemon juice** | ⅛ **teaspoon freshly ground pepper** |
| 1 **garlic clove, crushed through a press** | ⅛ **teaspoon salt** |
| 2 **tablespoons butter, softened** | |

**1.** Place fish in single layer in a nonreactive baking dish. In a small bowl, whisk oil, lemon juice, and garlic until combined. Pour over fish. Turn to coat. In small bowl, combine butter, parsley, lemon zest, and pepper. Stir until blended.

**2.** Prepare a medium-hot fire in a covered charcoal or gas grill. When coals are ready, remove fish from marinade and sprinkle both sides with salt. Reserve marinade. Place fish on oiled rack. Grill 8 to 10 minutes, turning once, brushing with some of the marinade, or until opaque throughout but still moist. Place on a serving platter and spread lemon butter immediately over hot fish.

---

## 246 EAST-WEST GRILLED ALASKAN SALMON

*Prep: 10 minutes    Chill: 1 hour    Cook: 10 to 11 minutes    Serves: 4*

1 tablespoon Asian sesame oil
¼ teaspoon crushed hot red pepper
2 tablespoons minced fresh ginger
1 garlic clove, minced
1 teaspoon grated orange zest
3 tablespoons hoisin sauce
3 tablespoons fresh orange juice
2 tablespoons soy sauce

1 tablespoon balsamic vinegar
1 teaspoon ground coriander
½ teaspoon Chinese five-spice powder
4 center-cut salmon fillets (about 6 ounces each)
2 scallions, cut in a fine julienne
2 teaspoons sesame seeds, toasted

**1.** In a small skillet, heat oil and hot pepper over medium heat until hot. Add ginger, garlic, and orange zest and cook until softened, about 2 minutes. Remove from heat. Add hoisin, orange juice, soy sauce, balsamic vinegar, coriander, and five-spice powder. Whisk until blended. Measure 2 tablespoons into a small bowl and set aside. Place salmon fillets in a heavy food storage bag. Pour remaining marinade over salmon. Seal bag and refrigerate at least 1 and up to 4 hours.

**2.** Prepare a medium-hot fire in a covered charcoal or gas grill. Brush grill rack lightly with oil. Place salmon on rack, skin side up. Grill 5 minutes. Carefully turn with spatula and grill 3 to 4 minutes, or until just opaque throughout but still moist, brushing with marinade.

**3.** Serve garnished with scallions and sesame seeds. Serve reserved marinade on the side to drizzle over salmon.

# 247 GRILLED STRIPED BASS WITH LIME-CHILI BUTTER

*Prep: 10 minutes    Cook: 8 to 12 minutes    Serves: 4*

This beautiful fish deserves the simplest of treatments.

|   |   |
|---|---|
| 2 tablespoons fresh lime juice | 1 small garlic clove, crushed |
| 1 tablespoon olive oil | through a press |
| 1½ teaspoons grated lime zest | ½ teaspoon chili powder |
| ¼ teaspoon salt | 2 tablespoons butter, softened |
| ¼ teaspoon freshly ground pepper | 4 pieces striped bass fillet (about 6 ounces each) |

**1.** Light a medium-hot fire in a barbecue grill or preheat broiler. In a shallow glass baking dish, stir 1½ tablespoons lime juice, olive oil, ½ teaspoon lime zest, ⅛ teaspoon salt, and ⅛ teaspoon pepper until blended. Add fish fillets, skin side up, and let marinate 15 minutes.

**2.** In a small bowl, combine remaining lime juice, lime zest, salt, and pepper with garlic, chili powder, and butter. Stir until blended.

**3.** Grill or broil fish 4 inches from heat, 8 to 12 minutes, turning once, or until opaque but still moist. Place skin side down on plates; spread with butter while hot.

# Chapter 10

# Vegetables, Beans, and Grains

Did Mom have to coax you to eat your vegetables, with threats of no dessert unless you cleaned your plate? Well, maybe if she had some of these tempting recipes to choose from, she wouldn't have had to. Here are fresh vegetables and side dishes so good that they could steal the attention from the main course at dinnertime.

Corn is a native American food, and we love it. There are many recipes here that use corn, such as succotash, which is a combination of corn and beans introduced to us by American Indians, and Iowa Corn Pudding, which is just one of the vegetable puddings that were very popular at one time. Corn Oysters, called so not because they contain oysters, but because it's the shape they make when spooned into a skillet, are another traditional American favorite. A relatively new variety of corn, which is great for eating on the cob, is butter and sugar corn, so sweet and good that it needs absolutely nothing on it. Just make sure to buy and eat it while it's fresh.

Beyond corn there is a vegetable patch full of recipes for a variety of American bounty: Baked French Fries, Fried Green and Red Tomatoes, Garden Fresh Peas, Roast Fresh Asparagus, and Baked Acorn Squash with Orange-Ginger Butter are just a few. You'll also find a pair of great American stuffings, for a holiday turkey or roasting chicken or to bake separately on the side.

---

## 248 ROAST FRESH ASPARAGUS
*Prep: 5 minutes    Cook: 10 to 12 minutes    Serves: 4*

This is a different way of preparing asparagus. Simple is best in this case, to let the taste of springtime asparagus shine through. The cooking time will vary depending on how thick the spears are.

1 **pound asparagus, trimmed**
1 **tablespoon olive oil**
⅛ **teaspoon salt**

⅛ **teaspoon pepper**
**Lemon wedges, as accompaniment**

**1.** Preheat oven to 425°F. Place asparagus on a jelly-roll pan. Drizzle with oil and sprinkle with salt and pepper. Toss to coat evenly. Spread in a single layer.

**2.** Bake 10 to 12 minutes, or until tender-crisp. Serve hot or at room temperature, with lemon wedges for squeezing over asparagus.

# 249   HARVARD-YALE BEETS
*Prep: 15 minutes    Cook: 36 to 46 minutes    Serves: 6*

According to James Beard, in his book *American Cookery*, Harvard beets are made with vinegar, and Yale beets with orange juice and lemon juice instead of vinegar. This is a combination of the two.

| | |
|---|---|
| 5  medium beets (about 2 pounds) | 1½ tablespoons red wine vinegar |
| 2  tablespoons sugar | 1  tablespoon lemon juice |
| 1  tablespoon cornstarch | 1  teaspoon grated orange zest |
| ½  teaspoon salt | 2  tablespoons butter |
| ½  cup fresh orange juice | |

**1.** Trim beets, leaving 2 inches of stem on. Place in a large saucepan, cover with water, and bring to a boil over high heat. Reduce heat to medium, cover, and cook until tender, 30 to 40 minutes. Drain and rinse with cold water. When cool enough to handle, rub off skins. Cut beets into ¾-inch dice.

**2.** In a nonreactive medium saucepan, combine sugar, cornstarch, and salt. Whisk to mix. Add orange juice, vinegar, and lemon juice. Bring to a boil over medium heat, whisking occasionally. Simmer 1 minute. Stir in beets. Cook until beets are hot, stirring occasionally, about 5 minutes. Stir in orange zest and butter, stirring until butter melts.

---

# 250   BROCCOLI WITH TWO CHEESES
*Prep: 10 minutes    Cook: 3 to 5 minutes    Serves: 4 to 6*

Instead of a thick cheese sauce, this has a spicy cheese butter, a quick way to dress up everyone's favorite vegetable—well, almost everyone's favorite. America consumes 1.2 *billion* pounds of broccoli per year!

| | |
|---|---|
| 1  head of broccoli (1¼ to 1½ pounds) | ⅛  teaspoon freshly ground pepper |
| 2  tablespoons butter, softened | 1  garlic clove, crushed through a press |
| 2  tablespoons grated Parmesan cheese | ⅓  cup shredded sharp Cheddar cheese |
| ⅛  teaspoon crushed hot red pepper | |

**1.** Trim and discard bottom 2 inches or so of tough stems from broccoli. Peel remaining stems with vegetable peeler and cut into ¼-inch-thick slices. Separate tops into small florets.

**2.** In a small bowl, combine butter, 1 tablespoon Parmesan cheese, hot pepper, and ground pepper. Stir to mix.

**3.** Place broccoli in a large skillet with ½ inch water. Sprinkle with garlic. Bring to a boil, cover, and cook 2 to 3 minutes, or until just tender. Drain broccoli, shaking colander. While hot return broccoli to skillet; stir in butter mixture.

**4.** Return to medium heat and sprinkle with remaining Parmesan cheese and Cheddar cheese. Cover and cook 1 to 2 minutes, or until cheeses melt. Serve hot.

---

## 251   GREEN BEAN CASSEROLE
*Prep: 15 minutes     Cook: 35½ to 37½ minutes     Serves: 6*

This is a scratch, homemade version of the back-of-the-box casserole that was—and still is—immensely popular.

| | |
|---|---|
| 1 **pound green beans, trimmed** | ½ **teaspoon chopped fresh rosemary or ¼ teaspoon dried** |
| 1 **tablespoon butter** | |
| ½ **pound Italian brown cremini or white button mushrooms, sliced** | ½ **teaspoon salt** |
| | ¼ **teaspoon freshly ground pepper** |
| 1 **cup milk** | 4 **large shallots, thinly sliced** |
| 3 **tablespoons flour** | ½ **cup vegetable oil** |

**1.** Fill a large skillet with water and bring to a boil. Add beans and cook until crisp-tender, 3 to 4 minutes. Drain and rinse under cold running water. Drain well and pat dry with paper towels.

**2.** In skillet, melt butter over medium-high heat. Add mushrooms and cook, stirring frequently, until tender and any moisture evaporates, about 2 minutes. Remove skillet from heat. In a small bowl, whisk milk and 1 tablespoon flour until smooth. Add to skillet. Add rosemary, salt, and pepper. Bring to a boil, stirring frequently, until sauce thickens, 1 to 2 minutes. Pour into a small bowl.

**3.** In a medium bowl, toss shallots with remaining 2 tablespoons flour, separating slices into rings and tossing until coated with flour. In a medium saucepan, heat oil over medium heat. When oil is hot, add one third of shallots to skillet, leaving excess flour in bowl. Fry, stirring constantly, until shallots are crisp and golden brown, about 1½ minutes. Remove with a slotted spoon to paper towels. Repeat in 2 more batches with remaining shallots.

**4.** Preheat oven to 400°F. Place green beans in a shallow 1½-quart baking dish. Pour sauce over and stir to mix.

**5.** Bake 23 minutes, or until hot and bubbly. Sprinkle shallots over casserole and bake 2 minutes longer.

# 252    CORN ON THE COB WITH CHILI BUTTER

*Prep: 2 minutes    Cook: 3 to 5 minutes    Serves: 4*

As purists say, the water's already boiling when the corn is picked, and in it goes. Most of us don't live next door to a cornfield, but for best, sweetest flavor, try to cook the ears as soon as possible after buying. I prefer the yellow and white butter and sugar variety.

| | |
|---|---|
| 2 tablespoons butter | 2 teaspoons sugar |
| ¼ teaspoon chili powder | 4 fresh ears of corn, husked |
| ⅛ teaspoon salt | |
| ⅛ teaspoon freshly ground pepper | |

**1.** Bring a large pot of water to a boil.

**2.** In a small saucepan, melt butter with chili powder, salt, and pepper over low heat. Reduce heat and keep chili butter warm.

**3.** Add sugar and corn to boiling water. Cook 3 to 5 minutes, or until corn is just tender. Remove corn and serve hot, brushed with chili butter.

# 253    CORN OYSTERS

*Prep: 15 minutes    Cook: 3½ minutes per batch    Serves: 6*

This is a contemporary version of an old recipe. There aren't any oysters here at all, but the little fritters are called oysters because of the shape they make when spooned into a skillet. They're sometimes served with maple syrup.

| | |
|---|---|
| 4 large ears of corn, husked | ½ teaspoon salt |
| 2 eggs, separated | ⅛ teaspoon pepper |
| ¼ cup flour | 2 tablespoons butter |
| 2 tablespoons cornmeal | 1 tablespoon olive oil |

**1.** Cut corn from cobs cutting halfway down into kernels into a large bowl. Using back of a knife, scrape down each cob to release all remaining pulp and milk. Stir into corn. There should be about 2 cups. Stir in egg yolks. Add flour, cornmeal, salt, and pepper. Mix until blended.

**2.** In a small bowl, beat egg whites with an electric mixer on medium-high speed until stiff but not dry. Fold into corn mixture.

**3.** In a large skillet, heat one third of butter and one third of oil over medium heat until hot. Spoon corn mixture by tablespoons into pan without crowding. Cook until browned on bottom, about 2 minutes. Turn carefully and cook until browned on second side, about 1½ minutes, adjusting heat if necessary. Remove to a paper towel–lined baking sheet and keep warm in a 250°F oven. Repeat with remaining butter, oil, and corn mixture. Serve hot.

# 254   IOWA CORN PUDDING
*Prep: 15 minutes    Cook: 30 to 35 minutes    Serves: 6*

This old-fashioned pudding is simple but good. Vegetable puddings were once very common, prepared with many different vegetables. You can also use 3½ cups corn removed from leftover cooked corn on the cob.

| | |
|---|---|
| 6 **large ears of corn, husked** | ¾ **teaspoon salt** |
| **and silk removed** | ⅛ **teaspoon pepper** |
| 2 **eggs** | 5 **tablespoons melted butter** |
| 1 **(12-ounce) can evaporated** | 1 **cup crushed saltine crackers** |
| **milk** | **(about 24)** |

**1.** Preheat oven to 325°F. Generously butter a shallow 2-quart baking dish.

**2.** Remove corn kernels from cobs; there should be about 3½ cups. Puree 2 cups in a food processor. In a large bowl, combine eggs and milk; whisk to blend. Add pureed corn, remaining corn kernels, salt, and pepper. Stir well.

**3.** In a small bowl, toss butter and cracker crumbs. Add ½ cup crumbs to corn mixture and blend well. Pour into prepared baking dish. Sprinkle remaining crumbs on top.

**4.** Bake 30 to 35 minutes, or until set but center is still jiggly. Let cool 10 minutes before serving.

---

# 255   GARDEN FRESH PEAS
*Prep: 20 minutes    Cook: 9 to 11 minutes    Serves: 6*

Take the trouble to buy fresh peas while in season, which is short. Sit outside while you shell them. They're worth the time.

| | |
|---|---|
| 1 **large carrot, peeled and cut** | 3 **tablespoons butter** |
| **into ¼-inch dice** | 2 **scallions, chopped** |
| 2 **pounds fresh peas, shelled** | ½ **pound sugar snap peas,** |
| **(about 2½ cups)** | **stringed** |
| 1 **tablespoon sugar** | ¼ **teaspoon salt** |

**1.** Bring a medium saucepan of salted water to a boil. Add carrot and return to a boil. Add peas and sugar. Cook 5 to 6 minutes, or until peas are tender. Drain, reserving ½ cup cooking water.

**2.** In same saucepan, combine butter, scallions, and sugar snap peas. Cook over medium-high heat, stirring constantly, until tender-crisp, about 2 minutes. Stir in peas and carrots, reserved liquid, and salt. Cook 1 minute, stirring, to heat peas through.

**3.** With a slotted spoon, remove vegetables to a serving dish. Boil juices in saucepan to thicken slightly, 1 to 2 minutes. Pour over peas. Serve hot in bowls.

## 256 SUMMER SUCCOTASH
*Prep: 5 minutes    Cook: 14 to 16 minutes    Serves: 6*

There are many variations on this traditional combination of corn and beans that was introduced to Colonial cooks by Native American Indians. This version contains onions, tomatoes, and fresh basil.

1 tablespoon butter
1 small onion, finely chopped
½ teaspoon salt
⅛ teaspoon pepper
  Dash of cayenne
1 plum tomato, seeded and finely chopped

¼ cup heavy cream
1 (10-ounce) box frozen lima beans
2 cups fresh corn kernels (from about 4 ears of corn)
1 tablespoon chopped fresh basil

**1.** In a small skillet, melt butter over medium heat. Add onion, salt, pepper, and cayenne. Cook, stirring occasionally, until onion is golden, 5 to 7 minutes. Stir in tomato and cream, bring to a simmer, and remove from heat.

**2.** In a medium saucepan, bring lima beans and 1 cup water to a boil. Reduce heat, cover, and simmer 6 minutes. Stir in corn. Return to a boil, reduce heat, and simmer until lima beans and corn are tender, about 3 minutes.

**3.** Drain off most of water, leaving a few tablespoons in pot. Stir in tomato-cream mixture and basil. Remove from heat, cover, and let stand 2 minutes. Serve hot in bowls.

## 257 HONEY-GLAZED CARROTS
*Prep: 10 minutes    Cook: 10 minutes    Serves: 4*

1¼ pounds carrots, peeled and cut into ½-inch-thick slices
2 tablespoons butter
2 tablespoons honey

2 teaspoons grated fresh ginger
⅛ teaspoon salt
⅛ teaspoon pepper
1 teaspoon grated orange zest

**1.** In a large skillet, combine carrots, butter, honey, ginger, salt, pepper, and ½ cup water. Bring to a boil. Reduce heat to medium, cover, and simmer until carrots are tender-crisp, about 5 minutes.

**2.** Uncover and stir in orange zest. Increase heat to medium-high. Cook, stirring constantly, until carrots are glazed and tender, about 5 minutes. Serve hot.

# 258 FRIED OKRA

*Prep: 10 minutes   Cook: 2 to 3 minutes per batch   Serves: 6 to 8*

| | |
|---|---|
| 1 pound fresh okra, preferably 2 to 3 inches long | ¾ cup cracker meal |
| | ¼ cup cornmeal |
| | 1 teaspoon salt |
| 2 eggs | ¼ teaspoon pepper |
| ¼ cup milk | Vegetable oil, for frying |

**1.** Trim okra stems without cutting into pods. In a pie plate, beat eggs and milk with a fork. Place cracker meal, cornmeal, salt, and pepper in large food storage bag and shake to mix.

**2.** In a large deep skillet, heat 1 inch of oil to 375°F. While oil heats, place okra in batches in egg mixture and toss to coat. Remove and let excess drip off back into plate. Transfer okra to bag and shake until coated. Place in single layer on a cookie sheet. Repeat until all okra is coated.

**3.** Fry okra in hot oil in batches until golden brown, turning with slotted spoon, 2 to 3 minutes per batch. Remove to paper towels and serve while hot and crisp.

# 259 SLOW-SIMMERED SOUTHERN GREENS

*Prep: 10 minutes   Cook: 1 hour 5 to 7 minutes   Serves: 4 to 6*

Collard greens are traditional, but it's nice to combine a few kinds of greens for contrast. Smoked pork, such as ham hocks, smoked neck bones, country ham, or slab bacon, is essential for the right flavor. The liquid the greens cook in is the "pot likker," and some people prefer this part to the greens themselves. Make sure to ladle some "likker" over the greens when serving, and pass a cruet of vinegar on the side.

| | |
|---|---|
| ¼ pound thickly sliced hickory-smoked slab bacon, cut into ½-inch pieces | ¼ teaspoon crushed hot red pepper |
| | 3 pounds greens (use any combination of collard, mustard, or kale) |
| 1 small onion, finely chopped | Salt |
| ½ teaspoon freshly ground black pepper | |

**1.** In a Dutch oven, cook bacon and onion over medium-low heat, stirring, until bacon is crisp and onion is golden, 5 to 7 minutes. Add black pepper, hot pepper, and 2 quarts water. Bring to a boil, reduce heat, cover, and simmer 30 minutes.

**2.** Meanwhile, remove green leaves from stems and tear into large pieces. Gradually add greens to pot, stirring to wilt.

**3.** Return to a simmer. Cook, uncovered, 30 minutes, or until greens are tender. Season with salt to taste.

## 260    FRIED ONION RINGS

*Prep: 15 minutes    Chill: 1 hour    Cook: 1½ to 2 minutes per batch*
*Serves: 4*

1 large Spanish onion (about
    1 pound)
½ cup buttermilk
¾ cup flour
2 tablespoons cornmeal
¾ teaspoon salt

¾ teaspoon paprika
¼ teaspoon cayenne
⅛ teaspoon freshly ground
    pepper
Vegetable oil, for frying

**1.** Cut onion into thin slices and separate into rings. Place onion rings and buttermilk in a large food storage bag. Seal bag and shake to mix well. Refrigerate 1 hour.

**2.** In a large bowl, combine flour, cornmeal, ½ teaspoon salt, paprika, cayenne, and pepper. Stir to mix.

**3.** Drain onion rings. In batches, toss rings in flour mixture until coated. Place on a cookie sheet. Line another cookie sheet with paper towels.

**4.** In a large deep skillet, heat 3 inches oil to 375°F. In batches, fry onion rings until golden brown and crisp, 1½ to 2 minutes per batch. Remove with tongs to paper towels. Season with remaining ¼ teaspoon salt. Serve while hot and crisp.

## 261    FIDDLEHEAD FERNS

*Prep: 10 minutes    Cook: 9 to 13 minutes    Serves: 4*

These are a wild spring delicacy that is showing up more and more frequently in farmers' markets and in the produce department of many supermarkets. Their season is brief. The flavor is similar to asparagus.

1 pound fiddlehead ferns
3 tablespoons butter
1 garlic clove, minced
2 teaspoons Dijon mustard
1 cup fresh coarse bread
    crumbs

2 tablespoons grated
    Parmesan cheese
1 tablespoon fresh lemon
    juice
¼ teaspoon salt
¼ teaspoon pepper

**1.** Trim brown ends off fern stems. Rinse well in cold water to remove brown membrane. Bring a large pot of water to the boil. Add fiddleheads and cook 3 to 5 minutes, until crisp-tender; drain.

**2.** In a large skillet, melt 2 tablespoons butter over medium heat. Add garlic and cook 1 minute. Stir in mustard and bread crumbs and cook, stirring, until bread crumbs are lightly toasted, 3 to 5 minutes. Remove skillet from heat; stir in Parmesan cheese and pour crumbs onto a plate to cool.

**3.** Return skillet to heat and melt remaining butter. Add lemon juice, salt, pepper, and ferns. Cook, stirring occasionally, until hot, about 2 minutes. Turn into a serving dish, sprinkle crumbs on top, and serve.

# 262    BAKED FRENCH FRIES
*Prep: 15 minutes    Cook: 40 minutes    Serves: 4*

French fries are not named for a country, but because the potatoes are frenched—cut into thin strips. These are every bit as crisp as deep-fat fried versions and much easier to cook. Let the professionals stick to making great deep-fat fried fries.

4  **large baking potatoes,**
   **scrubbed and cut**
   **lengthwise into ½-inch-**
   **wide sticks**

2  **tablespoons vegetable oil**
½  **teaspoon salt**
⅛  **teaspoon freshly ground**
   **pepper**

**1.** Preheat oven to 450°F. Place potatoes in a colander and rinse with cold water. Place on paper towels and pat dry.

**2.** In a large bowl, toss potatoes, oil, salt, and pepper. Spread on 2 greased jelly-roll pans in single layers.

**3.** Bake 40 minutes, or until browned and crisp, turning with a spatula after 20 minutes. Serve immediately while crisp and hot.

# 263    HASH BROWN POTATOES
*Prep: 20 minutes    Cook: 28 to 31 minutes    Serves: 6 to 8*

Serve these with eggs for breakfast or as a dinner side dish. Sometimes hash browns are shredded; in this case the potatoes are diced. For variety and extra color, I sometimes use 3 red potatoes and 2 medium sweet potatoes.

5  **large red potatoes, peeled**
   **and cut into ½-inch dice**
1¼ **teaspoons salt**
2  **tablespoons olive oil**
1  **medium onion, cut into**
   **½-inch dice**

1  **medium red bell pepper, cut**
   **into ½-inch dice**
2  **teaspoons Creole Seasoning**
   **(page 152)**
2  **tablespoons chopped**
   **parsley**

**1.** Bring a large saucepan of water to a boil Add potatoes and 1 teaspoon salt. Cook 3 to 4 minutes, until potatoes are partially cooked but still firm. Drain well.

**2.** In a large nonstick skillet, heat oil over medium heat. Add onion. Cook, stirring constantly, until softened, about 4 minutes. Add bell pepper and cook 3 minutes, or until softened. Add potatoes and increase heat to medium-high. Cook, turning occasionally with a spatula, until potatoes are tender and begin to brown, about 10 minutes.

**3.** Stir in remaining salt and Creole seasoning. Cook 8 to 10 minutes, turning occasionally with a spatula and reducing heat if necessary, until potatoes are browned. Sprinkle with parsley.

# 264    GARLIC MASHED POTATOES
*Prep: 15 minutes    Cook: 26 to 32 minutes    Serves: 4*

When you feel like splurging on calories, here's a slightly decadent version of mashed potatoes that's worth the expense.

| | |
|---|---|
| 1  **large head of garlic, cloves separated but not peeled** | 5  **tablespoons butter, softened** |
| 2  **pounds russet potatoes, peeled and quartered** | ½  **teaspoon freshly ground pepper** |
| 1½  **teaspoons salt** | ⅔  **to ¾ cup hot half-and-half** |

**1.** Bring a small saucepan filled with water to a boil. Add garlic and cook 2 minutes. Drain and rinse with cold water until cool. Peel garlic cloves.

**2.** In a medium saucepan, cover potatoes with water. Add garlic cloves and 1 teaspoon salt. Bring to a boil, cover, and reduce heat to medium-low. Cook until potatoes are tender, 20 to 25 minutes. Drain well.

**3.** Return potatoes and garlic to pot and place over low heat, shaking pot to dry potatoes, about 2 minutes. Remove from heat. Mash well with a potato masher. Add butter, remaining salt, and pepper. Mash until butter melts.

**4.** With an electric mixer on medium speed, gradually beat in ⅔ cup half-and-half. Beat until fluffy, adding remaining half-and-half if needed. Return to very low heat to heat through, stirring often, 2 to 3 minutes.

---

# 265    MOM'S MASHED POTATOES
*Prep: 15 minutes    Cook: 21 to 22 minutes    Serves: 6*

Follow these rules for perfect mashed potatoes: Dry the potatoes after draining; mash first with a potato masher and then beat with an electric mixer; and be generous with the butter. If you want evidence they're homemade, leave in a few lumps. I've made mashed potatoes with everything from leeks to goat cheese, and these are still the best.

| | |
|---|---|
| 3  **pounds Idaho potatoes (about 5 large)** | 4  **tablespoons butter, cut into 4 pieces** |
| 1¾  **teaspoons salt** | ¼  **teaspoon freshly ground pepper** |
| 1  **to 1¼ cups hot milk** | |

**1.** Peel potatoes and cut into quarters. Place in a large saucpan and cover with water. Add 1 teaspoon salt. Bring to a boil, reduce heat to medium, cover, and cook 20 minutes, or until tender. Drain potatoes and return while hot to pan. Place over low heat to dry potatoes, shaking pot, 1 to 2 minutes. Remove from heat.

**2.** Mash with a potato masher. Add ¾ cup milk and butter. Continue to mash until potatoes are smooth. Add ¼ cup milk and beat with an electric mixer on medium-high speed until fluffy. Beat in remaining milk if needed. Beat in remaining salt and pepper. Return to very low heat to reheat if needed.

# 266    POTATO PANCAKES
*Prep: 15 minutes    Cook: 5 to 7 minutes per batch    Serves: 4 to 6*

| | |
|---|---|
| 3 large baking potatoes (about 2 pounds), peeled | ¼ teaspoon freshly ground pepper |
| 1 small onion | 2 eggs, lightly beaten |
| 2 tablespoons flour | 2 tablespoons butter |
| 1 teaspoon salt | 3 tablespoons vegetable oil |

**1.** In a food processor, grate potatoes and onion with coarse shredding blade. Spread on a large clean dish towel. Roll up towel and twist to wring out as much moisture as possible. Place potato and onion in a large bowl. Add flour, salt, and pepper. Toss to combine. Add eggs and stir well.

**2.** In a large skillet, melt ½ tablespoon butter in 1 tablespoon oil over medium-high heat. When sizzling, add potato mixture by ¼-cupfuls. Press with a wide spatula to make 3-inch cakes. Reduce heat to medium and cook until well browned and crisp on bottom, 3 to 4 minutes. Turn and cook until browned on second side, 2 to 3 minutes. Repeat with remaining potato mixture, adding remaining butter and oil as needed. Serve hot.

# 267    SCALLOPED TWO-POTATOES
*Prep: 15 minutes    Cook: 1 hour 7 to 12 minutes    Serves: 8*

A surprise layer of bright orange sweet potato in the center of this casserole adds visual interest and a little twist to the classic. Serve these up with glazed baked ham and broccoli for the perfect Sunday supper.

| | |
|---|---|
| 1 garlic clove, crushed through a press | ¼ teaspoon freshly ground pepper |
| 2½ pounds all-purpose potatoes (about 4 large), peeled and thinly sliced | 1 large sweet potato (about 12 ounces), peeled and thinly sliced |
| 2 cups half-and-half | 1 tablespoon butter, cut into small pieces |
| ½ cup milk | |
| 1 teaspoon salt | |

**1.** Preheat oven to 350°F. Sprinkle garlic over bottom of a buttered shallow 2½-quart baking dish.

**2.** In a large pot, combine all-purpose potatoes, half-and-half, milk, salt, and pepper. Bring to a boil over medium-high heat, stirring frequently. Reduce heat and simmer until liquid thickens slightly, about 2 minutes.

**3.** Pour half of potato mixture into prepared baking dish and spread evenly. Top with sweet potato slices in a single layer. Pour remaining all-purpose potato mixture over all, spread evenly, and dot with butter.

**4.** Bake 1 hour 5 to 10 minutes, or until potatoes are tender when pierced with a paring knife and top is browned. Baste top twice with sauce in pan during the first 45 minutes of baking.

## 268    TWICE-BAKED POTATOES

*Prep: 10 minutes    Cook: 1 hour 15 to 20 minutes    Serves: 4*

These potatoes are so good they could make a meal on their own. If served as part of a meal with another vegetable, cut them in half and make 8. They reheat well. The secret is to mash the potatoes while hot.

| | |
|---|---|
| **4  large baking potatoes (about 2½ pounds total)** | **¾  cup grated Parmesan cheese** |
| **¾  cup milk** | **½  teaspoon freshly ground pepper** |
| **1  garlic clove, smashed** | **¼  teaspoon salt** |
| **3  tablespoons butter** | **1  tablespoon chopped parsley** |

**1.** Preheat oven to 400°F. Prick potatoes with a fork. Bake 1 hour, or until soft.

**2.** In a small saucepan, heat milk and garlic over low heat until warm. While potatoes are hot, hold with a pot holder and cut one-third lengthwise off tops. With a large spoon, scoop potatoes into a medium bowl, leaving a thin shell around skin. Scoop out potato from tops. While hot mash with a potato masher. Remove garlic from milk and discard. Add milk and butter to potatoes and mash until fluffy. Stir in ½ cup Parmesan cheese, pepper, and salt. Spoon into shells, mounding mixture on top. Place on a baking sheet.

**3.** In a small bowl, toss remaining ¼ cup cheese and parsley to mix. Sprinkle over potatoes. Bake 15 to 20 minutes, until hot and golden brown.

---

## 269    POPEYE'S CREAMED SPINACH

*Prep: 10 minutes    Cook: 11 to 14 minutes    Serves: 4*

| | |
|---|---|
| **1  tablespoon butter** | **2  (10-ounce) boxes frozen chopped spinach, thawed and squeezed dry** |
| **2  scallions, thinly sliced** | **2  tablespoons grated Parmesan cheese** |
| **1  tablespoon flour** | |
| **¾  cup milk** | |
| **¼  teaspoon salt** | |
| **⅛  teaspoon pepper** | |
| **1  (3-ounce) package cream cheese, cut into cubes, softened** | |

**1.** In a medium saucepan, melt butter over medium heat. Add scallions and cook 1 minute. Add flour and cook, stirring, 1 minute. Whisk in milk, salt, and pepper. Bring to a boil, whisking until sauce thickens, 1 to 2 minutes.

**2.** Reduce heat to medium-low. Gradually add cream cheese, whisking until smooth. Stir in spinach. Cover and cook 8 to 10 minutes, stirring occasionally, or until spinach is tender. Remove from heat, stir in Parmesan cheese, and serve.

# 270 SUMMER SQUASH CASSEROLE

*Prep: 15 minutes    Cook: 21 to 26 minutes    Serves: 6*

Summer squash is great cooked simply with a little butter, salt, and pepper, but sometimes that can get boring. This is a lightened version of a traditional casserole that was usually made with lots of cheese, butter, and cream. I'm of the old-fashioned school that likes summer squash well cooked, which really brings out its flavor—no crisp-tender here. It's pretty to use a combination of zucchini and yellow summer squash.

2 tablespoons olive oil
1 medium onion, thinly sliced
3 medium summer squash
   (1½ pounds), cut into
   ¾-inch cubes
1 ripe medium tomato,
   chopped
¼ cup heavy cream
¼ teaspoon salt

⅛ teaspoon pepper
⅓ cup crumbled feta cheese
2 tablespoons chopped fresh
   basil
½ cup coarse fresh bread
   crumbs
2 tablespoons grated
   Parmesan cheese

**1.** Preheat oven to 400°F. In a large skillet, heat 1 tablespoon oil over medium heat. Add onion and cook, stirring occasionally, until softened, 3 to 5 minutes. Add squash, increase heat to medium-high, and cook, stirring, until crisp-tender, about 4 minutes. Stir in tomato, cream, salt, and pepper. Cook, stirring constantly, until cream thickens slightly, about 2 minutes. Remove from heat. Stir in feta cheese and basil. Pour into a greased 2-quart shallow baking dish.

**2.** In a small bowl, toss bread crumbs, Parmesan cheese, and remaining 1 tablespoon oil. Sprinkle over squash.

**3.** Bake 12 to 15 minutes, or until crumbs are browned and squash is tender.

# 271 BAKED ACORN SQUASH WITH ORANGE-GINGER BUTTER

*Prep: 5 minutes    Cook: 35 minutes    Serves: 4*

2 medium acorn squash (1 to
   1¼ pounds each)
2 tablespoons butter, softened
2 teaspoons honey

¾ teaspoon grated fresh ginger
½ teaspoon grated orange zest
⅛ teaspoon salt
⅛ teaspoon pepper

**1.** Preheat oven to 400°F. Halve squash crosswise. Trim a thin slice off ends so squash will stand upright. Grease a baking pan large enough to hold squash. Place cut sides down in pan. Bake 30 minutes, or until tender.

**2.** In a small bowl, combine butter, honey, ginger, orange zest, salt, and pepper. Stir until blended. Turn squash over. Spread with butter. Return to oven and bake 5 minutes, or until butter melts. Serve hot.

## 272   BROWN SUGAR AND PECAN SWEET POTATO CASSEROLE

*Prep: 15 minutes    Cook: 55 to 60 minutes    Serves: 6*

If you can find them, use an assortment of sweet potatoes for this casserole, ranging from pale yellow to deep orange.

3  **pounds sweet potatoes, peeled and cut into ¾-inch-thick slices**
2  **tablespoons orange juice**
½  **teaspoon grated orange zest**
⅓  **cup packed dark brown sugar**

¼  **teaspoon salt**
¼  **teaspoon freshly ground pepper**
3  **tablespoons butter, cut into small pieces**
⅓  **cup chopped pecans**

**1.** Preheat oven to 400°F. Arrange half of sweet potatoes in a buttered 2-quart shallow baking dish. Drizzle with half of orange juice and sprinkle with orange zest. Sprinkle with half of brown sugar, salt, and pepper. Dot with half of butter. Repeat with remaining sweet potatoes, orange juice, sugar, salt, pepper, and butter. Cover with foil.

**2.** Bake 25 minutes. Uncover and bake 15 minutes.

**3.** Sprinkle pecans over top of casserole and bake 15 to 20 minutes, basting occasionally with juices in dish, or until potatoes are tender.

## 273   SCALLOPED TOMATOES

*Prep: 10 minutes    Cook: 23 to 25 minutes    Serves: 6*

If you have some ripe summer tomatoes and want to do something different with them, try this simple American classic. With grilled chicken and a tossed salad, it makes a wonderful summer meal.

½  **cup heavy cream**
1  **garlic clove, smashed**
4  **ripe medium tomatoes (1½ pounds)**
¼  **teaspoon salt**
⅛  **teaspoon pepper**

½  **cup shredded sharp Cheddar cheese**
1  **cup fresh bread crumbs**
1  **tablespoon grated Parmesan cheese**
1  **tablespoon butter, melted**

**1.** Preheat oven to 450°F. In a small saucepan, bring cream and garlic to a boil. Immediately reduce heat so cream doesn't boil over and boil 8 to 10 minutes, until reduced by half to ¼ cup. Remove and discard garlic; set cream aside.

**2.** Cut tomatoes into ½-inch-thick slices. Arrange in a buttered shallow 2-quart baking dish with slices overlapping to make a single layer. Sprinkle with salt, pepper, and Cheddar cheese. Drizzle cream evenly over tomatoes.

**3.** In a small bowl, combine bread crumbs, Parmesan cheese, and butter. Toss to mix. Sprinkle over tomatoes.

**4.** Bake 15 minutes, or until crumbs are brown and juices are bubbly. Let stand 10 minutes before serving.

---

## 274  BOSTON BAKED BEANS

*Prep: 15 minutes    Stand: 1 hour    Cook: about 6½ to 6¾ hours
Serves: 8*

There are many varieties of dried beans, some of which are regional, that can be used for baked beans. Navy or pea beans are traditional and, of course, can be used in this recipe, but for fun, give another variety a try.

1 **pound dried yellow eye, soldier, or Great Northern beans, rinsed and picked over**
½ **cup unsulphured molasses**
2 **tablespoons dark brown sugar**

2 **teaspoons dry mustard**
1 **tablespoon ketchup**
¼ **teaspoon freshly ground pepper**
¼ **pound chunk of salt pork**
1 **medium onion, halved**

**1.** Place beans in a large pot. Cover with 2 inches of water. Soak overnight or bring to a boil, remove from heat, cover, and let stand 1 hour.

**2.** Drain beans and return to pot. Cover with 2 inches fresh water. Bring to a boil, reduce heat to medium, and simmer until just tender but not soft, 30 to 45 minutes, depending on beans. Drain beans, reserving 4 cups cooking liquid.

**3.** Preheat oven to 275°F. In a small bowl, combine 2 cups of reserved cooking liquid with molasses, brown sugar, mustard, ketchup, and pepper. Stir to mix well. Place beans in a 3-quart bean pot or a deep casserole with lid. Remove rind from salt pork. Score salt pork without cutting all the way through. Push salt pork and onion halves into beans. Pour in molasses mixture. Add remaining bean cooking liquid, if necessary, so liquid just comes to top of beans. Cover pot with lid.

**4.** Bake 4 hours. Uncover and bake 2 hours, or until beans are tender, turn a rich brown color, and have absorbed cooking liquid. If necessary, add more reserved cooking liquid or water during baking if beans become dry.

## 275   OVEN-ROAST VEGGIES
*Prep: 20 minutes   Cook: 45 minutes   Serves: 8*

This makes a big batch of vegetables, but they're good leftover cold, made into a salad, tossed with pasta, or made into a frittata.

2 pounds small red potatoes, quartered
1 large sweet potato, peeled and cut into ¾-inch chunks
2 medium carrots, peeled and cut into ½-inch-thick slices
2 parsnips, peeled and cut into ½-inch-thick slices
4 garlic cloves, minced
¼ cup olive oil
1 teaspoon dried thyme

¾ teaspoon salt
½ teaspoon freshly ground pepper
1 fennel bulb, cored and cut into ¾-inch pieces
1 large red bell pepper, cut into ¾-inch chunks
1 medium zucchini, halved lengthwise, then cut crosswise into ¾-inch-thick slices
1 large red onion, cut into ¾-inch dice

1. Preheat oven to 400°F. In a large bowl, toss red potatoes, sweet potato, carrots, parsnips, garlic, oil, thyme, salt, and pepper. Divide between 2 jelly-roll pans.

2. Bake 15 minutes. Add fennel, bell pepper, zucchini, and red onion to pans, dividing vegetables evenly. Stir to combine.

3. Bake until vegetables are tender, about 30 minutes, stirring once. Serve hot, warm, or at room temperature.

## 276   FRIED GREEN AND RED TOMATOES
*Prep: 15 minutes   Cook: 17 minutes   Serves: 6*

¼ teaspoon cayenne
1 teaspoon salt
¾ teaspoon freshly ground pepper
2 medium green tomatoes, cored and cut in ¼-inch-thick slices

2 medium firm red tomatoes, cored and cut in ¼-inch-thick slices
1 cup cornmeal
1 slice of bacon, cut into ½-inch dice
½ cup olive oil

1. In a small bowl, combine cayenne, ¼ teaspoon salt, and ¼ teaspoon pepper. Stir to mix. Place tomatoes in a single layer on a baking sheet or wax paper. Season with spice mixture. In a pie plate, combine remaining salt and pepper with cornmeal. Stir until blended. Dredge tomato slices in seasoned cornmeal to coat both sides. Place back on sheet and let stand 10 minutes. Coat slices again with remaining cornmeal.

2. In a large skillet, cook bacon over medium heat until crisp, about 5 minutes. Drain bacon on paper towels. Pour bacon fat into olive oil.

**3.** Heat 3 tablespoons of oil in skillet over medium-high heat until hot. Fry tomatoes in batches without crowding and cook until golden brown, about 2 minutes per side. Remove to paper towels. Add remaining oil as needed. Reduce heat slightly if necessary. Sprinkle bacon over tomatoes and serve while hot and crisp.

---

## 277   BARBECUE PINTO PONY BEANS
*Prep: 10 minutes    Cook: 1 hour 50 minutes    Serves: 8*

These beans make a great side dish to serve with burgers, hot dogs, corn on the cob, and coleslaw for a classic summer barbecue.

8  slices of bacon, cut crosswise into ½-inch pieces
2  medium onions, chopped
1  (15-ounce) can chunky chili-style tomato sauce
⅓  cup cider vinegar
2  tablespoons molasses
2  garlic cloves, crushed through a press

½  teaspoon freshly ground pepper
4  (15½-ounce) cans pinto beans, drained and rinsed
1  tablespoon brown sugar
½  teaspoon ground cumin

**1.** In a large nonreactive skillet, cook bacon over medium heat until crisp, about 5 minutes. Drain bacon on paper towels. Pour off all but 2 tablespoons drippings from pan.

**2.** Add onions to skillet and cook over medium-low heat, stirring occasionally, until golden, about 10 minutes. Remove ⅓ cup onions to a small bowl.

**3.** Add tomato sauce, vinegar, molasses, garlic, and pepper to skillet. Simmer over medium heat 20 minutes. Stir in beans and half of bacon. Pour into a 2-quart deep casserole. Toss brown sugar and cumin with reserved onions and sprinkle over top.

**4.** Preheat oven to 350°F. Bake 1 hour 15 minutes, or until beans are hot and top is browned. Sprinkle with remaining bacon. Serve hot or warm.

# 278   RICE PILAF
*Prep: 5 minutes    Cook: 35 minutes    Serves: 4*

2   tablespoons butter
1   small onion, finely chopped
1   cup converted white rice

1   (13¾-ounce) can chicken broth
⅛   teaspoon pepper

**1.** In a medium saucepan, melt butter over medium-low heat. Add onion and cook, stirring occasionally, until lightly browned, about 10 minutes. Stir in rice. Cook, stirring occasionally, until golden, about 5 minutes.

**2.** Measure chicken broth and add enough water to equal 2¼ cups. Stir into rice. Bring to a boil, stir, reduce heat to low, cover, and simmer 20 minutes, or until liquid is absorbed. Stir in pepper and let stand, covered, 5 minutes before serving.

# 279   RED BEANS AND RICE
*Prep: 15 minutes    Cook: 2¾ to 3 hours    Serves: 6*

In New Orleans, Sunday was the traditional day for serving ham, making Monday the perfect day to use the leftover ham bone for red beans and rice. In lieu of a ham bone, I use ham hocks. Louis Armstrong signed his letters Red Beans and Ricely Yours, proving his love for this dish.

You may notice the beans are not soaked here, which saves a lot of time.

1   pound dried red kidney beans, rinsed and picked over
2   large smoked ham hocks
2   medium onions, chopped
3   medium celery ribs, chopped
½   medium green bell pepper, finely chopped
4   garlic cloves, crushed through a press
2   bay leaves

1   teaspoon dried thyme
½   teaspoon dried oregano
½   teaspoon freshly ground black pepper
¼   teaspoon crushed hot red pepper
½   teaspoon salt
3   to 4 cups hot cooked rice
    Sliced scallions
    White vinegar and hot sauce as accompaniments

**1.** In a large pot, cover beans with 6 cups cold water. Add ham hocks, onions, celery, bell pepper, garlic, bay leaves, thyme, oregano, black pepper, and hot pepper. Bring to a boil, reduce heat, and simmer, partially covered, 2½ hours, stirring occasionally. Add 1 cup water if necessary so beans are just covered with water. Remove ham hocks and let cool.

**2.** Uncover and simmer, stirring frequently, until beans are softened and creamy, 15 to 30 minutes. Meanwhile, cut meat off ham hocks and chop.

**3.** Season beans with salt. Stir meat into beans. Remove and discard bay leaves. Spoon beans over rice. Sprinkle with scallions. Serve vinegar and hot sauce on the side.

# 280  SAVANNAH RED RICE

*Prep: 10 minutes    Cook: 25 minutes    Serves: 6*

1 (16-ounce) can whole
  tomatoes in juice,
  drained, juice reserved
1 (13¾-ounce) can chicken
  broth
2 slices of bacon, finely diced
1 medium onion, finely
  chopped

½ cup diced green bell pepper
1 teaspoon paprika
1½ cups long-grain white rice
1 teaspoon hot pepper sauce
¼ teaspoon salt

**1.** Finely chop tomatoes. Combine tomatoes, reserved juices, and broth. Measure and add enough water to equal 3⅓ cups.

**2.** In a medium saucepan, cook bacon over medium heat until crisp, about 5 minutes. Remove bacon with slotted spoon and drain on a paper towel.

**3.** Add onion, bell pepper, and paprika to saucepan. Cook over medium heat, stirring occasionally, until vegetables soften, about 5 minutes. Stir in tomato mixture, rice, hot sauce, and salt. Bring to a boil. Reduce heat to low, cover, and simmer 15 minutes, or until liquid is absorbed and rice is tender. Remove from heat and stir in bacon. Cover and let stand 5 minutes before serving.

# 281  WILD RICE PILAF

*Prep: 10 minutes    Cook: 49 to 58 minutes    Serves: 4*

This simple side dish is adapted from a recipe in Marie Simmons's book *Rice, The Amazing Grain*, a cookbook filled with terrific recipes.

¾ cup wild rice
¼ teaspoon dried thyme
3 tablespoons chopped
  almonds
2 tablespoons butter
½ medium red onion, cut into
  ½-inch dice

1 small celery rib, finely
  chopped
1 cup seedless red or green
  grapes, halved
¼ teaspoon salt
⅛ teaspoon freshly ground
  pepper

**1.** Rinse rice. Place in a medium saucepan. Add thyme and 2½ cups water. Bring to a boil, reduce heat to medium-low, cover, and simmer 40 to 45 minutes, or until rice is tender. Remove from heat, uncover, and set aside.

**2.** In a large dry skillet, cook almonds over medium heat, stirring constantly, until toasted, 3 to 5 minutes. Transfer to a plate.

**3.** Add butter to skillet and place over medium heat. Add onion and celery. Cook, stirring occasionally, until softened, 6 to 8 minutes. Drain off any water from rice. Add rice and grapes to skillet. Cook, stirring occasionally, until hot. Stir in salt, pepper, and almonds and serve.

# 282    HOPPIN' JOHN

*Prep: 10 minutes    Cook: 36 to 45 minutes    Serves: 8*

A Southern tradition says that Hoppin' John served on New Year's Day will bring good luck all year long. The origin of the name is not certain, but the credit for creating this dish may go to the Gullahs, descendants of African slaves who settled in the coastal areas and islands of South Carolina.

2    ounces salt pork or bacon, cut into ½-inch dice
1    medium onion, chopped
2    medium celery ribs, chopped
3    scallions, thinly sliced
2    garlic cloves, crushed through a press
1    (13¾-ounce) can chicken broth

1    cup converted white rice
1    (10-ounce) box frozen black-eyed peas
¼    teaspoon dried thyme
¼    teaspoon crushed hot red pepper
2    tablespoons chopped flat-leaf parsley

**1.** In a medium saucepan, cook salt pork over medium-low heat, stirring occasionally, until golden and fat is rendered, 6 to 8 minutes. Remove with slotted spoon to a small bowl. Add onion, celery, scallions, and garlic to pan. Raise heat to medium and cook, stirring occasionally, until soft, 5 to 7 minutes.

**2.** Measure broth and add enough water to equal 2½ cups. Stir broth, rice, peas, thyme, and hot pepper into saucepan. Bring to a boil. Reduce heat and simmer, covered, 20 to 25 minutes, or until liquid is absorbed and rice is tender. Remove from heat and let stand 5 minutes. Stir in reserved salt pork and parsley and serve.

# 283    CHILI CHEESE GRITS

*Prep: 5 minutes    Cook: 43 minutes    Serves: 8*

You don't have to be Southern to love grits, even just plain with a lump of butter and some salt and pepper. This version, laced with chiles and cheese, some would say, is gilding the lily.

2    garlic cloves, crushed through a press
1¼    teaspoons chili powder
1    cup old-fashioned grits
1    (4½-ounce) can diced green chiles

½    teaspoon salt
3    tablespoons butter
3    eggs
1½    cups shredded Monterey Jack cheese

**1.** Preheat oven to 375°F. In a medium saucepan, bring 3 cups water, garlic, and chili powder to a boil. Reduce heat to low and gradually whisk in grits, sprinkling them over water to avoid lumps. Stir in chiles. Cook, stirring constantly, until thickened, about 3 minutes. Remove from heat and stir in salt and butter.

**2.** In a medium bowl, whisk eggs until blended. Mix in 1 cup hot grits. Stir into remaining grits in saucepan and whisk to mix well. Stir in 1 cup cheese. Pour into a greased 1½-quart deep baking dish. Smooth top and sprinkle with remaining cheese.

**3.** Bake 40 minutes, or until browned.

---

## 284 CORN BREAD AND WILD RICE STUFFING
*Prep: 20 minutes    Cook: 51 to 58 minutes    Makes: 15 cups*

1  cup wild rice
8  slices of stale Italian bread, cut into ½-inch cubes (about 4 cups)
1  (12-ounce) tube country-style pork sausage
4  tablespoons butter
1  large onion, chopped
3  medium celery ribs, chopped

3  cups packaged corn bread stuffing
1  cup dried cranberries, coarsely chopped
½  cup chopped parsley
¾  teaspoon dried thyme
¾  teaspoon freshly ground pepper
2  to 2½ cups reduced-sodium chicken broth

**1.** Preheat oven to 350°F. Bring a medium saucepan of salted water to a boil. Add wild rice and cook 35 to 40 minutes, or until tender; drain.

**2.** Meanwhile, spread cubed bread on a jelly-roll pan and bake, stirring once, until dry and lightly toasted, about 15 minutes.

**3.** In a large skillet, cook sausage over medium heat, stirring with a spoon to break up large pieces, until browned, about 10 minutes. With a slotted spoon, remove sausage to a large bowl.

**4.** Add butter, onion, and celery to skillet. Increase heat to medium-high and cook, stirring frequently, until vegetables soften, 6 to 8 minutes. Pour into bowl with sausage.

**5.** Add rice, bread cubes, corn bread stuffing, cranberries, parsley, thyme, and pepper. Toss to mix. Drizzle in 2 cups chicken broth, tossing until evenly moistened. Add remaining broth if needed.

# 285    SPOONBREAD

*Prep: 10 minutes    Cook: 32 to 37 minutes    Serves: 4 to 6*

3 cups milk
¾ cup cornmeal, preferably
    white
3 eggs
4 tablespoons butter,
¾ cup fresh or frozen corn
    kernels

¾ teaspoon salt
1 teaspoon sugar
2 teaspoons baking powder
⅛ teaspoon cayenne

**1.** Preheat oven to 375°F. In a medium saucepan, bring 2½ cups milk just to a boil. In a small bowl, stir together remaining milk and cornmeal. Gradually whisk cornmeal mixture into hot milk. Reduce heat to low and simmer, stirring constantly, until thickened, about 2 minutes. Remove from heat.

**2.** In a medium bowl, whisk eggs until blended. Gradually whisk 1 cup hot cornmeal mixture into eggs. Gradually whisk egg mixture into saucepan. Stir in butter until melted. Add ½ cup corn, salt, sugar, baking powder, and cayenne. Stir until well blended. Pour into a buttered shallow 2-quart baking dish. Sprinkle remaining ¼ cup corn over batter.

**3.** Bake 30 to 35 minutes, or until set and browned on top. Serve hot.

# 286    HOT AND SPICY HUSH PUPPIES

*Prep: 10 minutes    Cook: 1½ to 2 minutes per batch    Serves: 6*

Solid vegetable shortening,
    for frying
1½ cups cornmeal
½ cup flour
1 tablespoon baking powder
1 teaspoon salt
1 teaspoon freshly ground
    pepper

1 teaspoon sugar
¼ teaspoon cayenne
1 egg, lightly beaten
1½ cups buttermilk
3 scallions, minced
1 garlic clove, crushed
    through a press

**1.** Melt enough shortening to measure 3 inches in a deep fat fryer or large deep saucepan. Heat to 375°F.

**2.** While shortening heats, in a large bowl, combine cornmeal, flour, baking powder, salt, pepper, sugar, and cayenne. Stir well to mix.

**3.** In a small bowl, combine egg, buttermilk, scallions, and garlic. Beat with a fork to mix. Add to dry ingredients and stir just until dry ingredients are moistened.

**4.** Drop batter by rounded teaspoonfuls into hot oil, a few at a time without crowding. Cook, turning once, until well browned and cooked through, about 1½ to 2 minutes. Drain on paper towels. Serve hot.

# 287    SAGE AND ONION STUFFING
*Prep: 20 minutes    Cook: 16 to 20 minutes    Makes: about 13 cups*

This stuffing can be used to stuff a turkey or chicken. Any extra stuffing can be baked in a buttered baking dish: Drizzle with additional chicken broth, dot with butter, and bake in a 350°F oven for about 30 minutes, or until hot.

6   tablespoons butter
¼   pound thinly sliced pancetta or bacon, chopped
3   medium celery ribs, cut into ½-inch dice
3   medium onions, chopped
½   pound mushrooms, sliced
3   medium carrots, peeled and shredded
1   (14-ounce) bag cubed herb-seasoned stuffing

1½  teaspoons crumbled dried sage
½   teaspoon freshly ground pepper
1   (10-ounce) box frozen corn kernels, thawed
¼   cup chopped Italian flat-leaf parsley
1   (13¾-ounce) can reduced-sodium chicken broth

**1.** In a large skillet, melt 1 tablespoon butter over medium heat. Add pancetta or bacon and cook, stirring frequently, until it begins to brown, about 5 minutes. Drain on paper towels. If bacon was used, discard fat from pan.

**2.** Add remaining butter, celery, and onions to skillet. Cook over medium heat, stirring frequently, until onions are golden brown, 8 to 10 minutes. Add mushrooms and carrots and cook, stirring, until softened, 3 to 5 minutes. Remove from heat.

**3.** In a large bowl, combine pancetta, vegetable mixture, stuffing, sage, pepper, corn, and parsley. Stir until mixed. Drizzle in broth and ¼ cup water, tossing until evenly moistened.

*Chapter 11*

# Heirloom Cookies, Custards, Cobblers, . . . and More

Grab that glass of milk and pick one of America's favorite cookies: All-American Chocolate Brownies, Oatmeal Cookies, Peanut Butter Cookies, or America's Favorite Chocolate Chip Cookies. Or spoon into a comforting, creamy sweet like Butterscotch Pudding, Chocolate Pudding, or Banana Pudding, a Southern favorite spiked with a little bourbon.

Try one of the fruit desserts with a funny-sounding name. Grunt, buckle, slump, brown Betty, pandowdy, cobbler, and crisp are some great American classics. A crisp and a crumble are both basically fruit covered with a crunchy, buttery streusel topping, sometimes with nuts and oatmeal added. A brown Betty is usually apples, although other fruits can be used, topped or layered with buttered bread cubes or cookie crumbs. A grunt, slump, and cobbler are sweetened fruit covered with a biscuit topping in one form or another. A pandowdy is fruit topped with a pastry, biscuit, or cake topping. Its name is thought to come from its appearance or what was done sometimes, which was to push the topping down into the fruit, called dowdying. A buckle is a cake batter, usually with berries, with a streusel topping. Thoroughly confused now? Well, the lines have been crossed between these desserts, and one person's cobbler may be another's buckle. These special recipes have been around for a long time and are just as wonderful today as they were 100 years ago. They don't take long to make, and everyone will be impressed when you bring one of these warm, old-fashioned, fruit-filled desserts to the table.

# 288 AMERICA'S FAVORITE CHOCOLATE CHIP COOKIES

*Prep: 10 minutes    Cook: 12 minutes per batch    Makes: 48*

2¼ cups flour
 1 teaspoon baking soda
 ½ teaspoon salt
 2 sticks (8 ounces) butter, softened
 1 cup packed light brown sugar

 ½ cup granulated sugar
 1 tablespoon vanilla extract
 2 eggs
 2 cups (12 ounces) semisweet chocolate chips
 1 cup chopped walnuts

**1.** Preheat oven to 350°F. Set rack in upper third of oven. Sift flour, baking soda, and salt into a medium bowl.

**2.** In a large bowl with an electric mixer on medium speed, beat butter, brown sugar, granulated sugar, and vanilla until fluffy, 2 to 3 minutes. Beat in eggs 1 at a time, beating well after adding each. On low speed, beat in dry ingredients until blended. Stir in chocolate chips and walnuts.

**3.** Drop dough by rounded teaspoonfuls 2 inches apart onto ungreased cookie sheets.

**4.** Bake about 12 minutes, or until golden brown. Let stand 2 minutes on baking sheets, then remove cookies to a rack and let cool completely if you can.

# 289 GINGERSNAPS

*Prep: 10 minutes    Cook: 13 to 15 minutes per batch    Makes: 48*

 2 cups flour
1½ teaspoons ground ginger
 1 teaspoon cinnamon
 1 teaspoon baking soda
 ¼ teaspoon ground cloves
 ¼ teaspoon salt

 1 stick (4 ounces) butter, softened
1¼ cups sugar
 ¼ cup unsulphured molasses
 1 egg

**1.** In a small bowl, combine flour, ginger, cinnamon, baking soda, cloves, and salt. Stir until blended.

**2.** In a large bowl with an electric mixer on medium speed, beat butter, 1 cup sugar, molasses, and egg until light and fluffy. Beat in flour mixture on low speed until well blended. Refrigerate dough 15 minutes.

**3.** Preheat oven to 350°F. Roll dough into 1-inch balls. Roll balls in remaining ¼ cup sugar. Place 2½ inches apart on greased baking sheets.

**4.** Bake 13 to 15 minutes, or until flattened and browned. Let cookies stand on sheets 2 minutes, then remove to racks to cool completely.

# 290 OATMEAL COOKIES

*Prep: 10 minutes    Cook: 14 to 16 minutes per batch*
*Makes: about 36*

1½ cups flour
1 teaspoon baking soda
½ teaspoon cinnamon
½ teaspoon salt
2 sticks (8 ounces) butter, softened
1 cup packed dark brown sugar

¾ cup granulated sugar
1 teaspoon vanilla extract
2 eggs
3 cups quick-cooking oats
½ cup chopped pecans
½ cup raisins
½ cup flaked coconut

**1.** Preheat oven to 350°F. In a small bowl, combine flour, baking soda, cinnamon, and salt. Stir until well blended.

**2.** In a large bowl, beat butter with an electric mixer on medium speed until fluffy. Beat in brown sugar. Gradually beat in granulated sugar and vanilla. Add eggs 1 at a time, beating until well blended after adding each. Beat in flour mixture, half at a time. Stir in oats, then pecans, raisins, and coconut.

**3.** Drop dough by rounded tablespoons 3 inches apart on greased cookie sheets.

**4.** Bake 14 to 16 minutes, or until golden brown. Let stand 2 minutes on sheets before removing to a wire rack to cool completely.

# 291 CHRISTMAS SPRITZ COOKIES

*Prep: 5 minutes    Cook: 10 to 12 minutes per batch*
*Makes: about 70*

½ cup sliced almonds
1 cup powdered sugar
2 sticks (8 ounces) butter, softened

1 egg yolk
2 teaspoons vanilla extract
½ teaspoon almond extract
2 cups flour

**1.** In a food processor, process almonds and sugar until almonds are very finely ground, about 2 minutes. Add butter and process until smooth. Add egg yolk, vanilla extract, and almond extract. Process until blended. Add flour and pulse until combined.

**2.** Preheat oven to 350°F. Press dough through a spritz gun onto lightly greased cookie sheets, spacing cookies 1 inch apart.

**3.** Bake 10 to 12 minutes, or until edges are very lightly browned. Remove cookies to wire racks to let cool completely.

## 292 PEANUT BUTTER COOKIES

*Prep: 5 minutes    Chill: 2 hours    Cook: 8 to 10 minutes per batch*
*Makes: about 36*

1  stick (4 ounces) unsalted
   butter, softened
¾  cup packed light brown
   sugar
¼  cup granulated sugar
¾  cup creamy peanut butter
1  egg

1  teaspoon vanilla extract
1⅓  cups flour
½  teaspoon baking soda
¼  teaspoon salt
¼  cup roasted unsalted
   peanuts, chopped

**1.** In a large bowl, beat butter with an electric mixer on low speed until creamy. Gradually beat in brown sugar and then granulated sugar. Beat 1 minute. Add peanut butter and beat until blended. Add egg and vanilla and beat until mixed. In a small bowl, combine flour, baking soda, and salt. Add to peanut butter mixture half at a time, beating until blended. Cover dough and refrigerate 2 hours or overnight.

**2.** Preheat oven to 375°F. Lightly grease several baking sheets. Roll dough into 1¼-inch balls. Place 2½ inches apart on cookie sheets. Flatten with a fork dipped in sugar to make a crisscross pattern. Sprinkle with peanuts and press lightly to stick.

**3.** Bake 8 to 10 minutes, or until set and edges begin to brown lightly. Let stand 2 minutes before removing to racks to cool completely.

## 293 ALL-AMERICAN CHOCOLATE BROWNIES

*Prep: 5 minutes    Cook: 25 to 30 minutes    Makes: 16*

These not overly sweet, fudgy brownies are the answer to any chocolate lover's dream. To make them even more chocolatey, stir in ½ cup semi-sweet chocolate chips with the walnuts.

4  (1-inch) squares
   unsweetened chocolate,
   chopped
1  stick (4 ounces) butter
1⅓  cups sugar

1  teaspoon vanilla extract
3  eggs
¾  cup flour
   Pinch of salt
½  cup walnuts, chopped

**1.** Preheat oven to 350°F. Line a 9-inch square baking pan with foil. Grease foil.

**2.** In a medium saucepan, melt chocolate and butter over low heat, stirring frequently. Remove from heat and let cool 10 minutes. Stir in sugar and vanilla. Beat in eggs 1 at a time. Add flour, salt, and walnuts. Stir until blended. Turn into pan and spread evenly.

**3.** Bake 25 to 30 minutes, or until a toothpick comes out with moist but not wet crumbs. Let cool completely on a wire rack. To cut, lift out of pan using foil. Cut into squares.

# 294   BROWN SUGAR PECAN ICEBOX COOKIES

*Prep: 10 minutes    Chill: 4 hours    Cook: 18 to 20 minutes per batch*
*Makes: 68*

These are what is known as icebox, refrigerator, or slice-and-bake cookies. They are great to have on hand, refrigerated or frozen, when you need home-baked cookies in a flash.

2½ **cups flour**
1 **teaspoon cinnamon**
⅛ **teaspoon salt**
½ **cup granulated sugar**
2 **sticks (8 ounces) unsalted**
    **butter, softened**

¾ **cup packed dark brown**
    **sugar**
2 **teaspoons vanilla extract**
1½ **cups chopped pecans**

**1.** In a small bowl, stir together flour, ½ teaspoon cinnamon, and salt. In a small bowl, stir together remaining ½ teaspoon cinnamon and ¼ cup granulated sugar.

**2.** In a large bowl, combine remaining ¼ cup granulated sugar, butter, and brown sugar. Beat with an electric mixer on medium speed until fluffy. Beat in vanilla. Beat in half of flour mixture on low speed just until blended. Stir in remaining flour mixture and ¾ cup pecans.

**3.** Divide dough in half. Roll each half with hands on a lightly floured surface into an 8-inch log. Finely chop remaining ¾ cup pecans. Spread nuts on a flat surface and roll each log in pecans, pressing gently until logs are 10 inches long. Wrap each in plastic wrap and refrigerate at least 4 hours, or until firm. Logs can be refrigerated up to 2 weeks, or double wrapped and frozen 6 months.

**4.** Preheat oven to 325°F. Unwrap logs and cut into ¼-inch-thick slices with a sharp knife. Dip 1 cut side in cinnamon sugar and lay slices sugared side up 2 inches apart on greased cookie sheets.

**5.** Bake 1 sheet at a time 18 to 20 minutes, or until cookie edges are lightly browned. Let stand 1 minute before transferring cookies to racks to cool completely.

# 295   FIG BAR COOKIES

*Prep: 35 minutes   Chill: 1 hour   Cook: 16 to 18 minutes*
*Makes: 45*

6 tablespoons butter, cut into
  8 pieces, softened
⅔ cup packed dark brown
  sugar
1 egg
¼ cup milk
2½ cups flour
1½ teaspoons baking powder
¼ teaspoon salt

2 cups dried figs, stems
  removed
½ cup dried apricots
½ cup golden raisins
½ cup walnuts
¼ cup granulated sugar
2 tablespoons honey
¼ cup orange juice
1 teaspoon grated orange zest

**1.** In a food processor, process butter and brown sugar until blended. Add egg and milk. Process until combined. Add flour, baking powder, and salt. Pulse until blended and dough forms a ball. Remove dough to a bowl and refrigerate, covered, 1 hour.

**2.** In a food processor, combine figs, apricots, raisins, and walnuts. Process until very finely chopped. Add granulated sugar, honey, orange juice, and zest. Process until combined and filling forms a ball. Remove to a bowl.

**3.** Preheat oven to 350°F. Divide dough into 5 equal pieces. Work with 1 piece at a time, leaving remaining refrigerated. On a floured surface, roll dough to a 12 x 3¾-inch rectangle. Using fingers or a spoon, place scant ½ cup filling lengthwise down center of rectangle in a 1-inch-wide strip. Brush 1 edge of dough lightly with water. Fold other side up over onto filling, using a spatula. Fold moistened side over, pressing lightly to seal. Place on lightly greased baking sheets, seam side down. Repeat with another piece of dough and filling. Press each lightly so logs are 1½ inches wide. Repeat with remaining dough and filling.

**4.** Bake on upper oven rack 16 to 18 minutes, or until set and lightly browned at edges. Slide logs onto a wire rack to let cool slightly. Place on a cutting board and with a serrated knife cut each log crosswise into 9 pieces. Place on wire rack to cool completely. Store cookies in an airtight container.

# 296    ROLLED SUGAR COOKIES
*Prep: 15 minutes    Chill: 4 hours    Cook: 8 to 10 minutes per batch*
*Makes: about 70*

2  sticks (8 ounces) butter,
    softened
1½ cups powdered sugar, sifted
1  egg
2  teaspoons vanilla extract
2½ cups flour

½  teaspoon baking soda
½  teaspoon cream of tartar
⅛  teaspoon salt
    Granulated sugar, for
    sprinkling

1. In a large bowl, beat butter with electric mixer on low speed until fluffy. Beat in powdered sugar. Beat in egg and vanilla extract until blended.

2. In a small bowl, combine flour, baking soda, cream of tartar, and salt. Stir well to mix. Stir into butter mixture until well blended. Divide dough into quarters and wrap each piece in plastic wrap. Refrigerate dough 4 hours or overnight.

3. Preheat oven to 375°F. On a floured surface, using a floured rolling pin, roll dough 1 piece at a time to ⅛ inch thick. Cut with 2½-inch cookie cutters and transfer with spatula to lightly greased cookie sheets. Scraps can be rerolled once. Sprinkle tops lightly with granulated sugar.

4. Bake 1 sheet at a time 8 to 10 minutes, or until cookie edges are just beginning to brown. Transfer to wire rack to cool completely.

# 297    BLONDIES
*Prep: 10 minutes    Cook: 35 to 40 minutes    Makes: 16*

1  cup flour
½  teaspoon baking powder
1  stick (4 ounces) butter,
    softened
¾  cup packed dark brown
    sugar

1  egg
1½ teaspoons vanilla extract
¾  cup semisweet chocolate
    chips
¾  cup chopped pecans

1. Preheat oven to 325°F. In a small bowl, stir flour and baking powder until blended.

2. In a large bowl, beat butter with an electric mixer on low speed until fluffy. Add brown sugar, egg, and vanilla. Beat with electric mixer on medium speed 1 minute, or until fluffy. Add flour mixture and beat on low speed until blended. Stir in chocolate chips and nuts. Turn into a greased 9-inch square baking pan and spread evenly.

3. Bake 35 to 40 minutes, or until a toothpick inserted in center comes out clean. Remove pan to rack and let cool completely before cutting.

# 298    STRAWBERRY ICE CREAM

*Prep: 5 minutes    Cook: none    Freeze: 5 hours    Makes: 1½ quarts*

Here's a homemade ice cream you can make without an ice cream maker.

| | |
|---|---|
| 1½ **pints strawberries, hulled** | ¼ **cup whole milk** |
| 2 **tablespoons sugar** | 2 **teaspoons vanilla extract** |
| 1 **(14-ounce) can sweetened** | ⅛ **teaspoon salt** |
| **condensed milk** | 2 **cups heavy cream** |

**1.** In a food processor, puree ½ pint strawberries until smooth.

**2.** Halve remaining strawberries and place in a large bowl. Add sugar and crush well with a potato masher. Add pureed berries, condensed milk, whole milk, vanilla, and salt. Stir until blended.

**3.** In a medium bowl, beat cream with an electric mixer on high speed until stiff. Fold whipped cream into strawberry mixture until combined. Pour into a shallow 2-quart baking dish. Cover with plastic wrap.

**4.** Freeze until frozen solid, about 5 hours, stirring gently a few times as mixture begins to freeze. Scoop into an airtight container and freeze up to 2 weeks.

---

# 299    WHOOPIE PIES

*Prep: 25 minutes    Cook: 8 to 10 minutes per batch    Makes: 12*

These are big pies, almost enough for 2 people. If you'd like them smaller, make 36 cookies, which will make 18 sandwich cookies.

| | |
|---|---|
| 2 **sticks (8 ounces) unsalted** | 1 **cup granulated sugar** |
| **butter, softened** | 2 **eggs** |
| 4 **(1-ounce) squares** | ½ **cup milk** |
| **unsweetened chocolate,** | 1 **(8-ounce) package cream** |
| **chopped** | **cheese** |
| 2⅓ **cups flour** | 1¼ **cups powdered sugar, sifted** |
| 1 **teaspoon baking powder** | 1 **teaspoon vanilla extract** |
| 1 **teaspoon baking soda** | ½ **cup mini semisweet** |
| ¼ **teaspoon salt** | **chocolate chips** |

**1.** Preheat oven to 350°F. In a medium saucepan, combine 1 stick butter and unsweetened chocolate. Melt over low heat, stirring occasionally. Set aside to cool slightly.

**2.** In a small bowl, stir flour, baking powder, baking soda, and salt until well blended. In a large bowl, combine cooled chocolate mixture and granulated sugar. Beat with an electric mixer on medium speed 1 minute. Add eggs 1 at a time, beating well after adding each. On low speed, beat in flour mixture in thirds alternately with milk, beating until blended after each addition.

**3.** Spoon batter by rounded teaspoonfuls onto greased baking sheets 3 inches apart, making 24 mounds.

**4.** Bake 1 sheet at a time 8 to 10 minutes, or until tops spring back when lightly pressed. Remove cookies with a spatula to a wire rack and let cool completely.

**5.** In a small bowl, combine remaining 1 stick butter and cream cheese. Beat with electric mixer on medium speed until fluffy, about 2 minutes. Add powdered sugar and vanilla; beat until fluffy. Stir in chocolate chips.

**6.** Spread filling on bottoms of half of cookies. Top with remaining cookies bottom side down. Store cookies in refrigerator. If refrigerated, let come to room temperature before serving.

---

# 300 HERMIT LOGS
*Prep: 15 minutes    Chill: 30 minutes*
*Cook: 12 to 14 minutes per batch    Makes: 36*

| | |
|---|---|
| 3  cups flour | 2  eggs |
| 1½ teaspoons cinnamon | ⅓  cup unsulphured molasses |
| 1  teaspoon baking soda | 1  cup raisins, coarsely |
| 1  teaspoon baking powder | chopped |
| 1  teaspoon ground ginger | ¾  cup chopped walnuts |
| ½  teaspoon grated nutmeg | 3  tablespoons minced |
| ¼  teaspoon ground cloves | crystallized ginger |
| 1½ sticks (6 ounces) butter, | 2  cups powdered sugar |
| softened | 3  tablespoons milk |
| 1½ cups packed light brown | |
| sugar | |

**1.** Preheat oven to 375°F. In a medium bowl, combine flour, cinnamon, baking soda, baking powder, ginger, nutmeg, and cloves. Stir to mix well.

**2.** In a large bowl, beat butter with an electric mixer on medium speed until fluffy. Gradually beat in brown sugar. Add eggs 1 at a time, beating well after adding each. Beat in molasses. Beat in dry ingredients, half at a time, just until blended. Stir in raisins, walnuts, and crystallized ginger. Refrigerate dough 30 minutes.

**3.** Divide dough into 6 equal pieces. On a lightly floured surface, shape each into a 12-inch log. Place 2 logs about 3 inches apart on a large greased cookie sheet.

**4.** Bake in upper third of oven 12 to 14 minutes, until browned and set but still slightly soft. Let cool 10 minutes on cookie sheet. Slide with a wide spatula onto a wire rack. Repeat with remaining dough.

**5.** Sift powdered sugar into a small bowl. Stir in milk. If necessary, add additional milk to make a thin glaze. While logs are warm, spread glaze over tops. Let stand until cool and glaze sets. Cut logs crosswise into 2-inch-wide pieces. Store airtight.

# 301 ICE CREAM SANDWICHES

*Prep: 5 minutes    Cook: 12 to 15 minutes*
*Freeze: overnight plus 3 hours 15 minutes    Makes: 10*

These are not difficult to make, but they do require some gentle handling during assembly to keep the chocolate cookie crust intact. Be sure to allow time for all the freezing. Instead of vanilla ice cream, try these with your favorite flavor—mine is espresso chip.

¾ **cup sugar**
4 **tablespoons butter**
3 **(1-ounce) squares**
    **unsweetened chocolate,**
    **chopped**

¾ **cup flour**
¾ **teaspoon baking soda**
1 **egg**
2 **pints vanilla ice cream**

**1.** Preheat oven to 325°F. Coat a 15 x 10-inch jelly-roll pan with cooking spray. Line pan with foil, letting it extend at ends. Grease and flour foil; tap out excess flour.

**2.** In a medium saucepan, combine sugar and butter with 2 tablespoons water. Place over medium heat. Cook, stirring occasionally, until mixture comes to a boil. Remove from heat. Add chocolate and stir until melted. Let cool 10 minutes.

**3.** In a small bowl, mix together flour and baking soda. Beat egg into cooled chocolate mixture. Stir in flour mixture until blended. Pour bàtter into pan; carefully spread evenly. The layer will be very thin.

**4.** Bake 12 to 15 minutes, or until a toothpick comes out clean. Place pan on a wire rack and let cool completely. Refrigerate chocolate cookie in pan 15 minutes, or until firm but not brittle. While cookie layer chills, set ice cream in refrigerator to soften. Invert cookie onto a cutting board. Remove pan and carefully peel off foil. With a serrated knife and using a sawing motion, trim ¼ inch from edges. Cut cookie in half crosswise. Turn halves over so shiny sides are up. Working quickly, spoon ice cream onto one half, spreading it evenly up to edges. Top with other half, shiny side down. Press lightly and return to freezer. Freeze until firm, about 3 hours.

**5.** Using a serrated knife, cut in half from short side. Cut each half crosswise into 5 rectangular sandwiches. Wrap each in plastic wrap. Freeze overnight, or until ice cream is frozen solid.

# 302 LEMON BARS
*Prep: 20 minutes   Cook: 40 to 45 minutes   Makes: 16*

The recipe for these tart, lemony bars come from friend and caterer Marge Foster. She has made more pans of these than she can count. They've been a much requested favorite for a long time.

1 stick (4 ounces) unsalted butter, softened
¼ cup powdered sugar
1 cup plus 2½ tablespoons flour
1 cup granulated sugar

½ teaspoon baking powder
Pinch of salt
2 eggs
2 teaspoons grated lemon zest
¼ cup fresh lemon juice

**1.** Preheat oven to 350°F. Line an 8 x 8-inch square baking pan with foil. Spray foil with nonstick cooking spray.

**2.** In a medium bowl, with a wooden spoon, beat butter and powdered sugar until combined. Add 1 cup flour and stir until blended. Pat evenly into bottom of pan.

**3.** Bake crust 20 minutes, or until golden. In a bowl, combine granulated sugar, remaining flour, baking powder, salt, eggs, lemon zest, and lemon juice. Whisk until smooth. Pour over crust.

**4.** Bake 20 to 25 minutes, or until top is firm to the touch. Remove to a wire rack to let cool completely. Dust lightly with additional powdered sugar. Remove from pan and cut into squares.

# 303 STRAWBERRY COCONUT POPS
*Prep: 10 minutes   Cook: none   Freeze: 4 hours   Makes: 8*

1 (12-ounce) bag frozen unsweetened strawberries
1 (8-ounce) container low-fat strawberry yogurt

½ cup powdered sugar
1 (14-ounce) can reduced-fat unsweetened coconut milk
2 tablespoons lime juice

**1.** In a food processor, pulse strawberries to break up. Process until finely chopped. Add yogurt and sugar and process until smooth. Add coconut milk and lime juice and process until combined.

**2.** Pour into 8 (5-ounce) plastic disposable drinking cups, dividing mixture evenly. Freeze until partially frozen, about 2 hours. Insert a popsicle stick in center of each. Return to freezer and freeze until frozen solid, about 2 hours.

**3.** To remove cup, cut edge with scissors and peel off.

# 304   HOT FUDGE SAUCE

*Prep: 5 minutes   Cook: 6 minutes   Makes: 1½ cups*

This is the kind that gets slightly chewy when spooned over ice cream. I always seem to need to go back for seconds on sauce because it somehow disappears first before all the ice cream is gone.

⅓ cup unsweetened cocoa
  powder
⅔ cup sugar
¾ cup heavy cream
⅓ cup light corn syrup

1 (1-ounce) square
  unsweetened chocolate,
  chopped
3 tablespoons butter
1 teaspoon vanilla extract

**1.** In a medium saucepan, whisk cocoa and sugar until combined. Whisk in cream and corn syrup. Bring to a boil over medium heat, stirring frequently. Reduce heat to low and boil 6 minutes, stirring occasionally, or until slightly thickened.

**2.** Remove from heat. Add chocolate, butter, and vanilla. Stir until chocolate melts. Let cool slightly. Serve warm over ice cream. To reheat if refrigerated, heat in a double boiler.

# 305   BANANA PUDDING

*Prep: 15 minutes   Cook: 8 minutes   Chill: 4 hours   Serves: 6*

3 cups milk
¼ cup cornstarch
⅓ cup plus 1 tablespoon sugar
⅛ teaspoon salt
3 egg yolks
2 tablespoons butter

2 teaspoons vanilla extract
24 vanilla wafer cookies
2 tablespoons bourbon
3 large firm, ripe bananas
  Whipped cream (optional)

**1.** In a small saucepan, heat 2 cups milk over low heat until hot, about 5 minutes.

**2.** In a medium saucepan, combine cornstarch, sugar, and salt. Whisk until blended. Whisk in 1 cup cold milk until smooth. Whisk in egg yolks. Gradually whisk in hot milk. Cook over medium heat, stirring constantly with a heatproof rubber spatula, until mixture comes to a boil, about 2 minutes. Reduce heat to low and simmer 1 minute, stirring constantly. Remove from heat and stir in butter and vanilla until butter is melted. Strain into a medium bowl.

**3.** In a 2½-quart glass bowl with straight sides, layer half of vanilla wafers. Brush with 1 tablespoon bourbon. Peel and slice bananas. Top wafers with half of bananas. Pour half of pudding over bananas, spreading evenly. Top with remaining wafers and brush with remaining bourbon. Top with bananas and pudding, spreading pudding to cover bananas. Cover surface directly with plastic wrap and refrigerate until very cold, at least 4 hours. Top with whipped cream, if desired, before serving.

# 306 CHOCOLATE PUDDING
*Prep: 5 minutes    Cook: 7 to 8 minutes    Chill: 2 hours    Serves: 4*

⅓ cup Dutch-process cocoa
   powder
½ cup sugar
3 tablespoons cornstarch
2¾ cups milk

2 egg yolks
½ cup semisweet chocolate
   chips
1 teaspoon vanilla extract
2 tablespoons butter

**1.** In a medium saucepan, whisk cocoa, sugar, and cornstarch until well blended. Gradually whisk in milk until smooth. Cook over medium heat, stirring constantly with a heatproof rubber spatula, until mixture comes to a boil, 4 to 5 minutes. Boil, stirring constantly, 1 minute. Remove from heat.

**2.** In a small bowl, whisk yolks. Gradually whisk in half of mixture from saucepan. Stir back into pan. Return to low heat. Cook, stirring constantly, until pudding returns to a simmer. Simmer 2 minutes, stirring constantly. Remove from heat.

**3.** Add chocolate chips, vanilla, and butter. Stir until chocolate melts. Pour into a medium bowl. Let cool 15 minutes, stirring gently a few times. Cover surface with plastic wrap and refrigerate until cold, about 2 hours.

# 307 INDIAN PUDDING
*Prep: 10 minutes    Cook: 55 to 60 minutes    Serves: 6 to 8*

2 cups milk
⅓ cup packed dark brown
   sugar
¼ cup yellow cornmeal
1 teaspoon cinnamon
¾ teaspoon ground ginger

⅛ teaspoon salt
1 tablespoon butter
¼ cup light molasses
2 eggs
Vanilla ice cream, as
   accompaniment

**1.** In a medium saucepan, heat 1½ cups milk over medium heat until hot but not boiling. In a small bowl, combine sugar, cornmeal, cinnamon, ginger, and salt. Stir until mixed. Gradually add to hot milk, whisking constantly. Whisk until mixture comes to a simmer. Reduce heat and simmer 10 minutes, stirring frequently, until mixture thickens. Remove from heat. Stir in butter. Let cool 10 minutes, stirring occasionally.

**2.** In a small bowl, whisk remaining milk, molasses, and eggs. Gradually whisk into cornmeal mixture until smooth.

**3.** Preheat oven to 350°F. Pour cornmeal mixture into a buttered 1½-quart deep baking dish. Place dish in a shallow roasting pan. Place in oven and fill roasting pan with boiling water to come halfway up sides of dish.

**4.** Bake 45 to 50 minutes, or until set but still jiggly. Pudding will firm up as it cools. Remove dish from roasting pan and let cool on a wire rack. Serve warm or at room temperature with ice cream.

# 308    BUTTERSCOTCH PUDDING

*Prep: 5 minutes    Cook: 8 to 10 minutes    Chill: 2 hours*
*Serves: 4 to 6*

2¼  cups milk
4  tablespoons butter
¾  cup packed dark brown
  sugar

3  tablespoons cornstarch
4  egg yolks
1½  teaspoons vanilla extract

**1.** In a small saucepan, heat 2 cups milk and butter over low heat until butter melts, 5 to 7 minutes. In a medium saucepan, whisk sugar and cornstarch until blended. Whisk in ¼ cup cold milk. Whisk in egg yolks. Gradually whisk in hot milk mixture.

**2.** Cook over medium-low heat, stirring constantly with a heatproof rubber spatula, until pudding comes to a boil, about 2 minutes. Reduce heat to low and cook, stirring constantly, 1 minute. Remove from heat and stir in vanilla.

**3.** Strain into a medium bowl and let cool 15 minutes, stirring gently occasionally. Cover with plastic wrap and refrigerate until cold, about 2 hours.

# 309    BOURBON BREAD PUDDING WITH PRALINE SAUCE

*Prep: 10 minutes    Cook: 52 to 59 minutes    Serves: 6*

⅓  cup raisins
2  tablespoons bourbon
¼  cup pecans
⅓  cup granulated sugar
3  eggs
2  teaspoons vanilla extract
⅛  teaspoon cinnamon
⅛  teaspoon grated nutmeg

1  pint half-and-half
3  cups (½-inch) day-old
  French bread cubes
¼  cup packed light brown
  sugar
2  tablespoons unsalted butter
1  tablespoon dark corn syrup

**1.** Preheat oven to 325°F. Butter an 8-inch square baking dish. In a small bowl, combine raisins and bourbon. Let stand 15 minutes. Meanwhile, spread out pecans in a pie plate and bake 7 to 9 minutes, until toasted. Let cool, then chop.

**2.** In a large bowl, combine granulated sugar, eggs, vanilla, cinnamon, and nutmeg. Whisk to blend. Set aside 1 tablespoon half-and-half. Whisk in remaining half-and-half. Stir in bread cubes. Let stand 15 minutes, stirring occasionally. Add raisins and bourbon; stir well. Pour into prepared dish.

**3.** Bake 45 to 50 minutes, or until a knife inserted in center comes out clean. Place on a wire rack.

**4.** In a small saucepan, combine brown sugar and butter. Cook over medium heat until butter melts. Add reserved half-and-half and corn syrup. Bring to a boil, stirring occasionally. Reduce heat and simmer 2 minutes. Let cool until thickened, about 15 minutes. Drizzle over top of pudding. Sprinkle chopped pecans on top. Serve pudding warm.

---

# 310 CAPPUCCINO CHOCOLATE MOUSSE
*Prep: 15 minutes    Cook: 5 minutes    Chill: 2 hours    Serves: 6*

| | |
|---|---|
| 8 ounces bittersweet or semisweet chocolate, chopped | 1 teaspoon vanilla extract |
| | ¼ teaspoon cinnamon |
| | Pinch of salt |
| 3 tablespoons unsalted butter | 3 eggs, separated |
| 1 tablespoon instant espresso powder | ⅓ cup sugar |
| | 1¼ cups heavy cream, chilled |
| 3 tablespoons coffee liqueur | Cinnamon, for garnish |

**1.** In a medium saucepan, melt chocolate and butter over low heat, about 5 minutes. Pour into a large bowl.

**2.** In a small cup, combine espresso powder, 2 tablespoons coffee liqueur, vanilla, and cinnamon. Stir until coffee dissolves.

**3.** In a small bowl, with electric mixer on medium-high speed, beat salt and egg whites until soft peaks form. Add sugar, 1 tablespoon at a time, beating until stiff but not dry.

**4.** In a medium bowl, combine ¾ cup cream with coffee mixture. With electric mixer on high speed, beat just until stiff peaks form.

**5.** Add yolks to chocolate. Whisk to combine. Stir a spoonful of whites into chocolate mixture. Gently fold in remaining whites until almost blended in. Add cream mixture and fold gently just until no streaks of white remain. Spoon mousse into individual serving dishes or turn into a serving bowl. Cover and refrigerate until firm, 2 hours or overnight.

**6.** To serve, beat remaining ½ cup cream with remaining coffee liqueur until soft peaks form. Serve mousse garnished with cream and a sprinkle of cinnamon.

# 311   CREAMY RICE PUDDING

*Prep: 5 minutes    Cook: 50 minutes    Serves: 8*

¾ cup long-grain white rice
   (not converted)
¼ teaspoon salt
4 cups milk
½ cup plus 1 tablespoon sugar

2 egg yolks
1 teaspoon cornstarch
1½ teaspoons vanilla extract
⅛ teaspoon cinnamon

**1.** In a medium saucepan, bring rice, salt, and 2½ cups water to a boil. Stir, reduce heat to low, cover, and simmer 30 minutes, or until rice is soft and most of water is absorbed.

**2.** Stir 3 cups milk and ½ cup sugar into rice. Bring to a simmer. Simmer gently 20 minutes, stirring occasionally, or until thickened.

**3.** In a small bowl, whisk yolks, cornstarch, and remaining 1 cup milk until smooth. Stir into rice. Increase heat to medium and bring to a simmer, stirring occasionally. Remove from heat and stir in vanilla. Pour into a serving bowl.

**4.** In a small bowl, combine remaining 1 tablespoon sugar and cinnamon. Sprinkle over pudding. Let cool, then cover and refrigerate. Serve cold.

# 312   HONEY-SPICE BAKED APPLES

*Prep: 15 minutes    Cook: 45 to 55 minutes    Serves: 6*

6 large Golden Delicious, Ida
   Red, or Rome apples
¼ cup chopped walnuts
¼ cup packed light brown
   sugar
2 tablespoons butter, softened

½ teaspoon cinnamon
¼ cup dark rum
¼ cup honey
1 tablespoon lemon juice
1 tablespoon crystallized
   ginger, minced

**1.** Preheat oven to 350°F. Remove core from apples without cutting through to bottom, making a cavity about 1 inch wide. Using vegetable peeler, peel apples halfway down. In a small bowl, combine walnuts, brown sugar, butter, and cinnamon. Stir until blended. Stuff mixture into apple cavities. Spoon ½ teaspoon rum over filling in each apple.

**2.** Place apples in a 10-inch pie plate. In a small bowl, combine remaining rum, honey, lemon juice, and ginger. Whisk until blended. Drizzle over and around apples.

**3.** Bake 45 to 55 minutes, or until apples are tender when pierced with a knife, basting with pan juices a few times. Let cool and serve warm or at room temperature.

# 313   AMBROSIA

*Prep: 15 minutes    Cook: none    Chill: 2 hours    Serves: 8 to 10*

This Southern dessert is truly ambrosial when made with ripe pineapple, fresh coconut, and juicy oranges. It's traditionally served in a pretty cut-glass bowl.

6 **large seedless oranges**
1 **ripe medium pineapple**
   **(about 3 pounds)**

2 **cups shredded fresh coconut**
3 **tablespoons sugar**
¼ **cup orange liqueur**

**1.** Peel oranges with a small sharp knife, removing white membrane. Cut into ¼-inch-thick slices. Peel pineapple. Quarter, core, and cut into 1-inch chunks.

**2.** In a large glass bowl, layer one third of oranges, one third of pineapple, and one third of coconut. Sprinkle with 1 tablespoon sugar and 1 tablespoon orange liqueur. Repeat layering twice, sprinkling top with 2 tablespoons liqueur. Cover and refrigerate at least 2 hours before serving.

# 314   *APPLE BROWN BETTY*

*Prep: 20 minutes    Cook: 40 minutes    Serves: 8*

6 **slices homemade-type white**
   **bread**
5 **tablespoons unsalted butter,**
   **softened**
¼ **cup granulated sugar**
1 **teaspoon cinnamon**
½ **cup packed light brown**
   **sugar**
¼ **teaspoon grated nutmeg**

3 **Granny Smith apples,**
   **peeled, cored, and thinly**
   **sliced**
3 **Golden Delicious apples,**
   **peeled, cored, and thinly**
   **sliced**
1 **tablespoon lemon juice**
⅓ **cup apple cider**

**1.** Preheat oven to 375°F. Toast bread lightly in a toaster. In a small bowl, combine butter, 2 tablespoons granulated sugar, and ½ teaspoon cinnamon. Stir to mix. Spread over both sides of toast. Stack slices and cut into ½-inch cubes.

**2.** In a large bowl, combine remaining 2 tablespoons granulated sugar, ½ teaspoon cinnamon, light brown sugar, and nutmeg. Stir to mix. Add apples and lemon juice; toss well to combine.

**3.** Spread one third of bread cubes in a buttered 2-quart shallow baking dish. Add apples. Drizzle apples with cider and top with remaining bread.

**4.** Bake 40 minutes, or until apples are tender and bread is browned. Cover with foil after 30 minutes if bread is browning too quickly. Let cool on rack and serve warm.

## 315    APPLE-PEAR CRISP
*Prep: 10 minutes    Cook: 45 to 50 minutes    Serves: 6*

Use a combination of apples in this fall classic for the best flavor. The most common baking apples are Golden Delicious and Granny Smith. But some other bakers to try are Cortland, Paula Red, Winesap, Gala, Empire, or Northern Spy.

2  ripe pears, peeled, cored, and sliced
4  baking apples, peeled, cored, and sliced
½  cup dried cranberries
¾  cup packed light brown sugar
⅔  cup flour

¼  cup orange juice
¼  teaspoon grated orange zest
1  teaspoon cinnamon
¼  teaspoon grated nutmeg
1  stick (4 ounces) butter, cut into small pieces
½  cup oats

**1.** Preheat oven to 350°F. In a large bowl, combine pears, apples, cranberries, ¼ cup brown sugar, 1 tablespoon flour, orange juice, orange zest, cinnamon, and nutmeg. Toss well. Turn into a 2-quart shallow baking dish.

**2.** In a medium bowl, combine remaining brown sugar and flour, butter, and oats. Mix with fingers until crumbly. Crumble over fruit.

**3.** Bake 45 to 50 minutes, or until fruit is tender and top is browned. Let cool on wire rack. Serve warm or at room temperature.

## 316    THREE-BERRY GRUNT
*Prep: 10 minutes    Cook: 31 to 36 minutes    Serves: 6 to 8*

A grunt is sometimes made in a pot, with dumplings dropped on top and then simmered on the stove, the name coming from the sound that it makes as it cooks. I prefer mine baked in the oven.

3  cups blueberries
¾  cup plus 3 tablespoons sugar
1½  tablespoons cornstarch
1  cup blackberries
1  cup raspberries
1  tablespoon lemon juice

1¼  cups flour
1½  teaspoons baking powder
¼  teaspoon salt
4  tablespoons butter, melted
½  cup milk
⅛  teaspoon cinnamon
Vanilla ice cream

**1.** Preheat oven to 400°F. In a medium saucepan, combine 1 cup blueberries and ¾ cup sugar. In a small cup, dissolve cornstarch in ¼ cup cold water. Stir into blueberry-sugar mixture. Bring to a boil over medium-high heat, stirring occasionally. Reduce heat and simmer until thickened, about 1 minute. Remove from heat. Stir in remaining blueberries, blackberries, raspberries, and lemon juice. Pour into a 2-quart shallow baking dish.

**2.** In a medium bowl, stir 2 tablespoons sugar, flour, baking powder, and salt until well blended. Add butter and milk and stir just until dry ingredients are moistened. Spoon over fruit by tablespoonfuls, with spaces in between to make 8 biscuits. In a small bowl, mix remaining 1 tablespoon sugar and cinnamon. Sprinkle over biscuits.

**3.** Set baking dish in oven with a piece of foil underneath to catch drips. Bake 30 to 35 minutes, or until fruit is bubbly and biscuits are well browned. Let cool slightly on a wire rack. Serve warm in bowls with vanilla ice cream.

## 317    OREGON BLACKBERRY COBBLER

*Prep: 25 minutes    Cook: 32 to 34 minutes    Serves: 8*

4 large Golden Delicious apples (2 pounds), peeled and cored
½ cup plus 2 tablespoons sugar
1½ tablespoons cornstarch
1 stick plus 2 tablespoons (5 ounces) butter
3 cups fresh or frozen blackberries

1½ cups flour
3 tablespoons cornmeal
1 tablespoon baking powder
⅛ teaspoon salt
1½ teaspoons grated orange zest
½ cup milk
¼ cup seedless blackberry preserves

**1.** Cut apples into ¾-inch-thick slices. In a Dutch oven, combine apples and ½ cup water. In a small bowl, stir ½ cup sugar and cornstarch until well blended. Add to apples. Add 2 tablespoons butter. Bring to a boil over medium-high heat, stirring constantly. Reduce heat to low. Simmer, stirring occasionally, 4 minutes, or until apples soften slightly. Remove from heat. Stir in blackberries and pour into a 13 x 9 x 2-inch glass baking dish; spread evenly.

**2.** In a food processor, combine remaining 2 tablespoons sugar, flour, cornmeal, baking powder, and salt. Process until blended. Cut 7 tablespoons butter into small pieces and add to flour mixture. Process until the texture of meal. Add orange zest and process until blended. Add milk and process until dough begins to come together. Turn dough out onto a floured surface and shape into a ball.

**3.** Preheat oven to 425°F. Roll dough on a floured piece of wax paper to a 12 x 8-inch rectangle. Spread with jam up to ½-inch from edges. Use wax paper to roll dough up from a long side. Gently cut roll crosswise with a serrated knife into 12 slices, wiping knife occasionally. Place cut side down on fruit, spacing evenly. Melt remaining butter and brush over biscuits.

**4.** Bake 28 to 30 minutes, or until fruit is bubbly in center and biscuits are browned and cooked through. Let cool on wire rack and serve warm.

# 318  BANANAS FOSTER
*Prep: 5 minutes    Cook: 3 minutes    Serves: 4*

This fabulous and rich New Orleans classic, made famous by Brennan's restaurant, is served as a conclusion to their renowned brunch, and will even make converts of people who aren't crazy about bananas.

| | |
|---|---|
| **4 tablespoons unsalted butter** | **2 large firm, ripe bananas,** |
| **½ cup packed light brown** | **peeled, halved** |
| **sugar** | **lengthwise and crosswise** |
| **⅛ teaspoon cinnamon** | **¼ cup dark rum** |
| **¼ cup banana liqueur** | **1 pint butter pecan ice cream** |

**1.** In a large skillet, melt butter over medium heat. Stir in brown sugar, cinnamon, and banana liqueur. Cook, stirring, until thickened and bubbly, about 1 minute. Add bananas. Cook until slightly softened, turning to coat with sugar mixture, about 2 minutes. Remove pan from heat.

**2.** In a small saucepan, heat rum briefly just until warm. Remove pan from heat. Ignite with a long match. Pour over bananas and gently shake skillet until flames die out. Scoop ice cream onto plates and spoon bananas and sauce over.

# 319  RHUBARB TORTE
*Prep: 15 minutes    Cook: 56 to 63 minutes    Serves: 8*

This recipe comes from Sister Marlene Hetzel, a terrific baker who for years has baked for up to 300 people a day. This is like a rhubarb custard pie, only much easier.

| | |
|---|---|
| **1 cup plus 2 tablespoons flour** | **1 pound rhubarb, trimmed** |
| **2 tablespoons powdered** | **1¼ cups granulated sugar** |
| **sugar** | **¼ teaspoon salt** |
| **1 stick (4 ounces) cold** | **3 large eggs** |
| **unsalted butter, cut into** | **1 tablespoon vanilla extract** |
| **1-inch pieces** | |

**1.** Preheat oven to 350°F. In a food processor, combine 1 cup flour, powdered sugar, and butter. Process until dough begins to clump together. Press into bottom of a greased 9-inch square baking pan. Bake 16 to 18 minutes, until golden brown. Let cool on a wire rack.

**2.** Cut rhubarb into ½-inch pieces. In a large bowl, whisk granulated sugar, remaining 2 tablespoons flour, and salt until blended. Add eggs and vanilla; whisk until smooth. Stir in rhubarb. Pour over crust, spreading evenly.

**3.** Bake 40 to 45 minutes, or until top is browned and custard is firm. Let cool completely on a wire rack before serving. To serve, run sharp knife around edges, cut into squares, and lift out with a spatula.

# 320 NECTARINE BLUEBERRY BUCKLE

*Prep: 20 minutes    Cook: 35 to 40 minutes    Serves: 8*

A buckle is a cake batter with berries, sprinkled with a crumb topping. This is best served the same day it's made.

| | |
|---|---|
| 6 tablespoons unsalted butter, at room temperature | ½ teaspoon salt |
| ¾ cup granulated sugar | ⅔ cup milk |
| 1 egg | 1½ cups fresh blueberries |
| 1 teaspoon vanilla extract | 3 medium firm-ripe nectarines, peeled and sliced ½ inch thick |
| 2¼ cups flour | |
| 2½ teaspoons baking powder | Streusel (recipe follows) |

**1.** Preheat oven to 375°F. In a large bowl with an electric mixer on medium speed, beat butter until fluffy. Gradually beat in granulated sugar. Beat 2 minutes until fluffy. Beat in egg until well blended. Beat in vanilla.

**2.** In a small bowl, stir together flour, baking powder, and salt until well blended. On low speed, add dry ingredients to batter in 3 additions, alternating with milk, beginning and ending with flour and beating just until blended. Gently fold in blueberries.

**3.** Measure and reserve 1 cup batter. Turn remaining batter into a greased and floured 13 x 9 x 2-inch pan. Spread batter evenly. Place nectarines on batter in a single layer. Dot reserved batter over nectarines by half-teaspoonfuls (batter will spread). Crumble streusel over all.

**4.** Bake 35 to 40 minutes, or until a toothpick inserted in cake part of buckle comes out clean. Let cool on rack. Serve warm or at room temperature.

## STREUSEL

*Makes: about ⅔ cup*

| | |
|---|---|
| 3 tablespoons cold unsalted butter, cut into small pieces | ⅓ cup flour |
| | 1¼ teaspoons cinnamon |
| ⅓ cup packed light brown sugar | |

In a small bowl, combine butter, sugar, flour, and cinnamon. Mix with fingers until crumbly.

# 321   PLUM FULL OF PEACHES COBBLER

*Prep: 20 minutes    Cook: 40 to 45 minutes    Serves: 8*

For extra color and flavor, I like to add a couple of plums to my peach cobbler. Use ripe peaches, the kind where the juice runs down your chin. The combination of really ripe peaches and plums turns the fruit a gorgeous pink color.

3 **pounds ripe peaches (about 10)**
2 **ripe plums**
1 **tablespoon lemon juice**
¾ **cup plus 1 tablespoon granulated sugar**
1½ **cups plus 2 tablespoons flour**
3 **tablespoons light brown sugar**

1½ **teaspoons baking powder**
½ **teaspoon baking soda**
¼ **teaspoon salt**
6 **tablespoons cold butter, cut into small pieces**
¾ **cup buttermilk**
¼ **teaspoon cinnamon**

**1.** Preheat oven to 400°F. Bring a medium saucepan of water to a boil. Add peaches a few at a time and cook 30 seconds per batch. Remove with a slotted spoon and run under cold water until cool. Pat peaches dry and remove skin with a paring knife. Cut peaches into ¾-inch-thick slices and place in a large bowl. Slice plums ½ inch thick and add to peaches. Add lemon juice and stir gently.

**2.** In a small bowl, mix ¾ cup granulated sugar with 2 tablespoons flour. Add to fruit and stir well. Pour into a 13 x 9 x 2-inch baking dish. Bake fruit 10 minutes.

**3.** Meanwhile, make biscuits: In a large bowl, combine 1½ cups flour, brown sugar, baking powder, baking soda, and salt. Stir well to break up lumps of brown sugar. Add butter and cut in with a pastry blender or 2 knives until crumbly. Add buttermilk and stir just until a very soft dough forms.

**4.** Remove baking dish from oven and drop dough by 10 heaping spoonfuls onto fruit with spaces in between. In a small bowl, combine remaining 1 tablespoon granulated sugar and cinnamon and sprinkle over biscuits. Return pan to oven.

**5.** Bake 30 to 35 minutes, or until biscuits are well browned and fruit is bubbly. Let cool on a wire rack and serve warm.

# 322 PEAR-CRANBERRY PANDOWDY

*Prep: 15 minutes    Cook: 1 hour 10 to 15 minutes    Serves: 8*

7 firm-ripe juicy pears,
   preferably Anjou
   (3½ pounds)
1¼ cups fresh or frozen
   cranberries
1½ cups plus 2 tablespoons
   flour
¾ cup sugar

1 teaspoon grated orange zest
½ teaspoon ground ginger
2 teaspoons baking powder
¼ teaspoon salt
5 tablespoons cold butter, cut
   into small pieces
¾ cup plus 1 tablespoon heavy
   cream

**1.** Preheat oven to 375°F. Peel and core pears. Cut into 1-inch chunks. In a large bowl, combine pears, cranberries, 2 tablespoons flour, ½ cup sugar, orange zest, and ginger. Stir well. Pour into a 9-inch square baking pan. Bake 25 minutes.

**2.** Meanwhile, in a large bowl, stir remaining 1½ cups flour with 3 tablespoons sugar, baking powder, and salt until blended. Add butter and cut in with a pastry blender until the texture of meal. Add ¾ cup cream, stirring with a fork until dough holds together. If necessary, stir in remaining cream. Gather dough into a ball.

**3.** On a floured sheet of wax paper, roll dough to fit just inside baking pan, to an 8 x 8-inch square, about ½ inch thick. Invert dough over fruit; peel off paper. Make 2 (2-inch) crosswise slits in center. Fold back dough to expose fruit. Sprinkle dough with remaining 1 tablespoon sugar.

**4.** Bake 45 to 50 minutes, or until fruit is bubbly and crust is well browned. Let cool on a wire rack and serve warm.

# Chapter 12

# Blue Ribbon Pies and Cakes

The pies and cakes in this chapter would be sure to win first prize at the county fair. To me a homemade pie is a work of art and a real labor of love. What could be more American? There are enough pies here to include everyone's favorite. And it seems as if everyone has his own personal preference. If you like fruit-filled pies, pick Black and Blueberry Pie, Sour Cherry Pie, Ruby Red Raspberry Pie, Down-Home Spiced Peach Pie, or Classic Apple Pie. If cream pie is at the top of your list, then Chocolate Cream Pie, Banana-Coconut Cream Pie, or Florida Key Lime Pie would be a good choice. And if you're a nut lover, then give Georgia's Best Pecan Pie or Peanut Butter Pie a try.

In my beginning stages as a pie baker, years ago as a teenager, I must admit I had some pie anxiety. Sometimes the crust would be flaky, sometimes tough as shoe leather, sometimes so dry I had to throw the whole mess in the garbage, and I was following the recipe exactly! It really helps to understand some of the more technical things that go on, so you end up with a flaky crust and a great pie you'll be proud of. Flour and fat are blended together with some tiny pieces of butter still visible. The fat, if butter, should be cold. Cold water is gradually added just until the dough clings together. There is a minimum amount of water listed in the recipes, so start at that point. Remember that flour varies in moisture content, so the amount of water needed will not be the same each and every time. You will learn to know how the dough looks when it is the right amount. It should hold together but not be wet and sticky. Too much water and the crust will be tough; too little and it will crumble and not roll out. The dough is refrigerated to chill the fat. When baked, the fat melts and the water evaporates into steam and makes the flaky layers.

A few other notes on pies: I use a glass pie plate for pies; I think the crust browns better, plus you can see the bottom crust. Sometimes I bake pies on the bottom oven rack to ensure that the bottom does brown and become crisp. Remember to let pies cook long enough. The crust should be well browned and the fruit bubbly, two signs of a fully baked pie. Something I do when the rim is getting too brown before the pie is fully baked: Cut a circle of foil 2 inches larger than the pie plate. Cut a circle out of the center, big enough so just the rim of the pie will be covered. Place this over the pie and fold down the foil at the edges. It stays on much better than trying to piece together strips of foil, which always fall off.

A homemade cake is a beautiful thing to behold.

Here are a few tips to make sure your cake is the best you've ever made: Butter should be softened. Make sure to cream butter and sugar as long as it says in the recipe; this will make for a good-textured cake. Beat in dry ingredients just until blended, unless otherwise specified in the recipe. Overbeating can cause a cake to be tough. I grease and flour cake pans but also line them with wax paper to ensure that the layers don't stick to the pan; it's frustrating to turn out a cake and have half of the cake stay in the pan. Cakes are usually cooled for a few minutes in the pan and then turned out onto a rack to cool. This gives time for the cake's structure to set. It helps to use an oven thermometer—an oven that is off temperature can cause cakes to have poor texture. An oven takes about 15 minutes to preheat, so make sure to do this before you start mixing.

There are some real cake classics here. So pull out the mixer, turn on the oven, and choose from one of the dandy desserts like Devil's Food Cake with Fluffy Chocolate Frosting, for chocolate lovers. A true Southern favorite, Fresh Coconut Layer Cake is an absolute showstopper. A double-layer Butter Cake with Glossy Chocolate Frosting is probably the quintessential example of Americana. A surefire grand finale to any Fourth of July picnic would be Fourth of July Flag Cake, for a touch of red, white, and blue.

---

## 323   SINGLE CRUST PASTRY

*Prep: 15 minutes    Chill: 1 hour    Makes: 1 (9- or 10-inch) piecrust*

1⅓ cups flour
¾ teaspoon sugar
¼ teaspoon salt
4 tablespoons cold unsalted butter, cut into small pieces

¼ cup solid vegetable shortening
3 to 4 tablespoons ice water

**1.** In a food processor, combine flour, sugar, and salt. Process to combine. Add butter and shortening and pulse 8 to 10 times until mixture resembles fine crumbs with some very small pieces of butter about the size of half a split pea. Turn into a large bowl.

**2.** Gradually drizzle in ice water 1 tablespoon at a time, tossing with a fork, adding enough water until dough begins to clump together. Gather dough into a ball. Press into a ½-inch-thick disk and wrap in wax paper. Refrigerate 1 hour or overnight.

**3.** Roll out dough on a lightly floured surface with a floured rolling pin to a 13-inch circle for a 9-inch pie shell or a 14-inch circle for a 10-inch pie shell. Lift and turn dough as it's rolled, lightly flouring surface as necessary to prevent sticking. Drape over rolling pin and ease into pie plate. Press gently against sides and bottom of pan without stretching. Trim edge to 1 inch beyond pie plate and fold under. Press to form a rim and flute.

## PARTIALLY BAKED PIE SHELL

Preheat oven to 425°F. Freeze pie shell until firm, about 15 minutes. Line with foil and fill halfway with dried beans or rice. Bake in lower third of oven 12 minutes, or until edge is set and begins to brown. Remove foil and beans and bake 6 to 10 minutes longer, until crust is set and beginning to turn golden brown. As it bakes, check to see if pastry bubbles up and prick with a fork. Transfer to a wire rack to let cool completely before filling.

## FULLY BAKED PIE SHELL

Preheat oven to 425°F. Prick bottom and sides of pie shell with a fork. Freeze until firm, about 15 minutes. Line with foil, covering edge. Fill halfway with beans or rice. Bake in lower third of oven 12 minutes, or until edge is set and begins to brown lightly. Remove foil and dried beans and bake 12 to 15 minutes longer, pricking with fork if pastry bubbles up, or until bottom and sides are golden brown and fully baked. Transfer to a wire rack and let cool completely before filling.

---

## 324 DOUBLE CRUST PASTRY

*Prep: 15 minutes    Chill: 1 hour*
*Makes: 1 (9- to 10-inch) double crust pie*

2¼ cups flour
1½ teaspoons sugar
¾ teaspoon salt
1 stick (4 ounces) cold
    unsalted butter, cut into
    small pieces
⅓ cup solid vegetable
    shortening
5 to 6 tablespoons ice water

1. In a food processor, combine flour, sugar, and salt. Process until blended. Add butter and shortening. Using quick pulses, pulse 12 to 14 times, or until texture of meal with some very small pieces of butter about size of half a split pea. Turn into a large bowl.

2. Drizzle in ice water 1 tablespoon at a time, tossing with a fork, adding enough water until dough begins to clump together. Gather into 2 balls, one slightly larger than the other. Press each into a ½-inch-thick disk. Wrap in plastic wrap and refrigerate 1 hour or overnight.

# 325  CLASSIC APPLE PIE
*Prep: 20 minutes    Cook: 60 to 65 minutes    Serves: 8*

For best flavor and texture, use a combination of tart baking apples, such as Granny Smith, Northern Spy, Rhode Island Greening, or Newtown Pippin.

**Double Crust Pastry
  (page 231)**
3 **pounds tart baking apples,
  peeled and cored**
2 **tablespoons lemon juice**
¾ **cup sugar**

3 **tablespoons flour**
1 **teaspoon cinnamon**
¼ **teaspoon grated nutmeg**
2 **tablespoons butter,
  cut into small pieces**

**1.** Preheat oven to 425°F. Place a baking sheet on bottom of oven or lowest rack to catch drips. On a lightly floured surface, roll out larger pastry disk to a 13-inch circle. Drape over rolling pin and ease into a 9-inch ovenproof glass pie plate. Press pastry gently against bottom and sides; refrigerate.

**2.** Cut apples into ¾-inch-thick slices. Place in a large bowl. Toss with lemon juice. In a small bowl, combine sugar, flour, cinnamon, and nutmeg. Stir until combined. Add to apples. Toss well until evenly coated with all of sugar mixture.

**3.** Roll out remaining pastry disk to a 12-inch circle. Stir apples and turn into pie shell. Dot with butter. Fold pastry circle in half and place over filling. Unfold and trim edges to leave a 1-inch overhang. Turn excess under and press to form a rim. Crimp rim. Cut 3 (1-inch) slits in center of top pastry.

**4.** Bake pie in lower third of oven 15 minutes. Reduce oven temperature to 375°F. Bake 45 to 50 minutes, or until filling bubbles and crust is browned. Cover edge with foil last 10 minutes if browning too quickly. Place pie on a wire rack and let cool. Serve barely warm or at room temperature.

# 326  LEMON CHESS PIE
*Prep: 10 minutes    Cook: 40 to 45 minutes    Serves: 8*

Chess pie is the Southern version of custard pie, and the name is thought to have come from the word *cheese*. It can be flavored with brown sugar or chocolate, but lemon is a favorite.

1¼ **cups sugar**
1 **tablespoon yellow cornmeal**
1 **tablespoon flour**
¼ **teaspoon salt**
2 **whole eggs**
4 **egg yolks**

4 **tablespoons butter, melted**
¼ **cup buttermilk**
¼ **cup fresh lemon juice**
2 **teaspoons grated lemon zest**
1 **(9-inch) Partially Baked Pie
  Shell (page 231)**

**1.** Preheat oven to 350°F. In a large bowl, whisk together sugar, cornmeal, flour, and salt until combined. Whisk in whole eggs and egg yolks until well blended. Beat in butter, buttermilk, lemon juice, and lemon zest. Pour into pie shell.

**2.** Bake 40 to 45 minutes, or until top is lightly browned and filling is set but still slightly jiggly in center. Let cool completely on a wire rack.

---

## 327    DUTCH APPLE PIE
*Prep: 20 minutes    Cook: 60 to 65 minutes    Serves: 10*

**Single Crust Pastry**
    **(page 230)**
2¼  **pounds Granny Smith**
    **apples (about 6), peeled**
    **and cored**
1¼  **pounds Golden Delicious**
    **apples (about 3 ), peeled**
    **and cored**
2  **teaspoons fresh lemon juice**

¾  **cup granulated sugar**
3  **tablespoons flour**
¾  **teaspoon cinnamon**
2  **tablespoons butter, cut up**
⅓  **cup heavy cream**
2  **tablespoons apple butter**
    **Nut Crumb Topping**
    **(recipe follows)**

**1.** On a floured surface with a floured rolling pin, roll out pastry to a 14-inch circle. Drape over rolling pin and place in a 10-inch ovenproof glass pie plate. Ease against sides and bottom of pie plate. Trim pastry to leave ¾-inch overhanging edge. Turn edges under to make a rim and flute. Refrigerate while making filling.

**2.** Preheat oven to 400°F. Cut apples into ½-inch-thick slices and place in a large bowl. Toss with lemon juice. In a small bowl, combine granulated sugar, flour, and cinnamon. Stir to mix. Add to apples and toss well to coat. Turn apples into pie shell. Dot with butter.

**3.** Place pie with a piece of foil underneath to catch drips on bottom oven rack. Bake 30 minutes. In a measuring cup, mix cream with apple butter until smooth. Remove pie from oven. Drizzle cream mixture over apples. Crumble topping evenly over apples.

**4.** Reduce oven temperature to 350°F. Cover edge of crust with foil. Bake 30 to 35 minutes, or until bubbly and top is browned. Place pie on a wire rack and let cool. Serve warm or at room temperature.

### NUT CRUMB TOPPING
*Makes: 1½ cups*

½  **cup flour**
½  **cup packed brown sugar**
4  **tablespoons butter, cut up**

1  **teaspoon cinnamon**
⅓  **cup chopped walnuts**
⅓  **cup chopped pecans**

In a medium bowl, combine flour, sugar, butter, and cinnamon. Mix with fingers until crumbly. Stir in walnuts and pecans.

## 328 SOUR CHERRY PIE

*Prep: 30 minutes    Cook: 1 hour 5 to 10 minutes    Serves: 8*

5  cups pitted sour cherries
1  cup Bing cherries, halved
   and pitted
1  cup plus 1 tablespoon sugar
3  tablespoons cornstarch
1  teaspoon grated lemon zest

Double Crust Pastry
   (page 231)
2  tablespoons butter, cut into
   small pieces
1  egg

**1.** Preheat oven to 425°F. Butter a 9-inch ovenproof glass pie plate. Place sour cherries and Bing cherries in a large bowl. In a small bowl, combine 1 cup sugar, cornstarch, and lemon zest. Stir until well blended. Add to cherries and toss gently.

**2.** On a lightly floured surface with a floured rolling pin, roll larger pastry disk to a 13-inch circle. Drape over rolling pin and place in pie plate. Ease dough against sides and bottom without stretching. Trim edge, leaving ¾ inch hanging over rim. Roll remaining pie disk to an 11-inch circle. Cut into ¾-inch-wide strips with a fluted pastry cutter or a small knife. Stir cherries and turn into piecrust. Dot with butter. Lay half of strips over cherries side by side about ¾ inch apart. Lay remaining strips over crosswise. Trim off excess dough strips hanging over edge. Fold overhanging bottom crust up onto rim and press to make a smooth border. Crimp or flute border.

**3.** In a small bowl, beat egg with 1 teaspoon water. Brush glaze lightly over lattice but not rim. Sprinkle lattice with remaining tablespoon sugar. Cover rim of pie with foil and place on bottom oven rack with a sheet of foil underneath to catch drips.

**4.** Bake 15 minutes. Reduce oven temperature to 375°F and bake 20 minutes. Remove foil on rim and bake 30 to 35 minutes, or until crust is browned and filling is bubbly. Remove to a wire rack and let cool completely.

## 329 BANANA-COCONUT CREAM PIE

*Prep: 20 minutes    Cook: 9 to 11 minutes    Chill: 4 hours 15 minutes
Serves: 8*

¾  cup flaked coconut
2¾  cups milk
½  cup plus 2 tablespoons
   sugar
¼  cup cornstarch
1  tablespoon flour
⅛  teaspoon salt
4  egg yolks

2  tablespoons butter
2  teaspoons vanilla extract
3  medium bananas
1  cup heavy cream
2  teaspoons dark rum
1  (9-inch) Fully Baked Pie
   Shell (page 231)

**1.** Preheat oven to 350°F. Spread ½ cup coconut on a cookie sheet. Bake 5 to 6 minutes, stirring occasionally, until golden brown. Set aside.

**2.** In a small saucepan, heat 2 cups milk over medium heat. In a medium saucepan, whisk together ½ cup sugar, cornstarch, flour, and salt. Whisk in ¾ cup cold milk. Whisk in egg yolks. Gradually whisk in hot milk. Cook over medium heat, whisking gently, until mixture comes to a boil, 2 to 3 minutes. Reduce heat to low and simmer, whisking constantly, 2 minutes. Remove from heat. Add butter and vanilla, stirring until butter melts. Let filling cool 15 minutes, stirring gently a few times. Cover and refrigerate 15 minutes.

**3.** Sprinkle half of toasted coconut over pie shell. Thinly slice 2 bananas and arrange evenly over coconut. Sprinkle with remaining toasted coconut. Pour filling into shell. Cover and refrigerate pie until cold, about 4 hours.

**4.** Just before serving, in a medium bowl with electric mixer on high speed, beat cream with remaining 2 tablespoons sugar and rum until soft peaks form. Fold in ¼ cup untoasted coconut. Spread over filling. Slice remaining banana and garnish top of pie.

# 330    LEMON MERINGUE PIE
*Prep: 25 minutes    Cook: 19 to 21 minutes    Serves: 8*

Fresh lemon juice and lemon zest—the thin yellow part of the peel—make this American classic one of the most refreshing sweets ever.

| | |
|---|---|
| 1¾  **cups sugar** | 3  **tablespoons butter** |
| ⅓  **cup cornstarch** | 4  **egg whites** |
| ⅛  **teaspoon salt** | ¼  **teaspoon cream of tartar** |
| 5  **egg yolks** | 1  **(9-inch) Fully Baked Pie** |
| ½  **cup fresh lemon juice** |    **Shell (page 231)** |
| 2  **teaspoons grated lemon zest** | |

**1.** Preheat oven to 325°F. In a medium saucepan, whisk together 1¼ cups sugar, cornstarch, and salt. Gradually whisk in 1¾ cups cold water. Cook over medium heat, stirring constantly, until mixture comes to a simmer. Whisk in egg yolks, lemon juice, lemon zest, and butter. Bring to a boil, stirring constantly. Simmer 1 minute, stirring. Remove from heat and place plastic wrap directly on surface.

**2.** In a medium bowl, beat egg whites with electric mixer on low speed until foamy. Add cream of tartar. Beat on medium speed until soft peaks form. Gradually beat in remaining ½ cup sugar, 1 tablespoon at a time. Beat whites until stiff and glossy but not dry.

Pour hot lemon filling into pie shell. Dollop small teaspoonfuls of meringue around edge of pie just touching edge of crust. Using back of a teaspoon, spread meringue up to crust to seal. Spoon remaining meringue into center. Spread to completely cover filling. Swirl with back of spoon.

Bake 18 to 20 minutes, or until meringue is golden brown. Let pie cool completely on a wire rack before serving.

# 331   CHOCOLATE CREAM PIE
*Prep: 15 minutes    Cook: 21 minutes    Serves: 8 to 10*

This pie is a chocolate lover's delight. Follow directions for a fully baked pie shell, but do not prick shell. As shell bakes, prick the dough if it bubbles up.

⅓ cup sugar
1½ tablespoons cornstarch
½ cup milk
2 cups heavy cream
1¼ cups semisweet chocolate
  chips
1½ teaspoons vanilla extract

3 egg yolks
1 (9-inch) Fully Baked Pie
  Shell (page 231)
2 tablespoons powdered
  sugar
¼ teaspoon unsweetened
  cocoa powder

**1.** Preheat oven to 350°F. In a medium saucepan, whisk sugar and cornstarch until combined. Gradually whisk in milk until smooth. Stir in 1 cup cream. Refrigerate remaining cream. Place saucepan over medium heat. Cook, stirring constantly, until custard comes to a boil. Boil 1 minute, stirring constantly. Remove from heat. Add chocolate chips and vanilla; whisk until chocolate melts. In a small bowl, whisk yolks. Gradually whisk in half of chocolate mixture. Return mixture in bowl to saucepan and whisk until blended. Pour into pie shell.

**2.** Bake 20 minutes, or until just set. Pie will still be jiggly but will firm up as it cools. Place on a wire rack and let cool completely.

**3.** Shortly before serving, in a medium bowl with electric mixer on high speed, beat remaining 1 cup cream and powdered sugar until soft peaks form. Spread over chocolate filling. Sift cocoa over cream to dust lightly.

# 332   FLORIDA KEY LIME PIE
*Prep: 10 minutes    Cook: 36 to 40 minutes    Chill: 3 hours    Serves: 8*

1¼ cups graham cracker crumbs
½ cup sweetened flaked
  coconut
¼ cup plus 2 tablespoons
  slivered almonds
2 tablespoons granulated
  sugar
5 tablespoons melted butter
1 (14-ounce) can sweetened
  condensed milk

4 egg yolks
½ cup fresh lime juice
2 teaspoons grated lime zest
1 cup heavy cream
2 tablespoons powdered
  sugar
1 teaspoon dark rum

**1.** Preheat oven to 350°F. In a food processor, combine cracker crumbs, ¼ cup coconut, and ¼ cup almonds. Process until almonds are finely chopped. Add granulated sugar and butter and process until combined. Press into bottom and sides of a 9-inch pie plate.

**2.** Bake 12 to 15 minutes, or until golden brown. Let cool on a wire rack. Place remaining 2 tablespoons almonds on a baking sheet. Bake until lightly toasted, about 5 minutes. Remove and chop when cool. Place remaining coconut on baking sheet. Bake, stirring occasionally, until golden, 4 to 5 minutes. Add to almonds.

**3.** In a medium bowl, whisk together milk and egg yolks. Stir in lime juice and lime zest. Pour into crust. Bake 15 minutes, or until set. Let cool on a wire rack. Refrigerate until cold, at least 3 hours or overnight.

**4.** Just before serving, in a medium bowl with an electric mixer on high speed, beat cream with powdered sugar and rum until stiff. Pipe around edge of pie. Sprinkle with toasted almonds and coconut. Serve chilled.

---

# 333   BLACK AND BLUEBERRY PIE
*Prep: 35 minutes    Cook: 60 to 65 minutes    Serves: 8*

It's a good idea to taste fruit and berries before making a pie. If the fruit is especially tart, then up the sugar to 1 cup.

4  **cups fresh blueberries, rinsed and dried**
2  **cups fresh blackberries, rinsed and dried**
¾  **cup plus 1 tablespoon sugar**
3  **tablespoons quick-cooking tapioca**
1  **tablespoon lemon juice**
1  **teaspoon grated lemon zest**
  **Double Crust Pastry (page 231)**
2  **tablespoons butter, cut into small pieces**
1  **egg, beaten with 1 teaspoon water**

**1.** In a large bowl, combine blueberries, blackberries, ¾ cup sugar, tapioca, lemon juice, and lemon zest. Stir gently but thoroughly. Let stand 15 minutes, stirring twice.

**2.** Butter bottom of a 9-inch ovenproof glass pie plate. On a lightly floured surface with a floured rolling pin, roll out larger disk of pastry to a 13-inch circle. Drape over rolling pin and transfer to pie plate. Gently press dough against sides and bottom without stretching; refrigerate. Roll smaller disk to an 11-inch circle. Place on a small cookie sheet and refrigerate.

**3.** Preheat oven to 450°F. Adjust oven rack to lower third of oven. Remove pie shell and top crust from refrigerator. Stir berries to mix. Pour into pie shell. Dot berries with butter. Moisten edge of crust with water. Place top pastry on berries. Press edges to seal. With a sharp paring knife, trim dough using an up-and-down motion and running knife against pie plate. Press edge with a floured fork to decorate rim with tine marks and seal. Brush top but not rim lightly with egg glaze and sprinkle with remaining 1 tablespoon sugar. Make 5 (1-inch) slits in center of pie. Cover rim with foil.

**4.** Bake pie 20 minutes. Reduce heat to 375°F. Bake 15 minutes. Uncover edge, place a piece of foil underneath to catch drips, and bake 25 to 30 minutes, or until pie is well browned and juices are bubbly. Place pie on a wire rack and let cool completely before serving.

# 334    DOWN-HOME SPICED PEACH PIE

*Prep: 35 minutes    Cook: 50 to 55 minutes    Serves: 8*

Ripe juicy peaches make the best pie!

**Double Crust Pastry**
**(page 231)**
3 **pounds ripe peaches (about**
**10 medium)**
1 **tablespoon lemon juice**
1 **teaspoon grated lemon zest**
⅔ **cup granulated sugar**
¼ **cup packed light brown**
**sugar**

3 **tablespoons cornstarch**
½ **teaspoon cinnamon**
¼ **teaspoon ground ginger**
¼ **teaspoon grated nutmeg**
⅛ **teaspoon salt**
2 **tablespoons butter, cut into**
**small pieces**
1 **tablespoon milk**

**1.** Butter bottom of a 9-inch ovenproof glass pie plate. On a lightly floured surface with a floured rolling pin, roll out larger pastry disk to a 12-inch circle. Drape over rolling pin and ease into pie plate. Press gently against sides and bottom without stretching dough; refrigerate. Roll smaller disk to an 11-inch circle. Trim uneven edges. Cut with fluted pastry cutter or sharp knife into 1-inch-wide strips. Transfer strips to a small baking sheet and refrigerate.

**2.** Bring a large pot of water to a boil. Add peaches and boil 30 seconds. Remove to colander and run under cold water. Peel peaches and cut into ¾-inch-thick slices; place in a large bowl. Gently stir in lemon juice and lemon zest. Set aside 1 tablespoon granulated sugar. In a small bowl, combine remaining granulated sugar, brown sugar, cornstarch, cinnamon, ginger, nutmeg, and salt. Stir well. Add to peaches and stir gently but thoroughly.

**3.** Preheat oven to 425°F. Remove pie shell and strips from refrigerator. Stir peaches and pour into pie shell. Dot with butter. Brush edge of pie with water. Lay pastry strips diagonally on peaches side by side ¼ inch apart. Trim edge of crust to ½ inch beyond rim. Press strips and bottom crust together and fold under. Flute edge. Brush strips with milk and sprinkle with reserved 1 tablespoon sugar.

**4.** Bake pie in lower third of oven 20 minutes. Remove from oven. Cover rim with foil. Move oven rack to middle. Return pie to oven with a piece of foil on rack underneath pie to catch drips. Bake 30 to 35 minutes, or until pie is well browned and fruit is bubbly. Remove to a wire rack and let cool completely before serving.

## 335    PEANUT BUTTER PIE

*Prep: 10 minutes    Cook: 12 minutes    Freeze: 3 hours
Chill: 30 minutes    Serves: 10*

This pie is very rich, so serve it in small slices.

| | |
|---|---|
| 1½ **cups graham cracker crumbs** | 1 **cup powdered sugar** |
| 5 **tablespoons butter, melted** | 1½ **cups heavy cream** |
| 3 **tablespoons granulated** | ¾ **cup chocolate-covered** |
| **sugar** | **peanuts, coarsely** |
| 8 **ounces cream cheese, at** | **chopped** |
| **room temperature** | 1 **cup semisweet chocolate** |
| ¾ **cup creamy peanut butter** | **chips** |

**1.** Preheat oven to 350°F. In a medium bowl, combine graham cracker crumbs, melted butter, and granulated sugar. Stir well. Press into bottom and up sides of a 9-inch pie plate. Bake 12 minutes, or until crust is golden brown. Let cool completely on a wire rack.

**2.** In a large bowl, beat cream cheese, peanut butter, and powdered sugar until blended. Beat in ¼ cup cream. In a medium bowl with clean beaters, beat ¾ cup cream until stiff. Stir one fourth into peanut butter mixture. Gently fold in remaining whipped cream. Pour half of filling into pie shell and spread evenly. Sprinkle on ½ cup chocolate-covered peanuts. Pour on remaining filling, spreading evenly. Freeze pie until firm, about 3 hours.

**3.** In a small saucepan, heat remaining ½ cup cream over medium-low heat until hot. Add chocolate chips and remove from heat. Whisk until melted and smooth. Set glaze aside to cool.

**4.** Before serving, spread chocolate glaze over pie. Sprinkle with remaining peanuts. Refrigerate 30 minutes, or until glaze sets and pie softens slightly.

## 336    HOLIDAY PUMPKIN PIE

*Prep: 15 minutes    Cook: 55 minutes    Serves: 8*

| | |
|---|---|
| ¾ **cup packed brown sugar** | 2 **eggs, lightly beaten** |
| 1½ **teaspoons cinnamon** | 1 **(16-ounce) can solid-pack** |
| 1 **teaspoon ground ginger** | **pumpkin** |
| ¼ **teaspoon grated nutmeg** | 1 **(12-ounce) can evaporated** |
| ¼ **teaspoon salt** | **milk** |
| **Pinch of ground cloves** | 2 **teaspoons vanilla extract** |
| 3 **tablespoons unsulphured** | 1 **(9-inch) Partially Baked Pie** |
| **molasses** | **Shell (page 231)** |

**1.** Preheat oven to 375°F. In a large bowl, combine brown sugar, cinnamon, ginger, nutmeg, salt, and cloves. Stir well to mix, breaking up lumps of sugar. Whisk in molasses, eggs, and pumpkin. Stir in milk and vanilla until well blended. Pour filling into pie shell. Cover edge of pie with foil.

**2.** Bake 45 minutes. Uncover edge and bake 10 minutes, or until filling is just set. Let cool completely on a wire rack.

## 337  GEORGIA'S BEST PECAN PIE

*Prep: 10 minutes    Cook: 43 to 48 minutes    Serves: 8*

¾ cup packed light brown
    sugar
¾ cup light corn syrup
4 tablespoons butter
3 eggs
1½ teaspoons vanilla extract
¼ teaspoon salt

2 tablespoons bourbon or
    dark rum
½ cup chopped pecans
1½ cups pecan halves
1 (9-inch) Partially Baked Pie
    Shell (page 231)

**1.** In a medium saucepan, combine brown sugar, corn syrup, and butter. Cook over medium heat, stirring occasionally, until mixture comes to a boil, about 3 minutes. Remove from heat and let cool 15 minutes.

**2.** Preheat oven to 350°F. In a large bowl, whisk eggs. Whisk in brown sugar mixture, vanilla, salt, and bourbon until well blended. Stir in chopped pecans and pecan halves. Pour into pie shell.

**3.** Bake 40 to 45 minutes, or until pie is set but still slightly jiggly in center. Let cool completely on a wire rack before serving.

## 338  RUBY RED RASPBERRY PIE

*Prep: 35 minutes    Cook: 1 minute    Chill: 3 hours    Serves: 8*

This is a glorious pie. Make it in summer when fresh raspberries are at their peak. This pie is best served the day it is made.

½ cup granulated sugar
2 tablespoons cornstarch
1 (10-ounce) package frozen
    raspberries in light syrup,
    thawed
1 tablespoon unsalted butter

5 cups fresh raspberries
1 cup heavy cream
1 tablespoon powdered sugar
1 teaspoon vanilla extract
1 (9-inch) Fully Baked Pie
    Shell (page 231)

**1.** In a medium saucepan, combine granulated sugar and cornstarch; stir well. In a food processor, puree thawed raspberries. Strain through a sieve into saucepan with sugar mixture; discard seeds. Stir well to dissolve sugar mixture. Bring to a boil over medium heat, stirring. Boil 1 minute, stirring constantly. Remove from heat. Stir in butter until melted. Pour into a large bowl and let cool 15 minutes, stirring once.

**2.** Add 4½ cups fresh raspberries to puree and fold very gently to combine. Pour into baked pie shell and spread gently. Cover and refrigerate until cold and set, about 3 hours.

**3.** In a medium bowl, combine cream, powdered sugar, and vanilla. Beat with an electric mixer on high speed until soft peaks form. Fold in remaining ½ cup raspberries.

**4.** Before serving, garnish pie with spoonfuls of cream around edge of pie on filling. Serve chilled.

# 339    SWEET POTATO PIE WITH MAPLE PRALINE TOPPING

*Prep: 20 minutes    Cook: 1 hour 57 minutes to 2 hours 5 minutes*
*Serves: 8*

If you can find Grade B maple syrup, try it; it has more flavor than Grade A.

| | |
|---|---|
| 4  **medium sweet potatoes or yams (about 2 pounds), scrubbed** | ¼  **teaspoon grated nutmeg** |
| | ¼  **teaspoon salt** |
| | ⅛  **teaspoon ground cloves** |
| 4  **tablespoons butter** | 3  **eggs** |
| ½  **cup pecans** | 1  **cup plus 2 tablespoons half-and-half** |
| ¾  **cup packed light brown sugar** | |
| | 1  **(9-inch) Partially Baked Pie Shell (page 231)** |
| ¼  **cup granulated sugar** | |
| 1½  **teaspoons cinnamon** | 2  **tablespoons maple syrup** |
| ¼  **teaspoon ground allspice** | |

**1.** Preheat oven to 400°F. Prick sweet potatoes. Bake 1 hour, or until soft. Cut potatoes in half lengthwise and let stand until cool enough to handle. Scoop into a large bowl, add 2 tablespoons butter, and beat with an electric mixer on low speed until smooth. Let cool.

**2.** Reduce oven temperature to 350°F. Place pecans in a small baking dish and bake in oven until toasted and lightly browned, 5 to 7 minutes. Remove and chop when cool; leave oven on. In a small bowl, stir ½ cup plus 1 tablespoon brown sugar, granulated sugar, cinnamon, allspice, nutmeg, salt, and cloves. Add to sweet potatoes and stir until blended. In a small bowl, whisk eggs and 1 cup half-and-half. Whisk into sweet potatoes until well blended. Pour into pie shell.

**3.** Bake 50 to 55 minutes, or until filling is set. Remove pie to a wire rack and let cool completely.

**4.** Before serving, in a medium saucepan, combine remaining 2 tablespoons butter, 3 tablespoons brown sugar, 2 tablespoons half-and-half, and maple syrup. Bring to a boil over medium heat. Boil 2 to 3 minutes, or until slightly thickened. Remove from heat; let cool without stirring 10 minutes, or until thickened. Stir in pecans.

**5.** Spoon topping over filling around edges of crust, leaving about 4 inches in center uncovered.

# 340   FRESH COCONUT LAYER CAKE

*Prep: 45 minutes    Cook: 49 to 54 minutes    Chill: 3 hours*
*Serves: 12*

This is a wonderful Southern classic. Fresh coconut really makes a difference. It does take time to peel and grate, but if you love coconut, the flavor's worth it.

**Butter Cake batter (page 244,**
**step 2), made with**
**changes detailed in step**
**1 below**
½ **teaspoon coconut extract**

1 **large fresh coconut**
 **Seven-Minute Frosting**
 **(page 243)**
 **Lemon Filling (recipe**
 **follows)**

**1.** Preheat oven to 350°F. Grease 3 (9-inch) round cake pans. Line bottoms with wax paper. Grease paper and dust pans with flour, tapping out excess. Prepare butter cake batter, but reduce vanilla to 1 teaspoon and add coconut extract along with vanilla. Divide batter among pans, spreading evenly.

**2.** Bake 25 to 30 minutes, or until a toothpick inserted in center comes out clean. Let layers cool in pans on wire racks 10 minutes. Run knife around sides and invert onto racks to let cool completely.

**3.** With a hammer, drive a nail through 3 eyes in coconut. Drain off liquid. Place coconut on a baking sheet and bake 20 minutes. Wrap in a kitchen towel and hit with a hammer to crack and break into pieces. Remove shell. Remove brown skin with a paring knife. Finely grate coconut in a food processor with fine shredding disk. Reserve 3 cups; use remainder for another use.

**4.** Just before assembling cake, make frosting. Place 1 cake layer on a serving plate bottom side up. Spread with half of lemon filling. Top with another cake layer, bottom side up. Spread with remaining lemon filling. Top with third cake layer, rounded side up. Spread sides and then top with frosting. Gently press grated coconut onto sides and top of cake while frosting is soft.

## LEMON FILLING

*Makes: 1½ cups*

¾ **cup sugar**
3 **tablespoons cornstarch**
⅛ **teaspoon salt**
2 **egg yolks**

¼ **cup fresh lemon juice**
1 **teaspoon grated lemon zest**
1 **teaspoon grated orange zest**
3 **tablespoons unsalted butter**

**1.** In a medium saucepan, whisk sugar, cornstarch, and salt. Stir in 1 cup cold water until smooth. Cook over medium heat, stirring constantly, until mixture comes to a boil. Cook 1 minute, stirring constantly. Remove from heat.

**2.** In a small bowl, whisk yolks and lemon juice. Gradually whisk in half of hot cornstarch mixture. Whisk back into pan. Reduce heat to medium-low and cook, stirring constantly, 3 minutes. Remove from heat.

**3.** Add lemon zest, orange zest, and butter, stirring until butter melts. Pour into a small bowl. Let cool to room temperature, stirring a few times. Place a piece of plastic wrap directly on surface and refrigerate until cold, at least 3 hours.

---

# 341   SEVEN-MINUTE FROSTING
*Prep: 5 minutes    Cook: 7 minutes    Makes: about 5 cups*

|   |   |
|---|---|
| 3  **egg whites** | 2  **teaspoons light corn syrup** |
| 1½  **cups sugar** | 1  **teaspoon vanilla extract** |
| ¼  **teaspoon cream of tartar** | ¼  **teaspoon coconut extract** |

**1.** In top of a double boiler, combine egg whites, sugar, cream of tartar, corn syrup, and ⅓ cup cold water. Place over boiling water. Beat with an electric hand mixer on high speed 7 minutes, or until soft peaks form.

**2.** Remove top from heat and add vanilla and coconut extract. Beat until frosting is cool and thick, 4 to 5 minutes. Use immediately to frost cake.

---

# 342   FOURTH OF JULY FLAG CAKE
*Prep: 40 minutes    Cook: 30 to 35 minutes    Serves: 12*

|   |   |
|---|---|
| **Butter Cake batter, prepared as described in step 2 on page 244** | 1  **pint strawberries, sliced** |
| | 1  **cup blueberries** |
| | 2  **cups raspberries** |
| **Cream Cheese Frosting (page 245), made with lemon zest and lemon juice** | |

**1.** Preheat oven to 350°F. Grease a 13 x 9 x 2-inch baking pan; line bottom with wax paper. Grease paper and dust pan with flour; tap out excess. Pour cake batter into pan and spread evenly.

**2.** Bake 30 to 35 minutes, or until a toothpick inserted in center comes out clean. Place on a wire rack and let cool 10 minutes. Invert cake onto a wire rack. Carefully turn over to cool top side up.

**3.** With a serrated bread knife, cut cake in half horizontally. Remove top carefully with 2 large spatulas. Place bottom cut side up on a serving platter. Spread ½ cup frosting over bottom layer. Top with sliced strawberries in a single layer. Spread ½ cup frosting over berries. Replace cake top cut side down. Frost sides and top of cake with remaining frosting.

**4.** Arrange blueberries in a rectangle in upper left hand corner of cake. Arrange raspberries in 6 rows to resemble stripes of a flag. Refrigerate cake until serving.

# 343   BUTTER CAKE WITH GLOSSY CHOCOLATE FROSTING

*Prep: 15 minutes    Cook: 25 to 30 minutes    Serves: 12*

There is nothing like a homemade layer cake. This is a variation of the classic 1-2-3-4 cake, which has 1 cup butter, 2 cups sugar, 3 cups flour, and 4 eggs. I happen to like it less sweet, hence the change in the amount of sugar.

| | |
|---|---|
| 3  cups sifted cake flour | 4  eggs, at room temperature |
| 1  tablespoon baking powder | 2  teaspoons vanilla extract |
| ½  teaspoon salt | 1¼  cups milk, at room |
| 2  sticks (8 ounces) unsalted | temperature |
|    butter, softened | Glossy Chocolate Frosting |
| 1¾  cups sugar | (recipe follows) |

**1.** Preheat oven to 350°F. Grease 2 (9-inch) round cake pans. Line bottoms with wax paper. Grease paper and dust pans with flour; tap out excess.

**2.** In a small bowl, stir together flour, baking powder, and salt. In a large bowl, beat butter with an electric mixer on medium speed until fluffy. Gradually beat in sugar. Beat 2 minutes until fluffy. Beat in eggs 1 at a time, beating well after adding each. Beat in vanilla. On low speed, beat in flour mixture in 3 additions, alternating with the milk in 2 additions until just blended. Divide batter between pans, spreading it evenly.

**3.** Bake 25 to 30 minutes, or until a toothpick inserted in centers comes out clean. Let cool on a wire rack 10 minutes. Run knife around sides of pans and invert onto racks. Remove wax paper. Turn layers to cool upright. Let cool completely before frosting.

# 344   GLOSSY CHOCOLATE FROSTING

*Prep: 5 minutes    Cook: 5 minutes    Makes: 3 cups*

| | |
|---|---|
| 3  tablespoons unsweetened | 1  stick (4 ounces) unsalted |
|    cocoa powder | butter |
| 1⅓  cups sugar | 1  teaspoon vanilla extract |
| 1½  cups heavy cream | |
| 5  (1-ounce) squares | |
|    unsweetened chocolate, | |
|    chopped | |

**1.** In a medium saucepan, whisk cocoa and sugar until blended. Add cream. Bring to a boil over medium heat, stirring occasionally. Reduce heat to medium-low and boil 5 minutes. Remove from heat. Add chocolate and butter and whisk until chocolate is melted. Stir in vanilla.

**2.** Place saucepan in a bowl filled with ice water. Stir frequently until cool and thick enough to spread but still glossy.

# 345 CARROT CAKE

*Prep: 15 minutes    Cook: 25 to 30 minutes    Serves: 12*

2 cups flour
2½ teaspoons cinnamon
2 teaspoons baking powder
1 teaspoon baking soda
¾ teaspoon salt
1 cup packed light brown
  sugar
¾ cup granulated sugar
1¼ cups vegetable oil
4 eggs, at room temperature

2 teaspoons vanilla extract
4 cups shredded peeled
  carrots (1 pound)
1 cup chopped pecans
½ cup currants
  Cream Cheese Frosting
  (recipe follows,
  made with orange zest
  and juice)
12 pecan halves

**1.** Preheat oven to 350°F. Grease 3 (9-inch) round cake pans. Line bottoms with wax paper. Grease paper. Dust pans with flour; tap out excess.

**2.** In a small bowl, combine flour, cinnamon, baking powder, baking soda, and salt. Stir well. In a large bowl, combine brown sugar, granulated sugar, oil, eggs, and vanilla. Beat with an electric mixer on medium speed 1 minute. On low speed, beat in flour mixture until blended. Stir in carrots, chopped pecans, and currants. Divide batter among pans, spreading evenly.

**3.** Bake 25 to 30 minutes, or until a toothpick inserted in centers comes out clean. Let cakes cool in pans on wire racks 10 minutes. Run knife around sides and invert onto racks. Carefully turn layers right side up and let cool completely.

**4.** Remove wax paper from layers. Fill with cream cheese frosting, using ¾ cup between layers. Frost top and sides with remaining frosting. Decorate top with pecan halves.

# 346 CREAM CHEESE FROSTING

*Prep: 5 minutes    Cook: none    Makes: 3½ cups*

2 (8-ounce) packages cream
  cheese, at room
  temperature
1 stick (4 ounces) unsalted
  butter, softened

2¼ cups powdered sugar, sifted
1 teaspoon grated lemon or
  orange zest
1 teaspoon lemon or orange
  juice

In a large bowl, beat cream cheese and butter with an electric mixer on medium speed until fluffy. Gradually beat in powdered sugar until light and fluffy. Beat in lemon or orange zest and lemon or orange juice. Refrigerate frosting 10 minutes if too soft to spread.

# 347   BOSTON CREAM PIE

*Prep: 20 minutes    Cook: 32 to 37 minutes    Chill: 2 hours*
*Serves: 8 to 10*

This classic American dessert is not a pie at all, but a cake—filled with vanilla custard and topped with chocolate icing.

| | |
|---|---|
| 1   cup plus 2 tablespoons cake flour | 3   tablespoons melted butter |
| 1½   teaspoons baking powder | 1   teaspoon vanilla extract |
| ¼   teaspoon salt | Vanilla Custard Filling (recipe follows) |
| 3   eggs, at room temperature | Chocolate Glaze |
| ¾   cup sugar | (recipe follows) |

**1.** Preheat oven to 350°F. Grease 2 (9-inch) round cake pans. Line bottoms with wax paper. Grease paper and dust pans with flour; tap out excess.

**2.** Sift flour, baking powder, and salt into a small bowl. In a medium bowl with an electric mixer on high speed, beat eggs 3 to 4 minutes until thickened. Gradually beat in sugar until fluffy, about 3 minutes. On low speed, beat in butter, vanilla, and ⅓ cup hot water just until blended. Add dry ingredients and beat on low speed just until blended. Pour into prepared pans, dividing batter evenly.

**3.** Bake 25 to 30 minutes, or until a toothpick inserted in centers comes out clean. Let cool completely in pans on a wire rack.

**4.** Run a knife around edge of layers. Turn out onto a wire rack. Remove wax paper. Place 1 layer bottom side up on a serving plate. Stir vanilla filling and spread over cake up to ½ inch from edge. Top with a second cake layer top side up. Cover top with glaze. Use a serrated knife to cut. Refrigerate leftovers.

## VANILLA CUSTARD FILLING

*Makes: 1⅔ cups*

| | |
|---|---|
| ⅓   cup sugar | 3   egg yolks |
| 2   tablespoons cornstarch | 1½   teaspoons vanilla extract |
| ⅛   teaspoon salt | 1   tablespoon butter |
| 1¼   cups milk | |

**1.** In a medium saucepan, combine sugar, cornstarch, and salt. Whisk until blended. Gradually whisk in milk. Place over medium-low heat. Cook, stirring constantly, until mixture comes to a boil, about 3 minutes. Boil 1 minute, stirring constantly. Remove from heat.

**2.** In a small bowl, whisk egg yolks. Gradually whisk in half of milk mixture. Gradually whisk yolk mixture back into saucepan. Return pan to medium-low heat. Bring to a simmer and cook, stirring constantly, 2 minutes. Remove from heat.

3. Add vanilla and butter. Stir until butter melts. Cover surface with plastic wrap, poke a few holes in wrap with a sharp knife, and let cool 15 minutes. Refrigerate until cold, at least 2 hours.

## CHOCOLATE GLAZE
*Makes: ⅔ cup*

¼ cup heavy cream
1 teaspoon instant coffee
   powder
4 ounces semisweet
   chocolate, finely chopped

1 teaspoon light corn syrup
2 tablespoons powdered
   sugar, sifted

In a small saucepan, bring cream and coffee powder to a boil, about 1 minute. Remove from heat, add chocolate, and whisk until chocolate melts. Stir in corn syrup and powdered sugar. Let cool until slightly thickened.

---

# 348    FRESH STRAWBERRY PIE
*Prep: 35 minutes    Cook: 1 minute    Stand: 30 minutes*
*Chill: 4 hours    Serves: 8*

Use ripe, red strawberries for this pie. Wash strawberries before removing the stems, then lay them on paper towels and gently pat dry. This way the berries don't become waterlogged.

3 pints fresh strawberries
¾ cup sugar
2 tablespoons cornstarch
1 tablespoon lemon juice
1 tablespoon unsalted butter

8 drops of red food coloring
   (optional)
1¼ cups heavy cream
1 (9-inch) Fully Baked Pie
   Shell (page 231)

1. Rinse and dry strawberries. Set aside 1 perfect berry for garnish. Stem remaining berries. Measure 1½ cups strawberries and place in a medium saucepan. Mash well with a potato masher. In a small bowl, combine sugar and cornstarch; stir well. Add to strawberries. Stir until blended. Stir in lemon juice and 3 tablespoons cold water. Cook over medium heat, stirring, until mixture thickens and comes to a boil. Boil 1 minute, stirring constantly. Remove from heat. Stir in butter and food coloring, if desired. Pour into a medium bowl and let cool 30 minutes, stirring once. Measure 3 tablespoons strawberry filling into a medium bowl and set aside.

2. Cut remaining strawberries in half. Fill baked pie shell with half of berries, cut sides up. Evenly spoon half of filling over berries. Cover with remaining strawberries, cut sides down. Spoon on remaining filling. Cover loosely and refrigerate until set, about 3 hours.

3. One hour before serving, add cream to reserved filling. Beat with electric mixer on high speed just until stiff; do not overbeat. Uncover pie and spoon strawberry cream over filling up to 1 inch from edge. Refrigerate 1 hour. Garnish with strawberry. Serve chilled.

# 349  GRANDMA'S GINGERBREAD
*Prep: 10 minutes    Cook: 35 to 40 minutes    Serves: 8*

Serve this moist, spicy cake while just warm with lightly sweetened whipped cream. Measure the water that is stirred into the batter after it comes to a boil.

| | |
|---|---|
| 2  cups flour | ½  cup sugar |
| 2  teaspoons cinnamon | 2  eggs |
| 2  teaspoons ground ginger | ¾  cup unsulphured molasses |
| 2  teaspoons baking soda | ½  cup buttermilk |
| ¾  teaspoon grated nutmeg | ½  cup boiling water |
| ½  teaspoon ground cloves | |
| 1  stick (4 ounces) butter, softened | |

**1.** Preheat oven to 350°F. In a medium bowl, mix together flour, cinnamon, ginger, baking soda, nutmeg, and cloves.

**2.** In a large bowl, beat butter and sugar with an electric mixer on medium speed until fluffy, about 1 minute. Beat in eggs 1 at a time, beating well after adding each. Beat in molasses and buttermilk. Beat in flour mixture just until blended. Stir in boiling water just until blended. Pour into a greased 9-inch square baking pan.

**3.** Bake 35 to 40 minutes, or until a toothpick inserted in center comes out clean. Place pan on a wire rack and let cool.

# 350  DEVIL'S FOOD CAKE WITH FLUFFY CHOCOLATE FROSTING
*Prep: 15 minutes    Stand: 45 minutes    Cook: 30 to 35 minutes*
*Serves: 10 to 12*

Do not use Dutch-process cocoa in this recipe; it will not produce the same results.

| | |
|---|---|
| ¾  cup unsweetened cocoa powder | 2  sticks (8 ounces) unsalted butter, softened |
| 1¼  cups boiling water | 1¾  cups sugar |
| 2¼  cups cake flour | 3  eggs, at room temperature |
| 1  teaspoon baking soda | 2  teaspoons vanilla extract |
| ½  teaspoon baking powder | Fluffy Chocolate Frosting (recipe follows) |
| ½  teaspoon salt | |

**1.** In a medium bowl, whisk together cocoa powder and boiling water until smooth. Set aside at room temperature, whisking occasionally, until cool, about 45 minutes.

**2.** Preheat oven to 350°F. Grease 2 (9-inch) round cake pans. Line bottoms with wax paper. Grease paper and dust pans with flour; tap out excess. Sift flour, baking soda, baking powder, and salt into a medium bowl; set aside.

**3.** In a large bowl, beat butter with an electric mixer on medium speed until fluffy, about 1 minute. Gradually beat in sugar. Beat 2 minutes. Beat in eggs 1 at a time, beating well after each. Mix in vanilla.

**4.** With mixer on low speed, beat in dry ingredients in thirds, alternately with cocoa mixture, beginning and ending with dry ingredients; beat until blended. Turn into pans; spread evenly.

**5.** Bake 30 to 35 minutes, or until a toothpick inserted in centers comes out clean. Let cakes cool in pans on wire racks 10 minutes. Run a knife around sides and invert onto racks. Peel off wax paper. Turn again to cool top sides up. Let cool completely before filling and frosting with fluffy chocolate frosting.

---

# 351    FLUFFY CHOCOLATE FROSTING
*Prep: 10 minutes    Cook: 1 minute    Makes: 3 cups*

| | |
|---|---|
| 1½  cups sugar | 4  tablespoons unsalted butter |
| 1  tablespoon flour | 4  (1-ounce) squares |
| 3  egg yolks |     unsweetened chocolate, |
| ¾  cup milk |     chopped |
|    Pinch of salt | 1  teaspoon vanilla extract |

**1.** In a medium saucepan, whisk sugar and flour until blended. In a small bowl, whisk egg yolks. Gradually whisk in milk. Whisk milk mixture into saucepan. Add salt and butter. Cook over medium heat, stirring constantly, until mixture comes to a boil. Reduce heat to low and boil 1 minute, stirring. Remove from heat. Add chocolate and let stand 5 minutes. Whisk until chocolate is melted and mixture is smooth. Stir in vanilla. Let cool 30 minutes.

**2.** Place pot in a large bowl of ice water. Stir until icing is cool and begins to thicken, about 5 minutes. Beat with an electric mixer on high speed until light and fluffy and thick enough to spread. Use to fill and frost Devil's Food Cake (page 248).

## 352    APPLESAUCE RAISIN SPICE CAKE
*Prep: 10 minutes    Cook: 35 to 40 minutes    Serves: 8*

Moist and spicy, this is a perfect cake for snacking or packing in lunch boxes. I bet this cake came about when someone had an abundance of homemade applesauce to use up.

2 cups flour
2 teaspoons cinnamon
1½ teaspoons baking soda
½ teaspoon grated nutmeg
½ teaspoon ground ginger
¼ teaspoon salt
1 stick (4 ounces) butter, softened

1¼ cups packed light brown sugar
1½ cups unsweetened applesauce
2 eggs
1 cup golden raisins
1 cup chopped walnuts
Powdered sugar (optional)

**1.** Preheat oven to 350°F. Grease a 13 x 9-inch baking pan. In a medium bowl, combine flour, cinnamon, baking soda, nutmeg, ginger, and salt. Stir well.

**2.** In a large bowl, combine butter and brown sugar. With electric mixer on medium speed, beat 2 minutes until fluffy. Beat in applesauce and then eggs. Add half of flour mixture and beat until blended. Beat in remaining flour mixture. Stir in raisins and ½ cup chopped walnuts. Pour batter into pan and spread evenly. Sprinkle remaining ½ cup walnuts over batter.

**3.** Bake 35 to 40 minutes, or until a toothpick inserted in center comes out clean. Place on a wire rack to cool. Dust with powdered sugar before serving, if desired.

## 353    POUND CAKE
*Prep: 10 minutes    Cook: 1 hour 15 to 20 minutes    Serves: 12 to 16*

3 sticks ( 12 ounces) unsalted butter, softened
1 (1-pound) box powdered sugar
6 eggs, at room temperature

1 tablespoons grated lemon zest
2 teaspoons vanilla extract
¼ teaspoon salt
3 cups sifted flour

**1.** Preheat oven to 325°F. Grease and flour a 10-inch tube pan.

**2.** In a large bowl, beat butter with electric mixer on medium speed until fluffy. Gradually beat in sugar on low speed. Beat in eggs 1 at a time, beating well after adding each. Beat in lemon zest, vanilla, and salt. Fold in flour, half at a time, until blended. Turn batter into pan, spreading evenly.

**3.** Bake 1 hour 15 to 20 minutes, or until a toothpick inserted in center comes out clean. Let cool completely on a wire rack. To unmold, run knife around sides and bottom.

# 354 CHOCOLATE-COFFEE MARBLED ANGEL FOOD CAKE

*Prep: 10 minutes    Cook: 40 to 45 minutes    Serves: 12*

1½ cups sugar
1¼ cups cake flour
½ teaspoon salt
16 large egg whites, at
    room temperature
    (about 2 cups)
1 teaspoon cream of tartar

2 teaspoons lemon juice
2 teaspoons vanilla extract
½ teaspoon almond extract
½ ounce unsweetened
    chocolate, finely grated
1½ teaspoons instant espresso
    powder

**1.** Preheat oven to 350°F. In a food processor, process sugar 1 minute. Sift ½ cup sugar, flour, and salt onto a piece of wax paper. Repeat sifting 2 more times.

**2.** In a large bowl, beat egg whites with an electric mixer on low speed until foamy. Add cream of tartar, lemon juice, vanilla, and almond extract. Beat on medium-high speed until soft peaks form, about 2 minutes. Gradually beat in remaining 1 cup sugar, 2 tablespoons at a time, with electric mixer on medium speed. Beat 1 minute after each addition of sugar. Once all sugar has been added, beat 1 minute, or until whites form stiff peaks. Sift one fourth of flour mixture over egg whites. Fold gently into whites until almost blended. Fold in remaining flour mixture one fourth at a time, folding last addition in just until blended. Remove one third of batter to a large bowl and gently fold in chocolate and coffee powder just until combined; do not overfold.

**3.** Place large heaping spoonfuls of both batters into an ungreased 10-inch tube pan with a removable bottom, alternating kinds in a random pattern. Run a long knife through batter once and smooth top lightly.

**4.** Bake 40 to 45 minutes, or until cake begins to pull away from sides and springs back when pressed lightly with finger. Place pan upside down if pan has tabs or hang upside down on a bottle or funnel. Let cool completely.

**5.** To unmold cake, run a long sharp knife around sides and center of pan and remove. Run knife around bottom and turn cake out. Turn top side up to serve.

# 355    HOT FUDGE PUDDING CAKE
*Prep: 10 minutes    Cook: 30 to 35 minutes    Serves: 6*

This is the cake that magically forms its own sauce on the bottom as it bakes. Serve it warm with ice cream.

1  cup flour
¾  cup unsweetened cocoa
    powder, preferably
    Dutch-process
⅔  cup granulated sugar
2  teaspoons baking powder
¼  teaspoon salt
¾  cup milk
3  tablespoons butter, melted

1  teaspoon vanilla extract
½  cup semisweet chocolate
    chips
¼  cup chopped walnuts
¾  cup packed light brown
    sugar
2  teaspoons instant coffee
    powder
Vanilla ice cream

**1.** Preheat oven to 350°F. In a medium bowl, mix together flour, 6 tablespoons cocoa powder, granulated sugar, baking powder, and salt. Stir in milk, butter, and vanilla until blended. Turn into a greased 8-inch square baking pan, spreading batter evenly. Sprinkle chocolate chips and walnuts over batter.

**2.** In a medium saucepan, combine remaining cocoa powder, brown sugar, coffee powder, and 1¼ cups water. Stir and bring to a boil. Pour evenly over cake batter. Do not stir. Carefully transfer to oven.

**3.** Bake 30 to 35 minutes, or until a toothpick inserted in cake comes out clean. Remove to a wire rack and let cool. Serve warm or at room temperature, with a scoop of vanilla ice cream on top.

# 356    GERMAN SWEET CHOCOLATE CAKE
*Prep: 15 minutes    Cook: 30 to 35 minutes    Serves: 12*

½  cup boiling water
6  ounces sweet baking
    chocolate, chopped
2  sticks (8 ounces) butter,
    at room temperature
1½  cups sugar
4  eggs, separated

2½  cups cake flour
1  teaspoon baking soda
½  teaspoon salt
1  cup buttermilk
Coconut Pecan Frosting
    (recipe follows)

**1.** Preheat oven to 350°F. Grease and flour 3 (9-inch) round cake pans. Line bottoms with wax paper. Grease paper and dust pans with flour; tap out excess. In a medium bowl, pour boiling water over chocolate. Let stand 5 minutes. Whisk until chocolate is melted and smooth. Set aside to cool.

**2.** In a large bowl with an electric mixer on medium speed, beat butter until fluffy. Gradually beat in sugar. Beat 2 minutes. Beat in egg yolks 1 at a time. Beat in melted chocolate until blended. In a medium bowl, stir flour, baking soda, and salt until well blended. Beat in flour mixture on low speed alternately with buttermilk, beginning and ending with flour, just until blended.

**3.** In a medium bowl with clean beaters, beat egg whites on high speed until stiff but not dry. Fold whites into batter until blended. Turn batter into pans, dividing evenly. Spread batter until smooth.

**4.** Bake 30 to 35 minutes, or until a toothpick inserted in centers comes out clean. Let cakes cool in pans on wire racks 10 minutes. Run knife around sides and turn out layers onto racks. Remove wax paper. Let cool completely.

**5.** Place 1 cake layer on a serving plate. Spread top with one third of frosting. Top with another layer and half of remaining frosting. Top with last layer and spread with remaining frosting.

---

## 357    COCONUT PECAN FROSTING

*Prep: 10 minutes    Cook: 12 to 14 minutes    Chill: 1 hour*
*Makes: about 3½ cups*

| | |
|---|---|
| 1 **(5-ounce) can evaporated milk** | 2 **ounces sweet baking chocolate, chopped** |
| 3 **egg yolks** | 2 **teaspoons vanilla extract** |
| ⅓ **cup granulated sugar** | 1¼ **cups flaked coconut** |
| ⅓ **cup packed light brown sugar** | 1¼ **cups chopped pecans** |
| 1 **stick (4 ounces) butter, cut into 8 pieces** | |

**1.** In a medium saucepan, whisk evaporated milk and egg yolks until blended. Add granulated sugar, brown sugar, butter, and chocolate. Cook over medium heat, stirring constantly, 12 to 14 minutes, or until mixture thickens enough to coat back of a spoon.

**2.** Remove from heat and stir in vanilla, coconut, and pecans. Turn into a medium bowl. Cover and refrigerate until cold and thick enough to spread, about 1 hour.

# 358 CLASSIC CHEESECAKE

*Prep: 10 minutes    Cook: 1 hour 25 minutes    Chill: 6 hours*
*Serves: 8 to 10*

| | |
|---|---|
| 1¼ cups graham cracker crumbs | 2½ teaspoons vanilla extract |
| 4 tablespoons butter, melted | 4 eggs, at room temperature |
| 1¼ cups plus 2 tablespoons | 1½ teaspoons grated lemon zest |
| sugar | 1½ cups sour cream |
| 3 tablespoons flour | |
| 4 (8-ounce) packages cream cheese, softened | |

**1.** Preheat oven to 325°F. In a medium bowl, combine graham cracker crumbs, butter, and ¼ cup sugar. Stir well until crumbs are evenly moistened. Press firmly into bottom of a 9-inch springform pan. Bake 15 minutes. Let cool completely on a wire rack. Line outside of pan tightly with 2 sheets of heavy-duty foil.

**2.** In a small bowl, combine 1 cup sugar and flour. Stir to mix. In a large bowl with electric mixer on medium speed, beat cream cheese until smooth. Add sugar mixture and 2 teaspoons vanilla; beat just until blended. Add eggs 1 at a time, beating on low speed just until blended. Scrape sides of bowl after adding each egg. Beat in lemon zest and ½ cup sour cream just until blended.

**3.** Pour batter into pan. Place pan in a shallow roasting pan. Place roasting pan in oven. Fill roasting pan with boiling water so water is one third of way up sides of springform pan.

**4.** Bake 1 hour, or until set but slightly jiggly. Meanwhile, in a small bowl, combine remaining 2 tablespoons sugar, ½ teaspoon vanilla extract, and 1 cup sour cream. Stir until well blended. Spoon over cheesecake by small teaspoonfuls, starting at edge and carefully and gently spreading until smooth and top is covered.

**5.** Bake 10 minutes, or until topping is set. Remove cheesecake from water bath to a wire rack. Run a thin sharp knife around edge. Let cheesecake cool completely on rack. Remove foil and refrigerate, loosely covered, at least 6 hours or overnight. Remove side of springform pan just before serving.

*Variation:*

# 359 RED, WHITE, AND BLUE CHEESECAKE

Before serving: In a small saucepan, heat ¼ cup strawberrry jelly and 2 teaspoons orange liqueur or water over low heat until melted and smooth, stirring occasionally. Arrange ½ pint sliced strawberries, ¾ cup raspberries, and ½ cup blueberries on top of cheesecake. Brush with warm glaze.

*Variation:*

# 360    CARAMEL APPLE CHEESECAKE

Before serving: Spread ½ cup jarred butterscotch-caramel topping over top of cheesecake. Core and cut ½ Granny Smith apple and ½ Red Delicious apple into ½-inch dice. Sprinkle over topping. Sprinkle with ¼ cup coarsely chopped roasted peanuts. Drizzle with 2 more tablespoons butterscotch-caramel topping.

# 361    CITRUS CHIFFON CAKE
*Prep: 15 minutes    Cook: 1 hour 10 to 15 minutes    Serves: 12*

| | |
|---|---|
| 2 **cups flour** | 2¾ **teaspoons grated lime zest** |
| 1½ **cups granulated sugar** | 2¼ **teaspoons grated lemon zest** |
| 1 **tablespoon baking powder** | 1 **teaspoon grated orange zest** |
| ¾ **teaspoon salt** | ½ **teaspoon cream of tartar** |
| ½ **cup vegetable oil** | 2 **cups powdered sugar, sifted** |
| 8 **eggs, separated** | 2 **tablespoons butter, softened** |
| ¾ **cup plus 3 tablespoons fresh orange juice** | |

**1.** Preheat oven to 325°F. In a large bowl, stir together flour, sugar, baking powder, and salt until well blended. Add oil, egg yolks, ¾ cup orange juice, 2 teaspoons lime zest, 1½ teaspoons lemon zest, and orange zest. Beat with an electric mixer on low speed until smooth.

**2.** In a large bowl with clean beaters, beat egg whites on medium speed until foamy. Add cream of tartar and beat on medium-high speed until stiff but not dry peaks form. Pour yolk mixture over whites gradually, folding just until blended. Pour batter into an ungreased 10-inch tube pan with a removable bottom.

**3.** Bake 1 hour 10 to 15 minutes, or until top springs back when lightly pressed. Invert pan if it has tabs on side or invert on a funnel or bottle. Let cool completely.

**4.** Run a sharp knife around side and center to loosen; remove pan side. Run knife around bottom. Invert cake, turn top side up, and place on a plate. In a small bowl, combine powdered sugar, butter, remaining 3 tablespoons orange juice, and ¾ teaspoon each lemon zest and lime zest. Beat with an electric mixer on medium speed until smooth. Spread glaze over top of cake, letting some run down sides. Let stand until glaze sets before serving.

# 362    OATMEAL CAKE WITH COCONUT TOPPING

*Prep: 10 minutes    Stand: 30 minutes    Cook: 34 to 41 minutes*
*Serves: 12*

I hadn't made this cake in years, and what a delight it was to try it again. It's good—well worth remembering. The coconut topping would be great on almost any cake.

1¼ cups boiling water
1 cup old-fashioned or quick-cooking oats (not instant)
1 stick (4 ounces) unsalted butter, softened
1 cup packed light brown sugar
½ cup granulated sugar
1 teaspoon vanilla extract

2 eggs
1⅓ cups flour
1 teaspoon baking soda
1 teaspoon cinnamon
½ teaspoon baking powder
½ teaspoon salt
Coconut Topping (recipe follows)

**1.** In a small heatproof bowl, pour boiling water over oats. Let stand 30 minutes until cooled.

**2.** Preheat oven to 350°F. In a large bowl, beat butter with an electric mixer on medium speed until fluffy. Add brown sugar and granulated sugar and beat 1 minute. Beat in vanilla and eggs, 1 at a time, until well blended. Beat in cooled oatmeal. In a small bowl, stir flour, baking soda, cinnamon, baking powder, and salt until blended. Beat in flour mixture on low speed. Pour batter into a greased and floured 13 x 9 x 2-inch baking pan and spread evenly.

**3.** Bake 30 to 35 minutes, or until a toothpick inserted in center comes out clean. Let cool in pan on a wire rack for about 10 minutes.

**4.** While cake cools, preheat broiler and make topping. Spoon topping evenly over cake in pan, spreading to cover completely.

**5.** Broil cake about 6 inches from heat, watching carefully until topping is bubbly and golden brown, about 4 to 6 minutes. Let cake cool in pan on rack.

## COCONUT TOPPING
*Makes: 1⅓ cups*

5 tablespoons unsalted butter, softened
¾ cup packed light brown sugar

3 tablespoons milk
¾ cup chopped walnuts or pecans
¾ cup flaked coconut

In a small saucepan, combine butter, brown sugar, milk, walnuts, and coconut. Cook over low heat, stirring occasionally, until butter melts and mixture is blended.

# 363    PINEAPPLE UPSIDE-DOWN CAKE
*Prep: 15 minutes    Cook: 40 to 45 minutes    Serves: 8*

Traditionally baked in a skillet, this cake has a buttery brown sugar glaze and golden slices of pineapple.

2  **(8-ounce) cans sliced pineapple in juice, drained**
¾  **cup packed light brown sugar**
1½  **sticks (6 ounces) unsalted butter, softened**
7  **pecan halves**

¼  **cup cranberries**
¾  **cup granulated sugar**
2  **eggs, separated**
2  **teaspoons vanilla extract**
1½  **cups flour**
2  **teaspoons baking powder**
¼  **teaspoon salt**
½  **cup milk**

**1.** Preheat oven to 350°F. Lay pineapple slices on paper towels and pat dry.

**2.** In a 10-inch cast iron skillet, combine brown sugar and ½ stick butter. Heat over medium heat until butter melts, stirring until combined. Remove from heat. Cut 1 slice of pineapple into chunks. Lay 7 pineapple slices in brown sugar mixture in skillet. Place chunks in empty spaces between slices. Place pecans in centers of pineapple slices. Fill in empty spaces with cranberries.

**3.** In a large bowl with an electric mixer on medium speed, beat remaining 1 stick butter until fluffy. Gradually beat in ½ cup granulated sugar. Beat 2 minutes. Beat in egg yolks and vanilla. In a small bowl, stir flour, baking powder, and salt until blended. On low speed, beat in flour mixture in thirds alternately with milk, beginning and ending with flour, beating just until blended.

**4.** In a medium bowl with clean beaters, beat whites on medium-high speed until foamy. Gradually beat in remaining ¼ cup sugar, beating just until stiff but not dry peaks form. Stir one fourth of whites into batter. Gently fold in remaining whites. Pour batter over pineapple. Smooth top gently.

**5.** Bake 40 to 45 minutes, or until a toothpick inserted in center comes out clean. Let cool on a wire rack 5 minutes. Place a serving plate over skillet and carefully invert. Remove skillet. Let cake cool. Serve barely warm or at room temperature.

# 364    CHOCOLATE COOKIE CUPCAKES
*Prep: 15 minutes    Cook: 23 to 25 minutes    Makes: 18*

These cupcakes are made from a chocolate cake recipe made with mayonnaise. The idea came from the wife of a Hellman's sales distributor.

2   cups flour
½   cup unsweetened cocoa
       powder
1¼  teaspoons baking soda
⅜   teaspoon salt
1   cup mayonnaise
1   cup granulated sugar
3½  teaspoons vanilla extract

12  chocolate creme-filled
       cookies, such as Oreos,
       finely chopped
3   cups powdered sugar
4   tablespoons butter, softened
¼   cup plus 1 teaspoon milk
1   ounce semisweet chocolate,
       melted

**1.** Preheat oven to 350°F. In a small bowl, combine flour, cocoa, baking soda, and ¼ teaspoon salt. Stir well to mix. In a large bowl, combine mayonnaise, granulated sugar, and 2 teaspoons vanilla. Beat with an electric mixer on medium speed until smooth. Beat in flour mixture in fourths alternately with 1 cup cold water, beginning and ending with flour. Beat on medium speed 2 minutes. Stir in chocolate cookies. Let batter stand 10 minutes. Spoon batter into 18 paper-lined muffin cups 2¾ to 3 inches wide, filling cups three-quarters full.

**2.** Bake 23 to 25 minutes, or until a toothpick inserted in centers comes out clean. Let cool in pan on a wire rack 10 minutes. Remove cupcakes from pan to a wire rack and let cool completely.

**3.** In a medium bowl, combine powdered sugar, butter, ¼ cup milk, and remaining 1½ teaspoons vanilla and ⅛ teaspoon salt. Beat with electric mixer on medium speed until smooth and fluffy. Measure out 3 tablespoons frosting and set aside in a small bowl. Frost cupcakes with remaining frosting.

**4.** Stir melted chocolate and remaining 1 teaspoon milk into reserved 3 tablespoons frosting until smooth. Spoon chocolate icing into a small food storage bag. Snip one bottom corner to make a small hole. Drizzle in a thin swirled line across each cupcake. Let stand until frosting sets.

# 365    STRAWBERRY SHORTCAKE
*Prep: 20 minutes    Cook: 18 to 20 minutes    Serves: 8*

Here is a traditional sweetened biscuit version of strawberry shortcake, formed into a single large dessert for less work and a striking presentation.

3 pints strawberries
½ cup plus 3 tablespoons
   sugar
2 cups flour
1 tablespoon baking powder
¼ teaspoon salt

6 tablespoons cold unsalted
   butter, cut into small
   pieces
2 cups heavy cream
1 teaspoon vanilla extract

**1.** Reserve 2 large strawberries with stems for garnish; stem remaining berries. In a large bowl, combine ½ cup strawberries and ¼ cup sugar. Crush strawberries well with a potato masher. Halve, or if large slice, remaining strawberries and add to bowl. Stir to combine and let stand at room temperature while making shortcake. Place a medium bowl and beaters of an electric mixer in refrigerator to chill.

**2.** Preheat oven to 400°F. Generously butter 2 (8-inch) round cake pans. In a large bowl, combine flour, ¼ cup sugar, baking powder, and salt. Stir well. Add butter and cut in with a pastry blender or 2 knives until crumbly. Drizzle in ⅔ cup cream, tossing with a fork until dough is moistened and clumps together. Turn dough out onto a floured surface and knead lightly 4 times. Divide in half. Place in pans and press to cover bottom of pans. Brush with 1 tablespoon cream and sprinkle with 1 tablespoon sugar.

**3.** Bake 18 to 20 minutes, or until biscuit layers are golden brown on top. Place pans on wire racks to let cool.

**4.** Place remaining cream, 2 tablespoons sugar, and vanilla in chilled bowl. Beat with electric mixer and chilled beaters on high speed until cream thickens and soft peaks begin to form.

**5.** Place 1 biscuit layer on a serving plate. Top with half of strawberries. Top with second biscuit layer. Garnish top with whole strawberries. Place remaining strawberries and cream in serving bowls and pass at table. Cut strawberry shortcake into wedges with a serrated knife.

# Index

## Acknowledgments

To all of my family and neighbors, for their encouragement and tasting skills. To friends and fellow food professionals Paul Piccuito and Marge Foster, for their help and for being there.

To editor Susan Wyler, for her advice when needed and giving me space when needed.

A big thanks to a special friend, chef Joe Costanzo, for his recipe-testing talents, constant enthusiasm, and taste buds.

And a thank-you to my mom, for all of her support.